917.59 SOU 2009
Rubio, Paul.
South Florida Includes the Keys, Orlando, and the Tampa Bay Area./

INCLUDES THE KEYS,
ORLANDO, AND THE
TAMPA BAY AREA

**PALM BEACH COUNTY
LIBRARY SYSTEM**
3650 Summit Boulevard
West Palm Beach, FL 33406-4198

© 2009 BY PAUL RUBIO
All rights reserved
Manufactured in the United States of America

THIS TRADE PAPERBACK ORIGINAL IS PUBLISHED BY
Alyson Books
245 West 17th Street
New York, NY 10011

DISTRIBUTION IN THE UNITED KINGDOM BY
Turnaround Publisher Services Ltd.
Unit 3, Olympia Trading Estate
Coburg Road, Wood Green
London N22 6TZ England

Portions of the Fort Lauderdale section were originally written for *The Gay America Guide*, a division of Fun Maps.

FIRST EDITION: *February 2009.*

09 10 11 12   a   10 9 8 7 6 5 4 3 2 1

ISBN-10: 1-59350-103-X
ISBN-13: 978-1-59350-103-7

Library of Congress Cataloging-in-Publication data are on file.

Design by **VICTOR MINGOVITS**
Maps by **THE 411 MAGAZINE**

As the Editor in Chief of OUTTRAVELER.COM *and Travel Editor for Regent Media (the parent company of the publisher of this guide), I'm delighted at the launch of our new travel series.* OutTraveler *strives to inspire sophisticated readers like you by showcasing thoughtful and transformative travel experiences that set the standard of gay travel. These books, which emphasize the long-overlooked, but incredibly powerful cultural and historical traditions of our community throughout the world, help us reach this goal.*

—ED SALVATO
EDITOR IN CHIEF, OUTTRAVELER.COM
TRAVEL EDITOR, REGENT MEDIA

ABOUT THE AUTHOR

PAUL RUBIO is an economist and environmental policy analyst by training, who principally uses his power of prose as a grant writer for poverty alleviation and sustainable development projects. Paul's insatiable quest to learn and his passion for discovery have taken him to all corners of the world. Paul's first dabble in the professional travel writing arena came about during his double master's at Harvard, when he applied to write for the student-oriented *Let's Go* travel series. After his first travel publication in 2003 with *Let's Go: Spain & Portugal,* Paul continued to submit travel articles and journal entries to various travel magazines as a self-proclaimed stress relief during his five-year run as the head of an international nonprofit organization. On hiatus from the mayhem of donor funding and foreign aid projects, Paul has returned to his passion of travel writing to take readers on an unparalleled journey through his original home state of Florida. Outside of being a nerd, Paul is a global party animal and a family man, who now calls over a dozen cities in the world "home."

THE OUT TRAVELER PHILOSOPHY

Yes, we know: On your travels around the globe (or even close to home), you've plowed through your fair share of dry, Yellow Page-like guidebooks aimed at the most massive of mass markets. Sure, they may include a tiny gay section that makes a token nod to you, but little else. Moreover, many guides seem to rely so heavily on throwing as much soon-to-be-outdated information at you, that you are left wondering about the deeper aspects of a place. How is it unique from others? What's it like to live there? How is being gay there different from other places? What are the more meaningful things I need to know to really understand where I'm going?

With this guidebook, we aim to give you the expert tools that will not only lend practicality to your journey, but also cultural and historical insight, understanding, and intimate appreciation of where you're going—and of course, how to do it all in style.

THE LGBT TRAVELER

Loosened from the bonds of tradition and societal expectations, gay and lesbian people have been trailblazers throughout human history. And it's no different with our distinctive take on travel. Queer people have frequently had to sojourn to distant shores to find our true "homes." We often understand a place and discover its layers years before our heterosexual comrades do. As the globe opens up even further in the 21st century to welcome us, offering more places than ever for the LGBT traveler to visit, we still need to explore the world with our eyes wide open. Perhaps it's part of our special survival skill set: Queer people have to know where we are welcome, how to fit in, the vibe of a particular cultural or political climate—all things many straights take for granted. In a word, we are savvy. And innovative. And our authors strive to reflect that innate intelligence in our guidebooks. We want to impart to you the travel tools for deeper understanding. After all, even the slightest of vacations is meant to be transformative.

THE OUT TRAVELER GUIDES

Instead of throwing in the (shallow) kitchen sink, we present you with our knowledgeable, hand-picked recommendations. We cull, interview, visit, and delve deeply to find both the gay and mainstream establishments we feel fit well with sophisticated queer sensibility, with an emphasis on the luxurious, the classy, or at least the truly unique. You'll also find reference to our Web site, OUT-TRAVELER.COM, where loads more up-to-the-minute articles, listings, and information on a particular locale can be found. In our *Out Traveler* guidebooks, we spend time exploring the distinct history, politics, and the unexpected quirks of a place in order for you to become a sharp traveler, not just a fly-by-night tourist. If we can illuminate a locale's soul for you, then we have done our job.

No establishment has paid to be in our guides—you are getting our often opinionated take on what we feel is worthwhile. Our authors are personally involved in the places they write about, often having resided in the destination for years. Nothing beats local, on-the-ground insider expertise. Our authors give you pertinent knowledge on local laws and attitudes toward gays in our signature *Out Traveler* ratings boxes.

So sit back and let us take you on a trip. Travel is profoundly personal and frequently life changing. Let us help you discover the essence of what the journey is all about.

CONTENTS

FLORIDA AND ME xiii

CHAPTER 1
PUTTING LGBT FLORIDA IN PERSPECTIVE 3

PERSECUTION IN THE SUNSHINE STATE: 1950S AND 1960S 6

SIDEBAR: *Gay Life of the 1950s Remembered by Merrill Mushroom*

1970S ONWARDS 12

SIDEBAR: *The Yellow Brick Road to Victory*
SIDEBAR: *We've Got a Long Way to Go*

THE FUTURE OF HOMO FLORIDA POLITICS 14

FLORIDA ORGANIZATIONS, COMMUNITY CENTERS, AND HIV RESOURCES 17

CHAPTER 2
FLORIDA'S FLEDGLING CULTURE, ALLURE, AND ANOMALIES. 19

DOES FLORIDA HAVE CULTURE? 21
FLORIDA IN THE NEWS 23
   SIDEBAR: *Freaky Florida: Interesting, Random, and Useless Facts about the Sunshine State*
   SIDEBAR: *Debunking the Top Five Myths about Florida*
FLORIDA AND MUSIC 29
   The Conga Legacy and the Music Scene. 29
   Shake What Yo' Mama Gave Ya. 31
   Miami Freestyle 34
FLORIDA ON THE SMALL AND BIG SCREENS 35
   TV and Commercials 35
   Movie Glamour. 38
   The Porn Industry 41
FLORIDA'S CELEBRITIES AND D-LIST 41
FLORIDA PARTY ANTHOLOGY—R.I.P. AND NOSTALGIA 44
FEEDING THE FLORIDA STEREOTYPE: BEAUTY AND THE BEACH 47

CHAPTER 3

BASIC FLORIDA INFO 49
WHEN TO COME 51
WHAT TO BRING 52
GETTING HERE AND GETTING AROUND 52
   Air. 52
   From the Airport. 53
   Your Own Car 54
   Public Transportation 54
   Rental Car or Not? 54
   SIDEBAR: *Florida's Major Cities in a Nutshell*

UNDERSTANDING YOUR SECTIONS 55
A WORD ON PRICES 58
  SIDEBAR: *Facts and Figures*
LGBT EVENTS BIG AND SMALL 59
FOOD EVENTS 62
GAY PUBLICATIONS AND WEB SITES 62
RELIGIOUS ORGANIZATIONS 64
GYMS 65
PAMPERING: FLORIDA'S TOP SPAS 66
FLORIDA'S BEST MAINSTREAM SHOPPING . . . 69
FLORIDA'S BEACHES 71
TREASURES OFF THE BEATEN PATH 72

CHAPTER 4

MIAMI 87
  BIENVENIDOS A MIAMI 89
    SIDEBAR: *Essential Miami iPod Playlist*
  THE HOLLYWOOD OF LATIN AMERICA 94
    SIDEBAR: *Interesting, Random, and Useless Facts*
  POCKET GUIDE TO FLORIDA SPANGLISH . . . 97
  EVENTS (LGBT) 98
  EVENTS (NON-LGBT) 99
    SIDEBAR: *Great South Beach Reading*
    SIDEBAR: *Avoid Renting a Car in South Beach*
  TO DO AND SEE 102
  LODGING 109
    SIDEBAR: *Escape the World in Key Biscayne*
  DINING 113
    SIDEBAR: *Cuban Food in Little Havana*
  NIGHTLIFE 119
    SIDEBAR: *South Beach Remembered By Tara Solomon*

CHAPTER 5

FORT LAUDERDALE 125
   LIVING YOUR DEADLY SINS IN
      FORT LAUDERDALE 127
   FORT LAUDERDALE IN THE SPOTLIGHT 129
     SIDEBAR: *Interesting, Random, and Useless Facts*
   EVENTS (LGBT) 131
   EVENTS (NON-LGBT) 133
   TO DO AND SEE 134
   LODGING (LGBT) 138
   LODGING (MAINSTREAM) 140
   DINING 142
     SIDEBAR: *Food and Drink Orgasms*
   BEST 24-HOUR FIXES AND
      COFFEE SHOPS 147
   NIGHTLIFE 149

CHAPTER 6

THE PALM BEACHES 155
   THE POWER OF THE PALM BEACHES 157
     SIDEBAR: *Interesting, Random, and Useless Facts*
   EVENTS 159
   TO DO AND SEE 160
   LODGING 163
   DINING 164
   NIGHTLIFE 165

CHAPTER 7

THE KEYS 167
   CRACKED CONCH REPUBLIC 169

THE DRIVE UP FROM (AND DOWN TO) THE KEYS	172
SIDEBAR: *Interesting, Random, and Useless Facts*	
EVENTS	175
TO DO AND SEE	176
SIDEBAR: *What to Do When It Rains?*	
LODGING (LGBT)	182
LODGING (MAINSTREAM)	186
DINING	186
SIDEBAR: *Key Lime Rapture*	
NIGHTLIFE	190

CHAPTER 8

ORLANDO	195
HELP! I'M IN ORLANDO!	197
SIDEBAR: *Theme Park Attendance 2007*	
A COMPLETE GUIDE TO GAY DAYS: THE BEST GAY EVENT IN AMERICA	200
SIDEBAR: *The Straight Guy at Gay Days*	
TO DO AND SEE	210
LODGING	215
SIDEBAR: *Theme Park Rhapsody—Latest Thrills!*	
DINING	216
NIGHTLIFE	218

CHAPTER 9

TAMPA BAY AREA	221
A TALE OF TWO CITIES	223
SIDEBAR: *Interesting, Random, and Useless Facts*	
EVENTS	227

TO DO AND SEE: TAMPA 228
  SIDEBAR: *A Day of Rehab*
TO DO AND SEE: ST. PETERSBURG 234
  SIDEBAR: *Day Trips from Tampa Bay*
LODGING: TAMPA 241
LODGING: ST. PETERSBURG 242
DINING: TAMPA 244
DINING: ST. PETERSBURG 247
NIGHTLIFE: TAMPA 248
NIGHTLIFE: ST. PETERSBURG 251

MAPS 253
INDEX 259
PHOTO CREDITS 269

FLORIDA AND ME

The son of a Cuban immigrant father and a New York native mother, my conception in the suburbs of Kendall in the late 1970s was a classic South Florida tale of post-Communist opportunity, forbidden love, and cross-cultural perseverance. My Spanglish upbringing was a defining factor of the newly assimilated Cuban communities of South Florida. We lived in a cookie-cutter development, prone to severe flooding, and drove a brown Caprice Sedan with only AM radio and torn plastic seats. My diligent and overly intelligent parents worked long hours, and I spent most of my time with my Cuban nanny, YaYa, my dog, Shadow, and my idol—my big sister.

I was, no doubt, an odd child—a nine-year-old mini-entrepreneur who preferred cutting coupons and reading the *Wall Street Journal* to playing baseball. I was also a solitary child whose best friend was nature. While the normal kids played, I collected critters in the intertidal pools behind the Casa Marina in Key West, and dreamt of roaming the African savannah and fishing in the Amazon to complete my aquarium collection. I wanted to own a trailer and live in the Everglades, engage in the nomadic lifestyle of ancient Seminoles, and use an airboat as a primary means of transportation.

Growing up "straight," I had two "out" gay role models at home—my mother's brother, Uncle Ira—a gifted and witty rehab regular—and my mother's first cousin, Susan—a MENSA member, inspirational literature teacher extraordinaire, and World War II expert who taught me all I know about being butch. Even with the burgeoning gay momentum in South Beach in the early 1990s, it seemed from their experiences that, outside of miniscule pockets of the Sunshine State, perceived homosexuals were still met with incredible homophobia and persecution.

I was not gay in high school mostly because I had not yet realized my path of sexuality. However, my erudition and tolerance already confused the larger ignorant population who relentlessly accused me of being a "fag." By the time I graduated at 17, this salutatorian was desperate to trade life in the ghetto suburban wasteland for a world of sophistication and scholarship in Boston and Cambridge. Beyond family and nature, I hated Florida and never wanted to return.

However, my attitude toward Florida began to change in the summer of 1997, when I returned home for summer classes and began exploring my homosexuality via the dial-up demigod AOL and innocent jaunts at the local club, the Warsaw. After my best friend revealed her possible bisexual tendencies, it was no-holds-barred for a supportive friend to escort her to gay establishments on her sexual pursuits.

The places we discovered that summer blew me away; I could hardly recognize the city I had always called home. Miami was a gay Mecca—scenesters, hipsters, and gender illusionists. It was the world of beautiful men from Madonna's *Sex* book: muscle queens in high-cut Speedos rollerblading down A1A in a true period of gay cultural celebrity. By July 1997, I was intoxicated with South Florida gay life.

Thirty miles north, Fort Lauderdale lacked the glamour of Miami, but presented comparable fun at the Saint, Club Electra, and Cathode Ray. There was less pretension and a bit more age discrepancy among the crowd but a greater feeling of warmth and acceptance. It was a welcoming arena for "coming out" and, well, getting laid.

After the summer of 1997, my experiences with Gay Florida were sporadic and intermittent. I moved abroad in 1998 during my junior year and commenced what would become a 10-year sojourn to more than 50 countries and extended interactions with societies in Ecuador, Kenya, Malaysia, Madagascar, Spain, Portugal, France, the United Kingdom, and Costa Rica, to name a few. Though I lived abroad for most of these 10 years, long breaks during graduate school at Harvard and trips home for the holidays allowed me to return to the old Florida watering holes and to try new ones. Serendipity and honed writing skills landed me a few fantastic freelance writing jobs, which I would complete during sabbaticals from my work in the nonprofit arena.

By the end of 2006, I decided it was time to come "home." That critical year of 30 was fast approaching, my Aunt Bonnie had cancer, I was now an uncle, and after ending a three-year relationship, I was once again single and back on the prowl.

I took some time off when I returned to truly enjoy Florida. I picked up a writing gig describing the contrasts between the United States and Europe and documented my re-introduction. I bought four books about Florida. I wanted to rediscover my homeland.

I spent a lot of time visiting old friends, such as the Everglades and the Loggerhead Turtles, while making new ones. I went swimming with the manatees, witnessed the launch of a space shuttle, and sat among the wading herons. I was so enthused by my discoveries that I began plans for a book called *Forgotten Florida: Treasures Off the Beaten Path*.

Returning to Florida after the fast pace of London and the far corners of the Third World, I can arguably title Florida as one of the most special and beautiful places on Earth. It's hardly as cultured as New York City or Europe, or as exotic as Hawaii or Madagascar. Yet it is undeniably *the* zenith of leisure and the most visited destination in the world—a sensational juxtaposition of commercialization and nature, a contrast of glamour and tackiness, an unparalleled melting pot of the Americas.

—PAUL RUBIO

PUTTING LGBT FLORIDA IN PERSPECTIVE

1

PUTTING LGBT FLORIDA IN PERSPECTIVE

Whereas Disney World stakes claim as the happiest place on Earth, Florida holds arguable grounds for declaration as the gayest state on Earth. Florida's metamorphosis from a land of McCarthyism and persecution to a modern-day homo sanctuary has undoubtedly painted the green landscape pink. In all facets of everyday life, LGBT presence is ubiquitous. We are the bag boys at the grocery store, the pilot of your aircraft, your neighborhood mechanic, and your municipal mayor. We have a large and undeniably powerful presence.

Nevertheless, we still live in a state dominated by a Republican legislature and governor, where the law works against us and even harms us. Out of 67 counties throughout the state, only seven offer gays the basic protection of human rights and decency we believe to be standard in the United States. Outside of South Florida and the more populous areas in Central Florida, a gay person can be legally fired, asked to leave a restaurant, denied a hotel room with a partner, and be denied housing as a renter or homeowner. While this rarely happens, courts can legally support active discrimination on the basis of sexual orientation.

The homo-hypocrisy and dichotomies that define present-day Florida are both puzzling and peculiar. Gays do not just live in Florida. They thrive there. But political and legal struggles plague the community at the macro level to the detriment of eager would-be parents wanting to adopt children. To the chagrin of the national and local civil rights groups that work so hard for our protection, the battle for political and legal freedoms trails behind our social acceptance, and the realization of a more enlightened state policy still seems distant.

PERSECUTION IN THE SUNSHINE STATE: 1950S AND 1960S

Homosexuality is, and for too long has been, a skeleton in the closet of society. The [Florida Legislative Investigation] Committee claims no corner on understanding the history or prognosis of homosexuality. It is, however, convinced that many facets of homosexual practice as it exists in Florida today pose a threat to the health and moral well-being of a sizable portion of our population, particularly our youth.

—Homosexuality and Citizenship in Florida (1964)

Gay bars had clandestinely appeared by the late 1940s throughout Florida, nestled among corners in Miami Beach, the Tampa Bay area, Key West, and Jacksonville. The allure of sun, swim, and fun had put Florida on the map as a premier vacation destination. A fledgling gay life followed suit, most notably on Miami Beach with a dozen underground bars and a rumored gay beach. However, by the end of 1953 the "new" homosexual lifestyle was targeted as a media scapegoat for recent sensationalized cases of child molestation and murder. Referred to as "maniacs" by the Greater Miami Crime Commission Chief, and "sex perverts and degenerates" by the chief of police, the crusade had begun to suppress and crush this alternative lifestyle. Gay bars were raided and closed. Female impersonators were banned. Those who braved the gay beach were harassed by police and often arrested.

The prestigious *Miami Herald* took endless opportunity to partake in the smear campaign against gays. They published one editorial after the next, with headlines such as "Just Execute Them All," and socially sanctioned those arrested on charges of homosexual suspicion, printing their names, photos, and addresses in the newspaper. By the end of 1954, the hysteria had culminated in a Miami city ordinance that banned two or more homosexuals from congregating, sparked countless raids, and ushered in a wave of public paranoia declaring that people were not safe from homosexuals. McCarthyism had taken on a new dimension in Florida, centered on the gay community.

The Florida Legislative Investigation Committee was then formed in 1956 with a mission to investigate potentially subversive activities in government and state education, validating a government-sponsored brigade that effectively terrorized and tormented suspected homosexuals. Led by State Senator and Former Governor Charley Eugene Johns, the Johns Committee spread trepidation and anxiety across Florida's universities among both students and staff. Homosexual acts were considered lewd, lascivious, and constituted moral turpitude. They were grounds for interrogation, public humiliation, dismissal, and expulsion. Universities in Tampa, Tallahassee, and Gainesville were breeding grounds for homosexuals. Gays were less than second-class citizens.

The Johns Committee successfully destroyed lives for over a decade. During this time, hundreds of students were expelled based on the word of secret "student" informants. Over 100 professors, college physicians, deans, and public school teachers were dismissed

GAY LIFE OF THE 1950S REMEMBERED BY MERRILL MUSHROOM

Merrill Mushroom grew up on Miami Beach in the 1940s and 1950s and then began college at the University of Florida in 1958. As an adult she documented her experiences of coming out, dealing with her sexuality in a hostile political climate, and her first-hand persecution by the Johns Committee through books, articles, and short stories. Her experiences were chronicled a decade ago in the documentary *Behind Closed Doors: The Dark Legacy of the Johns Committee* by UF graduate student, Allyson A. Beutke.

A close childhood friend of my cousin Susan, Merrill was kind enough to discuss her experiences with me and to send me a collection of quotations from some of her works, including *Brothers & Sisters, The Gay Kids and the Johns Committee:1956,* and *The Coming Out Stories.*

"We knew that we had to be silent about our proclivities. Being gay was not safe. We read the newspapers, listened to the radio, and overheard discussions among our parents. We heard ... that adult gays were being arrested, incarcerated, given electroshock treatments, and lobotomized; were losing their jobs and families and freedoms; and were committing suicide.

in horrific, media-hyped spectacles devastating to the psyche and spirit. Some public school teachers "disappeared" for a year and returned the following fall with married names. The work of the Committee climaxed in 1964 with publication of *Homosexuality and Citizenship in Florida,* the so-called "Purple Pamphlet," which

GAY LIFE OF THE 1950S REMEMBERED BY MERRILL MUSHROOM

"The hetero kids always could go 'parking,' do it in their cars, and run not much more of a risk than to have the police give them a warning and make them move on, were they to be discovered. We gay girls would never dare to do that. We'd heard too many stories from bar dykes who were caught together necking in a car and had to give the police blow jobs to not get beat up, and maybe they got beat up anyway."

An account of a "gay beach" raid:

With what am I being charged, officer?
Vagrancy.
Vagrancy? But I have a job, a home, a family, a reputation. I have money and identification in my wallet. I was only sunbathing on a public beach on a Sunday. I am not a vagrant.
We have 27 different counts of vagrancy we can charge you with. We can book you and put you in a jail cell and hold you for 24 hours on suspicion. We can do with you as we please. You filthy queer!

warned the public of "frequent homosexual fixation on youth," and urged felony sentences for homosexual acts. The Committee disbanded in 1965 only when the government withdrew funding after word had spread that the Pamphlet was being sold as soft-core gay pornography for its racy photos.

THE YELLOW BRICK ROAD TO VICTORY

1964 The Johns Committee uses hot and racy photos in its scathing pamphlet on gay life. The photos are so risqué for the time that the pamphlets are sold on the black market as soft-core porn!

1965 Miami issues licenses to gay bars following disbandment of the Johns Committee.

1969 Ongoing violent riots between the New York City police and the LGBT community occur at Stonewall, marking the beginning of the modern-day movement toward rights for LGBT people.

1977 Anita Bryant has a pie thrown in her face during a live newscast. This delightful video can be viewed on YouTube (search: "Anita Bryant pie in the face"). Gay activists organize a juice boycott to protest Bryant. Endorsers include Barbra Streisand and Bette Midler.

1978 Gay bars all over North America take screwdrivers off of their drink menus and replace them with the "Anita Bryant" (vodka and apple juice).

1982 A magazine for lesbians, *Womyns Words,* is published in the Tampa area. Key West throws its first annual Pridefest.

1983 Richard Heyman becomes one of the first openly gay elected officials as mayor of Key West.

1987 The March on Washington delivers the message down to the local level, and gay activism takes on a new dimension in Florida at the community level. Equality Florida is formed.

THE YELLOW BRICK ROAD TO VICTORY

1991 Disney World's Magic Kingdom holds its first Gay Day and receives an immense amount of media attention.

1992 The Human Rights Ordinance is amended in the City of Tampa to include sexual orientation, inspiring others in more conservative cities to follow suit.

1995 Broward County amends its Human Rights Ordinance.

1996 The Supreme Court in Colorado rejects an antigay amendment to prevent future human right's ordinances that create classifications based on sexual orientation or sexual preference in *Romer v. Evans*. Alachua County's antigay Amendment 1 is defeated soon after in Central Florida.

1997 Anita Bryant files for bankruptcy.

2001 Anita Bryant files for bankruptcy for the second time.

2003 The Supreme Court declares gay sodomy statutes unconstitutional in *Lawrence v. Texas*.
Key West becomes the first city in Florida to amend the Human Rights Ordinance to include gender identity and expression.

2004 Professional organizations such as the American Academy of Pediatrics and the American Psychological Association issue policy statements to help repeal the ban on gay adoption.

2008 Miami-Dade County votes for Domestic Partner Protections. St. Petersburg Pride grows to nearly 100,000 attendees; Gay Days Orlando to 150,000.

1970S ONWARDS

As a mother, I know that homosexuals cannot biologically reproduce children; therefore, they must recruit our children. If gays are granted rights, next we'll have to give rights to prostitutes and to people who sleep with St. Bernards and to nail biters.

—Anita Bryant (1977)

While the legacy of the Johns Committee lived on, the Florida LGBT community fell out of the spotlight in the wake of the Stonewall Riots in New York. McCarthyism had died. Individuals were taking a stance to protest gay discrimination. The Marlin Beach Resort in Fort Lauderdale had been transformed into an all-inclusive gay refuge. The Parliament House Resort had opened in Orlando. Key West hosted its first Pridefest. The growing and more accepted gay presence in Miami finally led to Florida's first equal rights ordinance spearheaded by County Commissioner Ruth Shack, which prohibited housing and employment discrimination based on sexual orientation.

But unfortunately, for every Glenda there's always been an Elphaba. Within months of Shack's progressive legislation, her former BFF Anita Bryant led a highly publicized crusade to repeal the ordinance. Through the "Save Our Children" campaign the former Miss America runner-up and failed pop singer played on the fresh yet embedded fear of "homosexual recruitment." Bryant's role as spokeswoman for the Florida Citrus Commission prepared her for her greatest role as Queen Homophobia, preaching about the unabashed sinfulness of homosexuality and gays' insatiable desire for youth. Six months after the ordinance was passed the Queen reigned supreme, and the ordinance was repealed in June 1977 by a margin of 69 to 31%.

The blows continued. By the end of the disco decade, Bryant had taken her campaign to new heights, developing and promoting legislation to outlaw adoption by gays and lesbians—a law that haunts Florida to this day. Her "Save Our Children" campaign, ironically, had hurt many children over the long run by preventing loving and willing families from providing a home for them.

A personal and professional downward spiral began for Bryant in 1979 due to the very radicalism that had made her victorious. The aftermath of her social "death" brought an explosion of life to the LGBT community of Florida, a movement that mirrored Spain's *La Movida* in the wake of Franco's death. After decades of totalitarian-like repression, Gay Florida burst out laughing and crying in a breathtaking, state-wide release of inhibition. Isolated as the southernmost region in the United States, Key West led this movement of arts, culture, and lifestyle in one of the foremost accepting arenas for gay life. Miami and Fort Lauderdale followed suit, and then Tampa and Orlando.

Gay life never died during the nightmare years, but numerous attempts to starve and repress it caused innumerable setbacks. Nevertheless, the resilience of the gay community and the gay spirit resonated in the 1980s and 1990s as South Florida grew to become the foremost gay destination in the world. Today, Florida continues to serve as winter's playground for the snowbirds and a permanent home to one of the largest LGBT communities in the world. People flock to Florida for change and opportunity, to savor life and all its offerings. It's not as cosmopolitan as New York nor as charming as California, but it is undeniably the gay vacation capital of the world . . . the wild, pulsating heart of leisure, an enchanted land of indulgence and beauty.

WE'VE GOT A LONG WAY TO GO

1996 President Bill Clinton signs the federal Defense of Marriage Act (DOMA) into law, upholding states' rights to ban same-sex marriages and to refuse recognition of same-sex couples.

1997 Florida legislature adopts DOMA as state law, actively banning marriage and any other form of partnership recognition for same-sex couples.

2004 Sixty-five percent of Floridians oppose same-sex marriages according to *Miami Herald* and *St. Petersburg Times* polls.

2004 The U.S. Circuit Court of Appeals upholds the ban on gay adoption.

2004 President Bush declares support for a federal marriage amendment banning same-sex marriage.

2005 A Tampa man is convicted of killing his three-year-old son because he believed his son was too effeminate.

THE FUTURE OF HOMO FLORIDA POLITICS

As liberal states celebrate legal and political strides for gay couples and families across the United States, Florida struggles to change conservative policy. While gay marriage becomes recognized throughout the Northeast and California, Florida is fighting the Marriage Protection Amendment to keep the few existing rights of the LGBT community. Only seven (Broward, Miami-Dade, Pinellas, Leon, Monroe, Orange, Palm Beach) of Florida's 67 counties currently provide non-discriminatory policies based on sexual orientation. Thankfully these populous counties represent over 50% of the state's population.

WE'VE GOT A LONG WAY TO GO

and would grow up to be gay. He bludgeoned him to death with his fist.

2006 The county commissioner of Hillsborough County, Rhonda Storms, prevents the county from promoting gay pride events.

2007 Lisa Pond tragically passes away without saying goodbye to her partner, Janice Langbehn, and their jointly adopted children, when Jackson Memorial Hospital refuses Janice and the children permission to visit after Lisa suffers a brain aneurysm (on the grounds of DOMA). The family was in Florida for a family vacation on the Rosie O'Donnell Cruise.

2007 Twenty-five-year-old Ryan Skipper is killed for being gay. He is stabbed more than 20 times and has his throat slit in a town north of Orlando. The murderers brag about killing "a fag." The Polk County sheriff

Sadly, Florida remains the only state in the United States with a statutory ban on gays and lesbians adopting children. Regardless of finance, credence, or qualification, homosexuals have no legal rights to adopt. The law that dictates this blatant adoption discrimination, circa 1977, is a legacy of the one and only Anita Bryant. However, the courts have upheld this legislation on three separate appeals, most recently in 2004, dealing a devastating blow to the community. While there is no velvet glove on this iron fist of discrimination, the positive news is that in 2004 a hearing was held on the repeal of the adoption bill. This was the first time in 20 years that the courts allowed the bill to be heard; this can only be viewed as a sign of progress. The irony

WE'VE GOT A LONG WAY TO GO

publicly regurgitates lies of the assailants to paint a false, negative picture of Ryan (which he later retracts but not publicly). The media fails to cover the story.

2007 Steve Stanton, city manager of Largo, Florida, plans to undergo gender-reassignment surgery. He is then fired by the city, which declares him an untrustworthy leader.

2008 Right-wing activists of the political group Florida4-Marriage gather enough support to place on the ballot "The Marriage Protection Amendment," which enshrines discrimination in the Florida Constitution and bans financial, employment, and healthcare benefits for all unmarried partners. Amendment 2 passes.

2008 Pinellas County specifically excludes GIE (gender identity and expression) when amending its human rights' ordinance to include sexual orientation.

of the law is that gay couples are simply leaving the state to adopt and returning with their new families to Florida. The biggest losers become the children languishing in Florida's system.

As Nadine Smith, director of Equality Florida, points out, "Massachusetts once had the demographic of public attitudes that we now see in Florida." Polls show that while Floridians do not support same-sex marriage, a vast majority (67%) support civil unions. And it seems that almost nobody agrees with the outdated adoption law. "Change is on the way," Nadine assures us. We can only hope that by the second edition of this book some of this change will already be upon us.

FLORIDA ORGANIZATIONS, COMMUNITY CENTERS, AND HIV RESOURCES

CARE RESOURCE (HIV resources and free confidential testing) 3510 Biscayne Boulevard, Suite 300, Miami, (305) 576-1234; 830 E. Oakland Park Boulevard, Fort Lauderdale, (954) 567-7141 CARERESOURCE.ORG

CENTRAL FLORIDA GAY, LESBIAN, AND BISEXUAL COMMUNITY CENTER, 946 N. Mills Avenue, Orlando, (407) 228-8272, GLBCC.ORG

COMPASS: GAY AND LESBIAN COMMUNITY CENTER WEST PALM BEACH (ranked #7 GLCC in the country) COMPASSGLCC.COM

EQUALITY FLORIDA 3150 5th Avenue N., Suite 325, St. Petersburg, (813) 870-EQFL (3735), EQFL.ORG

FT. LAUDERDALE GAY AND LESBIAN COMMUNITY CENTER, 1717 N. Andrews Avenue, Fort Lauderdale, (954) 463-9005, GLCCSF.ORG

KEY WEST GAY AND LESBIAN COMMUNITY CENTER, 513 Truman Avenue, Key West, (305) 292-3223, GLCCKEYWEST.ORG

ORLANDO YOUTH ALLIANCE (321) 279-8041, ORLANDOYOUTHALLIANCE.ORG

PALM BEACH COUNTY HUMAN RIGHTS COUNCIL (561) 845-6545, PBCHRC.ORG

FLORIDA'S FLEDGLING CULTURE, ALLURE, AND ANOMALIES

2

DOES FLORIDA HAVE CULTURE?

Florida and culture in the same sentence—you probably misheard. Or you were eavesdropping on a common diatribe by the educated and enlightened, complaining about the lack of culture in Florida as defined by the *American Heritage Dictionary:* "intellectual and artistic activity and the works produced by it." Compared to New York City, the epicenter of U.S. culture and home of Florida's largest constituency of vacationers, it's true. Florida's "cultural" scene pales in comparison. It's like comparing Jersey beaches to Florida's. What's the point of splashing in a cold, polluted cesspool of jellyfish (aka the Jersey Shore), when you could glide through the lucid, placid, and majestic waters that line a subtropical peninsula?

Indeed, Florida's greater arts community has labored to change this tarnished reputation and foster a paradigm where Florida is more than beautiful beaches and theme parks. From world-renowned exhibits at new art museums to top tier performances at performing arts centers, Florida is gaining a cultural identity and shifting the thought patterns of cynics. Museums across South and Central Florida have upped their collections with flagship pieces to draw new visitors, and cultural events are on the calendar across the state. Miami hosts Art Basel in December, arguably the most prestigious art show in the country; Palm Beach presents the world-renowned Palm Beach Jewelry, Art, and Antique Show each February; and Fort Lauderdale welcomes visitors to the biggest boat event in the world, the Winterfest Boat Parade and the International Boat Show. Sometimes you just have to search a bit farther than the next borough for culture, but it definitely exists, and indeed thrives.

St. Petersburg, in particular, shines as the cultural hub of Florida. The myriad museums of the city are on par with some of the best in the Northeast. The Dalí museum boasts the most comprehensive collection of the genius artist and outshines its counterpart in Figueres, Spain. Sure it's not the same holistic experience to enter the mental dimensions of Dalí in central Florida, but it's a prime example of outstanding art and an understated cultural gem in the tropics. The next street showcases the Museum of Arts and Georgia O' Keefe's signature piece *Poppy*. A few blocks south, enter the immaculate Holocaust museum, on par with the Holocaust museum in Washington, DC, in emphasizing not only the atrocities of the World War II era but genocides across the world. But while in Florida, it's always a tough sale to break away from the fabulous beaches and water sport activities.

Approaching culture as the secondary definition of the *Unabridged Dictionary,* "the behaviors and beliefs characteristic of a particular social, ethnic, or age group," Florida is one of the most culturally diverse spots in the world—a sanctuary for gay culture, a melting pot of Latin cultures, an anchor for boating culture, and a stronghold of Jewish culture. And most importantly, Florida's cities have developed their own distinct cultures and idiosyncratic aspects shaped by geography, immigration, emigration, and history, such as Miami's Spanglish, Fort Lauderdale's drinking culture, Key West's iconoclasm, the Palm Beaches' leisure culture, and Orlando's Disney culture.

Conversely, Florida's presence as the largest vacation destination in the world has also shaped what has been perceived by most as a lack of true culture. Palm Beach, for example, was founded as the first resort town in the United States in 1894, and the legacy of leisure remains. Harboring an employment market saturated with service industry roles, Florida's work force tends to be more transient. Many come to Florida simply for quick cash or escape. Whatever the case, Florida is not a prime habitat for Renaissance men. Most of the men and women you will meet here are indeed literate, but that does not mean that they read.

But once you shake off this phenomena, it's time to embrace the distinguishing factors that make Florida unique, special, and flavorful, including our culture, whichever way you want to define it. The north of Florida feels like a part of the Deep South, Central Florida more Midwest, and South Florida a bit more Northeast-meets-Latin America. Regardless, Florida is still about fun in the sun. And it's only (the few) nontransient residents who truly long for a more robust arts scene or a good symphony orchestra. A day may arrive when travelers ignore the waves and the diesel bodies for the new Monet on exhibit at the Museum of Fine Arts, but that day is far from soon!

FLORIDA IN THE NEWS

Hurricane devastation, election debacles, deadly wildlife attacks, deportations, drug cartels, and first degree murder—the media takes joy in sensationalizing Florida as the Wild Wild Southeast! While some smear and slander has been warranted, other tales have been exaggerated. Regardless, sensational headlines have captured the world over the past decades.

HANGING CHADS

The presidential election of 2000 between George W. Bush and Al Gore was not decided until 36 days after Election Day. The entire controversy was the result of what happened in Florida. First, the major networks announced that Vice President Al Gore, the Democratic candidate, had won Florida; that news was retracted shortly thereafter. Bush and Gore were separated by an extremely close margin that resulted in partial recounts, the birth of new terms such as hanging chads and pregnant chads, 47 lawsuits, and a ruling by the U.S. Supreme Court to stop the recount in Florida. At this point, Gore conceded the election even though he had more popular votes than Bush; he did not win enough electoral votes.

DEATH OF A FASHION ICON

On the morning of July 15, 1997, Gianni Versace stepped outside his Ocean Drive mansion for his routine morning visit to News Café and returned to his home, whereupon he was shot twice in the face, dying a few moments later. The killer, Andrew Phillip Cunanan, had been linked sexually to Versace at some point in time. Versace was one of five victims on a five-person, three-month killing spree. Eight days after shooting Versace, Cunanan committed suicide on board a Miami houseboat to avoid capture by the police. In a morbid twist, for several years tourists literally swarmed the steps of Versace's home for snapshots at the crime scene. Though the mansion no longer belongs to Versace's straw-haired sister, first time visitors to Miami still insist on posing for tasteless photos on the front steps.

ANNA NICOLE SMITH FOUND DEAD

On February 8, 2007, the Seminole Hard Rock Hotel and Casino in Hollywood, Florida, received unprecedented media coverage over the tragic death of Vickie Lynn Hogan Marshall better known as Anna Nicole Smith. Less than one year after the unexpected death of her son, Smith was found unresponsive in room 607 from an accidental overdose of sleeping pills and benzodiazepines.

HILLARY'S DUFF

Hillary Clinton was not punished for imitating J. Lo's big booty style. But the former first lady and once presidential hopeful lost out big time when Florida was stripped of its delegates in 2008 for defying the national leadership and holding its primary too early. Under Democratic National Committee rules, no state may hold their primaries or caucuses before February 5 with the exceptions of New Hampshire, South Carolina, Iowa, and Nevada. Florida held its primary on January 29. In May 2007, Florida Governor Charlie Crist (R) had signed a bill, in violation of Democratic Party rules, to up the date of Florida's primary. This prompted a response from the Democratic National Committee to void Florida of delegates for the National Convention. Clinton won by a large margin in the voided Florida primary.

LIGHTNING CAPITAL OF THE UNITED STATES

Once known as the Lightning Capital of the World, Florida has now been demoted to Lightning Capital of the United States since it has been proven by NASA satellites that Rwanda, Africa, has the most lightning strikes on planet Earth each year. However, it is still the lightning strike capital of the world in terms of injuries and fatalities: Over a 35-year period (1959–1994), 1,523 injuries and fatalities were reported in the state of Florida.

Here are a few safety tips to protect yourself. If you see lightning and hear thunder less than 30 seconds later, stop screaming like a drama queen and take shelter! If you are outside, get away from bodies of water, never stand under a tree or near a tall object, stay away from metal objects such as golf clubs and umbrellas, and get indoors or in a hard-topped vehicle.

SPACE SHUTTLE *CHALLENGER* TRAGEDY

Space Shuttle *Challenger* completed nine successful missions before the tragedy that occurred on January 28, 1986. On this fateful day, *Challenger* broke apart 73 seconds into its flight, killing all seven crew members aboard including Christa McAuliffe, who was supposed to be the first school teacher to participate in a space shuttle mission. It was later discovered that an O-ring seal in its right solid rocket booster failed at liftoff from Cape Canaveral, Florida.

THE ELIAN GONZALEZ INCIDENT

One day in November 1999, a six-year-old boy named Elian Gonzalez, his mother, and 12 others left Cuba on a small boat with dreams of reaching freedom on the shores of the United States. Only Elian and two of the other 12 survived the journey by floating on an inner tube across the Florida Straights; they were subsequently found by two fishermen and were turned over to the U.S. Coast Guard. Shortly thereafter, all hell broke loose in a custody battle between Elian's Miami relatives and his father who lived in Cuba. Ultimately, Elian returned with his father, Juan Miguel Gonzalez, to Cuba on June 28, 2000. Activities that preceded this included court cases, mass local media coverage, demonstrations in the streets of Miami, and a predawn invasion of the home of Elian's Miami relatives by eight federal SWAT-equipped agents of the Border Patrol (with a frightening picture of a machine gun in Elian's face and an even scarier picture of Janet Reno!).

WHEN SHARKS ATTACK

Deaths from unprovoked shark attacks are rare anywhere in the world. However, the thought of being attacked or eaten by a shark evokes panic in the minds of many, if not all. In 2005 there were many headlines regarding this subject because a shark killed a 14-year-old girl near the Florida Panhandle; two days later a 16-year-old boy was bitten by a shark 40 miles southeast of Panama City. Media began to focus on something most Floridians already knew—Florida is shark attack capital of the world.

We endure 63.9% of confirmed and reported unprovoked shark attacks in the United States, and more shockingly, 39% in the world. The catch here is that most developing countries have no reporting system, so these percentages do not represent reality. You actually have a better chance of winning the lottery than being killed by a shark.

WHEN GATORS ATTACK

On May 10, 2006, a 28-year old woman, Yovy Suarez Jimenez, went out for an evening jog in the City of Sunrise (Greater Fort Lauderdale). Witnesses last saw her dangling her feet over the water of a canal along the jogging path; the next morning her partially eaten body was found in the canal. The media had a field day when four days later the body of a 43-year-old woman was found in a canal in Pinellas County, the victim of a gator attack. On the same day, in Ocala National Forest in Central Florida, a 23-year-old woman was pulled out of the mouth of an 11-foot alligator. These three fatalities over four short days actually represent 30% of all gator attacks since the dawn of the millennium. Attacks have risen in recent years as humans encroach on previously virgin wetlands, and more commonly, as morons carry out their Betty White *Lake Placid* fantasies by feeding and habituating

FREAKY FLORIDA: INTERESTING, RANDOM, AND USELESS FACTS ABOUT THE SUNSHINE STATE

- Florida is the first state in the country to receive a statewide budget for gay travel (which began in 2008).
- The tallest point in the state is on the Florida Panhandle at Britton Hill, standing only 345 feet high. It is the lowest state highpoint in the United States.
- Pollo Tropical introduced the concept of Cuban "fast food" in 1988 at its first store in Miami. Now the hormone-pumped chicken empire serves 24 million pounds of chicken and 4.6 million pounds of rice annually.
- Burger King Corporation was founded in 1954 in Miami. Over 10,000 stores later, 11 million guests grace the BK palace on a daily basis, with the possibility of ordering an Original Whopper Sandwich 221,184 different ways.
- Cher visited Florida 20 times during her three-year Farewell Tour.
- The Gatorade name comes from the University of Florida football team, the "Gators." Gatorade Thirst Quencher

gators (note that this is illegal). Since 1948, there have been a total of 463 alligator attacks (156 of which were provoked!) and 22 fatalities. In 2007 a python actually attacked and swallowed a large gator, causing the python to explode! Again, you actually have a better chance of winning the lottery than being killed by an alligator.

FREAKY FLORIDA: INTERESTING, RANDOM, AND USELESS FACTS ABOUT THE SUNSHINE STATE

was invented at the University of Florida to assist their athletes in combating the dehydration that limited their performance—hence "Gator . . . ade."

- Stone crabs are found only in Florida. Fishermen, by law, detach the crab's claws and return the critters to the water to regenerate the lost claws for next year's amputation.
- Besides alligators, crocodiles also live in Florida. They are classified as an endangered species with only 400 to 500 remaining in the state.
- The trash-talking guilty pleasure the *National Enquirer* is published in Lantana.
- Stephen Foster wrote Florida's state song, "Old Folks at Home (Suwannee River)," despite the fact that he had never even seen the Suwannee River, nor stepped foot in Florida.
- With more than 1,250 trimmed green expanses, Florida has more golf courses than any other state.

FLORIDA AND MUSIC

THE CONGA LEGACY AND THE LATIN MUSIC SCENE

The Miami Sound Machine's juggernaut—the "Conga"—exploded on the scene in 1985, revolutionizing Miami's status in the global music scene. Equipped with '80s hair (teased and pulled to the side) and a sequined white blazer overlaying lavender stirrup pants (scandalously stripped off at the end of the video), Gloria's voice sways over synthesized beats throughout the song and video while the Sound Machine diligently blows into saxophones and other Fisher-Price instrument props. While the song suited the '80s, the "Conga" and the accompanying "Conga train" have continued to plague weddings and bar mitzvahs until present day, making it arguably the single most destructive force to the sanctity of traditional American marriage (we can only hope that gay marriages will be spared).

Miami's organized dance debacles did not end with the "Conga," however. The sensation was reborn in the 1990s with the Los del Rios's "Macarena," which in fact became the second longest running #1 song in the history of *Billboard* magazine (14 weeks), the best-selling debut single of all time in the United States, and the longest-running song on the Billboard Hot 100 (60 weeks). Though Spanish in origin, the Spanglish remix by Miami's own Bayside Boys made 1996 the year of the Macarena. Over a decade later, VH1's "#1 Greatest One-Hit Wonder of all Time" is still a favorite on hetero cruises, while a semblance of the song greets visitors at baggage claim at Fort Lauderdale airport (accompanied by neon lights, of course).

Fortunately, in the mid to late 1990s, the Latin scene expanded beyond organized dance. At a mere 73 years old, Celia Cruz, the queen of Calle Ocho, released her biggest single "La Vida Es Carnaval." Gloria ditched the Miami Sound Machine, went solo, and became a gay favorite with homo-thumping remixes, the dancing sensation "Oye," a video that only included female impersonators of her ("Everlasting Love"), and mild vocal eloquence vis-à-vis several Spanish albums. With a more mature style, she quickly became a cultural icon for Latino newbies, including the homoerotic sexual conundrum Ricky Martin, the now moleless and ubersexy Enrique Iglesias, nipple-tweaked and posse followed Jennifer Lopez, and the bleach-blonde goddess who clearly took hair coloring tips from Heather Locklear—Shakira.

The English-speaking Latin sensations dominated the charts at the dawn of the millennium, but none maintained the staying power of our favorite hip-shaking, mud-crawling Shakira, who has truly ruled both the English and Spanish markets in the past decade. In 2003, Miami hosted the Latin Grammys at the American Airline Arena, where Juanes swept the night with five awards, including Album, Record, and Song of the Year. Though other crossovers such as Paulina Rubio (no relation to the author) and Thalia were less well received, Daddy Yankee and the entire Reggaeton clan earned their very own radio station in 2006 (Mega 94.9—Latino and Proud), which now caters to all types of Latin music flavors.

SHAKE WHAT YO' MAMA GAVE YA

Shake it. Don't break it. It took yo' mama nine months to make it.
—From 2 Live Crew's "Pop that Coochie"

Urban communities of South Florida proudly boast Liberty City/Overtown as a cradle of hip-hop civilization—the birthplace of the 1980s/1990s booty music sensation (also known as Miami bass). Luther "Luke Skyywalker" Campbell of 2 Live Crew, or Uncle Luke as he is locally known, became the poster child for this ass-shaking revolution, consisting of rhythmic convulsions of the butt cheeks, intense and rapid gyration in compromising positions, and even stimulated doggy-style sex to the tune of based-out jams, heavy on the Roland TR-808 rhythm composer. The booty

DEBUNKING THE TOP FIVE MYTHS ABOUT FLORIDA

MYTH 1. FLAMINGOS LIVE IN FLORIDA.
The only flamingos that live in Florida are in zoo-type settings. Flamingos are not native to Florida. The closest habitat range for the Caribbean Flamingo is the Bahamas; Hispaniola, Cuba; and Turks and Caicos.

MYTH 2. LOVE BUGS ARE THE PRODUCT OF A GENETICS EXPERIMENT FROM THE UNIVERSITY OF FLORIDA TO CONTROL THE MOSQUITO POPULATION OF FLORIDA.
Plecia nearctica is common to the southern United States, especially along the Gulf Coast. At some point over 50 years ago, the species migrated to the state.

MYTH 3. THERE IS AN UNDERGROUND JAIL AT DISNEY WORLD.
No, Goofy is not going to arrest you. And he did not

music movement gained serious recognition with the release of "Me So Horny" and the wild Pac-Jam sessions held in Liberty City, where sexual acts would reportedly take place on stage and in the audience. The crass and crude lyrics classifying women with the derogatory terms "bitches and ho's" and detailing sexual crusades of vaginal and anal imperialism were instant South Florida classics!

Booty music dominated the air waves of Miami in the early to mid 1990s with songs such as "Shake What Yo' Mama Gave Ya" and

DEBUNKING THE TOP FIVE MYTHS ABOUT FLORIDA

arrest so-and-so's sister 15 years ago for shoplifting. There are underground areas for costume changes and plumbing but no secret prison.

MYTH 4. WALT DISNEY WAS PLACED IN CRYONIC STORAGE IN ORLANDO AFTER HIS DEATH.
As far as Disney's family is aware, Walt was laid to rest and cremated two days after his death. Moreover, the primitive technology to perform such a feat in 1966 debunks this urban legend.

MYTH 5. IT HAS NEVER SNOWED IN MIAMI.
In January 1977 snow fell as far south as Homestead during the coldest Florida winter of the 20th century. In 1982 snow flurries fell on Miami Beach for the only time in recorded history, a day referred to as "Cold Sunday."

"It's Your Birthday," and my personal favorite "Funky Y2C," rapped by a bunch of fourth graders. Booty music was taken to another level when it hit the Atlanta scene with jams such as "Dunkie Butt," when 12 Gauge sang of unrequited lust, pleading with his lover, "Gimme that dunkie butt and them big old legs. I ain't too hard to beg. Ain't no shame in this game. I'm gonna break it down and beg like James."

Whereas LA and Compton famed the hydraulic cars that

seemingly bopped up and down to Snoop Dog and Dr. Dre, the Miami bass predecessor consisted of equally sized hoopties that would shake from excessive bass, nearly shattering fully-tinted windows and creating a regal glow from pink and green neon rims. It was a favorite early '90s South Florida pastime to drive around Coconut Grove or suburban shopping mall parking lots to showcase such synchronicity of car and music.

The same radio stations that captured our hearts and souls with the sensation of booty music (Rhythm 98 and Power 96) also popularized another form of Miami bass, which contained all the boom but less hip-hop influence. DJ Laz, Miami's own "Pimp with the Limp," piloted the Latin Miami bass crossover "Mami El Negro" and the unforgettable "Journey into Bass." Though good booty music has effectively died out in 2009, Laz's "Move Shake Drop Remix" has kept Miami bass alive and thriving on his radio station, Power 96. Fergie sampled a few classics of Miami bass in her 2007 *The Dutchess* album, combining JJ Fad's "Supersonic" and Afro Rican's "Give It All You Got (Doggy Style)" to produce the unoriginal but fan favorite "Fergalicous." Coliseum nightclub in Fort Lauderdale kept the fun and craziness of booty music alive in the gay community until it closed its doors in December 2007, famous for mini-jam sessions on Friday nights that mixed "Scarred," "Mix It Up," and "Peanut Butter & Jelly."

MIAMI FREESTYLE

Though freestyle originated in New York in the early 1980s, it quickly spread to Miami and catalyzed a new musical genre of electronic beats with Latin flavor and '80s cheese. Debbie Deb and Trinere are noted as some of the pioneers of the '80s freestyle movement, with roller-rink hits such as "When I Hear Music," and "I'll Be All You'll Ever Need." Stevie B, Linear, Will to Power,

Company B, and Exposé followed suit, crossing over to pop radio and defining the decade of Miami freestyle.

The highlight of fourth grade was waiting at Peaches Records and Tapes in South Miami for a personally signed copy of Expose's debut album, *Exposure* (which I still own). Even then I was aware of the cattiness of girl groups, conscious of the rumors and truths of all three original members quitting and/or being replaced during recording (there was never apparently a Beyoncé in this group).

The love for Miami freestyle never died out in South Florida. Not surprisingly, Debbie Deb, Trinere, and Exposé reunited in late 2006 for the "Freestyle Explosion" concert with a first stop at the American Airlines Arena in Miami. In 2007, Exposé pulled a Deborah Cox and started hitting the gay circuit, performing at Voodoo Lounge and then Parliament House in Orlando for Gay Days 2008.

FLORIDA ON THE SMALL AND BIG SCREENS

Media outlets have defined Florida culture, fashion, and lifestyle from retirement to spring break; from violence and crime to telenovela drama and glamour. In South Beach, for example, Florida's global visibility and media presence have shaped the visitor expectations for siliconed DD goddesses and pumped Latin beach gods against a backdrop of flamingo flocks and neon lights.

TV AND COMMERCIALS

MIAMI VICE Capitalizing on the excess of the '80s, *Miami Vice* was all about the hot cars, fast boats, big-breasted women, cash, and crime juxtaposed with synthesized beats, gunfire, and minimal but classic dialogue. Sagas of drug trafficking and prostitution for undercover cops James "Sonny" Crockett and Ricardo "Rico" Tubbs defined Miami in its heyday of violence and crime, transforming the city's fashion, style, music, and culture. Heavy on the pastels and the art deco, viewers were awestruck with the glitz and glamour of everything Miami 1987. The show single-handedly institutionalized the casual sports coat over the T-shirt and white linen pants and popularized the five-o'clock shadow. Though the 2006 movie failed to capture the nostalgia of the original vice squad, Colin Farrell looked hot as ever in the role of Detective Crockett (though we still prefer watching Colin eat "breakfast, lunch, and dinner" on his sex tape).

GOLDEN GIRLS Before *Sex and the City,* gay men and women were likening themselves to these four fabulous old broads, living the famed retired life of Miami Beach. With nearly 180 classic episodes over seven seasons, the amazing comedy and dynamic between Blanche, Dorothy, Rose, and Sophia kept viewers at home on Saturday nights from 1985 to 1992, long before Tivo, DVDs, and Lifetime television repeats. Flash forward to *Sex and the City* 20 years after cosmos and New York sophistication, Blanche/Samantha (the archetypal slut), Dorothy/Carrie (the archetypal professional/center of attention), Rose/Charlotte (the archetypal naïve and virginal), and Sophia/Miranda (the archetypal voice of reason) duke it out with wit, friendship, and love. *Golden Girls* was so progressive for its time that the pilot episode featured a gay character, Coco, who was then dropped from future episodes. R.I.P. Estelle Getty (July 25, 1923–July 22, 2008).

THE JACKIE GLEASON SHOW From 1964 to 1970, Gleason's quasi-career revival featured the antics of Gleason himself and an eclectic cast of comedic creations vis-à-vis the familiar comedy-variety format. As the only prime-time show not filmed in Los

Angeles or New York, Gleason shamelessly promoted Florida tourism and helped put Miami on the map.

THE MICKEY MOUSE CLUB REVIVAL Following the glory of the 1950s classic variety show for kids and teens and the disappointment of the 1970s revival, the Disney Channel revamped the Mickey Mouse Club in 1989, for eight new seasons focusing on the musical and comedic talents of the new Mouseketeers. Before K. Fed and amphetamines, Britney Spears was part of the all-star cast that met regularly at Disney MGM studios in Orlando for seasons 6 through 7, with other then-unknown teens including sex god Justin Timberlake, WB all-star Keri Russell, Academy Award-nominated Ryan Gosling, diva Christina Aguilera, and the tackiest dresser of life, JC Chasez.

CSI: MIAMI Seven seasons strong in the Nielsen Top #15, this *Crime Scene Investigation* spin-off tracks the work of forensic scientists in Miami-Dade as they assemble the puzzle pieces to bizarre and curious crimes. Naturally the main characters come with severe emotional baggage and an innate ability to solve murders. While some location shots are filmed in South Florida, the majority of shooting takes place in California.

"I'M GOING TO DISNEY WORLD" The world famous Disney advertising slogan and accompanying commercial captures celebrities in moments of triumph and glory, positing the question, "What's next?" in the immediate aftermath of a career pinnacle. Venturing to Disney was the "next" step for Super Bowl heroes from 1981 to 2009 and other sports icons such as Michael Jordan after leading the Chicago Bulls to victory in the NBA Finals 1991. The response "I'm Going to Disney World" has since become mainstream in society, and even served as Ellen DeGeneres's response when she came out on her show after being asked "What's next?" Placing the campaign on hold in 2005, Disney revamped it in 2006 and extended its celebrity appeal by including American Idol winner David Cook in 2008.

MOVIE GLAMOUR

WHERE THE BOYS ARE (1960) Fort Lauderdale's infamous reputation as the ultimate spring break destination stems from this coming-of-age adventure for four college students. Even in the 1960s, spring break drama revolved around—you guessed it—sex and alcohol! The movie chronicles the spring break flings of the four girls over a week of lust, passion, heartbreak, and despair. The legacy of the film stretched until recent years when the City of Fort Lauderdale took an active stance against the masses of underaged drinkers and partygoers and told them to seek refuge elsewhere.

THERE'S SOMETHING ABOUT MARY First Alf used spit to style his hair, then Cameron Diaz pioneered the use of a sticky load to create a similar style with that extra hold and shine. The unforgettable "cum in the hair scene" exemplified the campy plot of numerous predictable losers vying for the attention and love of the gorgeous Cameron Diaz. Real-life examples of living leather, similar to the unnaturally tanned Magda, are currently on display along Fort Lauderdale's gay beach, Sebastian Beach.

THE BIRDCAGE Set in South Beach, the 1996 American remake of *La Cage aux Folles* features an all-star cast, including Robin Williams and Gene Hackman, in a hysterical, gay-twisted tale of meet the parents. The movie explores both straight and gay stereotypes, climaxing in the dichotomous meeting of the überconservative parents and the flamboyant homosexual parents (including Nathan Lane dressed in drag as the groom's mother). Best in show still goes to Hank Azaria for his role of the sassy Guatemalan housekeeper, Agador Spartacus, and his uncannily accurate portrayal of a Miami Latin queen.

SCARFACE A Cuban exile who arrives during the Mariel Boatlift, Tony Montana (Al Pacino) rises to fame as a gangster in Miami's blossoming criminal and drug underworld against the backdrop of the 1980s cocaine boom. The film's most memorable scene gave birth to John Wayne Bobbitt's favorite pickup line, "say hello to my little friend."

TRUE LIES While Jamie Lee Curtis's striptease stole the movie, the big budget chase scenes across the Overseas Highways in the Florida Keys showcased some of the most awesome special effects and action sequences of the time. With final scenes shot throughout the city of Miami, Arnold Schwarzenegger provides that predictable "feel-good" ending, a far cry from his loin cloth battle days in *Conan the Barbarian* or his current political clout.

WILD THINGS Deceit, deception, greed, and threesomes with minors—did anyone really pay attention to the fact that the movie took place in Davie, Florida? The steamy scene between Neve Campbell and Denise Richards in the hotel would turn any gay man straight and even created a deluge among straight, female audience members.

MARRIED TO THE MOB A rare chance to catch Michelle Pfeiffer as a brunette who gets caught up in some cheesy, complicated mess trying to distance herself from the mafia in the wake of her husband's death. The house used as the set of the movie was crushed in a crane accident in early 2008.

FROM JUSTIN TO KELLY As much as *Where the Boys Are* attracted moviegoers to experience Fort Lauderdale spring break in the flesh, *From Justin to Kelly* probably would have dissuaded any future Fort Lauderdale spring breakers, had anyone actually seen the film. The appalling plotline and choreography, on par with Mariah Carey's *Glitter,* earned the film a special Golden Raspberry "Governor's Award" as the worst musical in the history of Razzies.

FLIGHT OF THE NAVIGATOR An instant Disney cult classic about a 12-year-old boy living in Fort Lauderdale who is unknowingly abducted by aliens for a few hours on Independence Day in 1978 and then wakes up in the year 1986. The mystery of his ageless skin and stunted development connects him to a downed extraterrestrial spacecraft in NASA's possession and to a robotic pilot named Max (voiced by the one and only Pee-wee Herman) who needs to retrieve information he planted in David's brain. After befriending Sarah Jessica Parker, performing time dilation and spacecraft metamorphosis, and cruising through few high-speed chases, David finally returns to 1978 to resume his life.

ACE VENTURA, PET DETECTIVE Before assuming roles as a "serious actor," Jim Carrey was at his comedic best with fart and sex jokes on the trail of a kidnapped dolphin, Snowflake, in an overtly simple plot to sabotage the Miami Dolphins' chance of winning the Super Bowl. The movie takes a bizarre twist at the end when sound cues "The Crying Game" and the murderer is revealed as a hot trannie mess—literally. And lest we forget, Courtney Cox's fabulous role as publicist Melissa Robinson, only second to her performances in *He-Man* and *Scream 3*.

THE PORN INDUSTRY

It's no coincidence that in one and a half years of living in Fort Lauderdale I unknowingly befriended a number of "porn stars," under the guise of their real names and lives. As homemade Internet videos and mobile cameras surpass the more traditional studio setting, Fort Lauderdale has begun replacing Los Angeles as the gay porn capital of the United States. While Bel Ami still does not film in South Florida, Lukas Ridgeston and Sebastian Bonnet are annual regulars at Boardwalk Strip Bar in Fort Lauderdale.

With the arrival of Helix Studios in Fort Lauderdale, the popularity of local sites such as MIAMIBOYZ.COM, PAPI.COM, and the gay explosion in Florida, it's hard to meet someone in South Florida who is either not in a porno themselves or has friends who have participated in porn. (I recently found out that my former best friend did three videos, after I discovered one online.) In fact, a favorite pastime for South Florida locals is to find out if their new trick is listed on RENTBOY.COM.

Gay porn icons and local residents such as Chi Chi LaRue regularly host events in South Florida, with scouts continuously on the lookout for new hires. A quick few hundred dollars of easy cash and your next porn star is created. Those looking to be discovered, look no further than your "Models Application" on your favorite site or pack your bags and come to South Florida.

FLORIDA'S CELEBRITIES AND D-LIST

Once upon a time, the greats of music (Madonna), fashion (Versace), and politics (Janet Reno and Rosie O' Donnell) proudly called Florida home. While Florida's real estate appeal has dwindled, some

A-list and D-list celebrities still shop at the local Publix and make the odd appearance at their favorite diner.

Celebrity stalking in Florida is not as formalized nor as cool as in Los Angeles, where you can buy an invasive map and drive to a celebrity's personal driveway (can we say trespassing?). There are no formal "celebrity home" tours advertised through the convention and visitors bureaus. Nevertheless, a favorite pastime of boaters and captains includes pointing out the different celebrity homes along the waterfront (where the majority are located) in hopes of a backyard glimpse into the lifestyles of the rich and famous. These tours even prompted Rosie to transplant a section of the Amazon jungle into her backyard to fence off the world and any possible onlookers.

In most cases, it's hard to tell who lives where—I received six different stories about the same houses on six different boat tours in South Florida! I was told that the same house belonged to Sonny and Cher and Tom and Nicole. I guess the common theme was nasty divorce or giant women/small men.

Regardless, some of our favorite celebrities still reside in Florida, including Anna Kournikova, Jennifer Lopez, Julio Iglesias, Shakira, Billy Joel, Matt Damon, P. Diddy, and Gloria Estefan. More interestingly, a vast number of D-list celebrities have chosen to either prematurely retire or search for a career change in the Sunshine State. These include Ingrid Cassaras, Hulk Hogan, Jon Secada, and O. J. Simpson. Florida's top D-list celebrities are ranked below.

VANILLA ICE Though a Texas native, this real *Surreal Life* star claimed fame and street cred though a false association with a Miami Lakes high school gang in his riveting biography, *Ice by Ice: The Vanilla Ice Story in His Own Words*. In total D-List fashion, "Ice Ice Baby" sampled the 1982 Queen and David Bowie hit "Under

Pressure" without credit or permission, or providing royalties. Outside of time spent on reality shows and domestic violence disputes, Ice and family now reside in the suburb of Wellington, Florida.

DENNIS RODMAN More famous for his outrageous hair colors and alleged bisexual tendencies than his basketball skills, the 6-foot, 8-inch former Chicago Bulls player frequents Fort Lauderdale's Voodoo Lounge gay/straight mixer on Sundays as a former co-owner of the establishment. With his frequent appearances around town, everyone in Fort Lauderdale (including me) seems to have some outlandish story to tell about Dennis, usually sexual and kinky.

MATTHEW RUSH There was a time when being a Falcon exclusive paid the bills. But apparently the advent of Internet porn fostered thousands of new stars; Matthew has since settled for a life of personal training and frequent club appearances across South Florida.

MISS CLEO A real-life "Oda Mae Brown," Youree Dell Harris, aka "Miss Cleo," settled down in Lake Worth, Florida, following a series of notorious television ads where she sported a faux Jamaican accent and relayed psychic abilities for 99 cents a minute. Since officially coming out in *The Advocate,* Cleo has been active in the Palm Beach gay community, hosting Pridefest of the Palm Beaches in 2008 and often appearing at Open Mic Night at Les Beans café in Lake Worth on Thursday nights.

BROOKE HOGAN Her one-hit-wonder career apparently cost her parent's marriage soon after the Hogans moved to Miami in part to promote Brooke's career. Her debut CD was aptly titled *Undiscovered.*

FLORIDA PARTY ANTHOLOGY— R.I.P. AND NOSTALGIA

It seems that we always long for "the days that were." We made fun of our parents as children when they recounted stories with nostalgic grins, and wondered if we would ever grow up to live in the past. In the competitive world of gay bars, clubs, and nonstop partying, it's simply too easy to become a part of "the past." However, some of these places touched our hearts while the crowds inside touched everything else. The gay bar has long served as the central social institution of gay life. In the gay cemetery below, we pay homage to a few special bars and nightclubs no longer with us, but which still deserve remembrance and posthumous fame.

CEMETERY OF KEY WEST

Beginning in the 1970s, Key West's progressive acceptance of gay life fostered a breeding ground for nonbreeders. A world of constant nudity, bareback sex, and an abundance of cocaine, the liberated gay world lived without limits. Ask any "conch," and they will delight you with outrageous stories from the time before AIDS and life in this pocket of tolerance during a climate of nonacceptance. Gays ruled in the years of the **COPA** (which locals say stood for Cocaine on Premises Always), the **MONSTER**, and the **LIGHTHOUSE COURT**. The spirit that defined gay life in the 1980s continued with the gay **ATLANTIC SHORES RESORT** and their infamous Sunday Tea Dance, until the resort closed in 2007.

CEMETERY OF FORT LAUDERDALE

Nobody in the gay community ever imagined that **CATHODE RAY** would close its doors in 2006, 23 years after planting roots in downtown Fort Lauderdale. Cathode Ray had stood the test of time, re-inventing nightly themes but always remaining true to its neighborhood bar roots despite location on the exclusive Las Olas Boulevard. But the unprecedented South Florida real estate boom and accompanying prices drove Fort Lauderdale's nightclub businesses to a quick bust after reaching its peak in 2006. The double-story decadence of **CHINA WHITE** revolutionized the gay scene of Fort Lauderdale for a hot minute, standing room only on Hump Wednesdays and Fagtabulous Fridays. Scene queens from Miami, Orlando, and even New York would endure lengthy car and plane rides to indulge in the symphony of DJ Chaos and the mayhem of Mizz Corri, or sipping Grey Goose inside the Moulin Rouge–inspired elephant among the fashion and style with a backdrop of eclectic mirrors and chandeliers. For a moment in time, Fort Lauderdale had its own Studio 54. By the end of 2007, the notorious dance hall the **COLISEUM** was the next to go. Still mourning the loss of raunchy Sunday shenanigans at the **SEA MONSTER** (now reopened), it was time for the hard-core party crowd to bid farewell to packed Saturdays at Coli featuring international guest DJs, and for the teenyboppers to lose college night Fridays.

CEMETERY OF MIAMI

There was a time when gays ruled South Beach. That time is over, but the 1990s undoubtedly put Miami Beach on the map as the premiere global gay destination. Night and day, the streets teemed with perfect bodies, scene queens, hipsters, and trannies. The beach on 12th Street showcased a real life wet dream. **THE WARSAW** hosted thousands on a nightly basis, and relentless, unapologetic partygoers carried on to **PUMP** for after hours. Drug-induced Saturday nights transitioned to Sunday mornings at **SALVATION,** followed by the raucous Sunday foam parties at **AMNESIA**. The South Beach club scene lost its luster post-millennium with the close of the Warsaw (now Jerry's Deli) but attempted to retain the glam with **CRO-BAR SUNDAYS** and **BACKDOOR BAMBI MONDAYS**.

CEMETERY OF TAMPA BAY

In 2006 the owners of MCFilmFest in Tampa, power couple Mark and Carrie, began compiling a simple list of the "Bars That Were" in the Tampa Bay Area (MCFILMFEST.COM/BARS_THAT_WERE). By 2008 they had compiled the most comprehensive archive of gay bars and nightclubs in a city to date, detailing over 220 former gay watering holes. Peppered with anecdotal stories and descriptions, readers have contributed to the literary eulogies of some of Tampa Bay's most beloved establishments, including the **PLEASURDOME** (formerly **EL GOYA** in the 1970s and **TRACKS** in the 1980s), which hosted the likes of Grace Jones and Debbie Harry in the early 1990s. The site pays special homage to the **SUNCOAST RESORT,** a former hotbed of hedonism housed in a post Soviet-esque compound. In 2008, the twink dome, **CHAMBERS,** closed its doors following a chicken run.

CEMETERY OF ORLANDO

Sometimes the dead are brought back to life, and sometimes they are buried forever. **SOUTHERN NIGHTS** rose from the dead in 2004, only to die again and be resuscitated in 2008 as Revolution Nightclub. Orlando nightlife suffered grave losses in the summer of 2007 when 30% of the city's nightclubs closed their doors (**LAVA LOUNGE, FACES, FULL MOON SALOON** and **SOUTHERN NIGHTS**). Since then the city has not quite recovered, but **PULSE** and **PARLIAMENT HOUSE** have seen huge upswings in business. The latest to join the Cemetery of Orlando—**MANNEQUIN'S THURSDAYS AT PLEASURE ISLAND**. What began as "cast night" several years ago instantly became an unofficial "gay night" at Pleasure Island's largest and most contemporary dance club. Partying the night away on the revolving dance floor to pop tunes with Goofy, Tiger, and Donald Duck (out of costume) at Disney-regulated decibels was not enough to prevent Disney from bulldozing PI in September 2008 for more family-oriented shops and restaurants.

FEEDING FLORIDA'S STEREOTYPE: BEAUTY AND THE BEACH

Even as the tacky usurp the stylish and society strives to be less image conscious, visitors still expect Florida to be a North American Ipanema. Rock-hard abs, bulging pecs (or insanely perky breasts), and sun-kissed skin, all eyes remain wide open in search of Florida's

GONE BUT NOT FORGOTTEN, DISNEY'S PLEASURE ISLAND

hottest hotties. Homoerotic Abercrombie catalogs come to life as the living divinity travel in packs and make frequent appearances at the following events and establishments:

- **AQUA GIRL,** Miami (Event in May)

- **ARABIAN NIGHTS II** (Saturday night) during Gay Disney weekend

- **BEACH BALL** (Typhoon Lagoon) in Orlando during Gay Disney weekend

- **BEACH ON 12TH AND COLLINS,** South Beach

- **FORT LAUDERDALE BEACH** during Spring Break

- **G. BAR** in Tampa on Saturday nights

- **INTERNATIONAL SWIMMING HALL OF FAME,** Fort Lauderdale

- **LINCOLN ROAD,** South Beach

- **MUSCLE BEACH PARTY** during White Party

- **PENSACOLA,** Memorial Day Weekend

BASIC FLORIDA INFO

3

WHEN TO COME

Florida is a popular destination year-round. However, a distinct rainy season in South Florida from late May to late October tends to keep away the masses. South Florida "high season" runs from mid-December to mid-April, peaking in February and March. This is when snowbirds flock down, the beaches are packed, the hotels full, and restaurant waits run over one hour. It's also the most pleasant time of year—often crisp enough for "good hair" days but warm enough for beach tanning. Hurricane season (June 1–November 30) coincides with "low season." During this time, hotels offer fantastic specials, restaurants participate in dining events to entice business, and locals tend to venture out more, embracing the humidity and afternoon showers. This is also when most Europeans mistakenly come to Florida, without realizing that their summer is our rainy season. Outside of the main hurricane path, Orlando and Tampa swell with visitors in summer when kids are out of school and hankering for some diversion.

WHAT TO BRING

Depending on the time of year you choose to visit, your packing list will change slightly with the addition of a light jacket or two (between December and March) or an umbrella-ella-ella (May to November). Average lows during winter in Central Florida run roughly 54 degrees in the evening (approximately 62 degrees F in South Florida). But remember, the same season will often boast a daytime temperature well into the 70s F.

Beach gear, skimpy Speedos and two-pieces, suntan lotion, sunglasses, condoms, flip-flops, jeans, T-shirts, and sleeveless shirts are Florida essentials. Given Florida's relaxed atmosphere, jeans and polos are dressy enough for most upscale restaurants. Trendier places on South Beach warrant more Euro sophistication and less Abercrombie & Fitch.

Variable weather is a way of life in the subtropics, so a glance at the forecast on weather.com is definitely in order. You may be arriving during one of the two annual cold spells or during an erratic storm pattern.

GETTING HERE AND GETTING AROUND

AIR

The most economical and most popular flights to Florida enter through the airports of Miami International (MIA), Fort Lauderdale/Hollywood International (FLL), Orlando International (MCO), and Tampa International (TPA). Orlando Sanford International (SFB), West Palm Beach (PBI), Key West (EYW), and St. Petersburg (PIE) also serve regions covered in this guide. For international travelers, long lines at immigration in Miami can be a frustrating start to your holiday but a decent conversation piece, since foreign travelers love to critique American immigration policy. With American Airline's hub in Miami, Spirit's in Fort Lauderdale, and Air-Tran's in Orlando, flights between Florida and other parts of the United States and Central America are still reasonably priced even with astronomical fuel prices ($200 round-trip to New York, DC, San Francisco, or San Jose, Costa Rica). Take warning, however. Flights on Spirit Airlines from their Fort Lauderdale hub sport the longest and slowest lines in perhaps the entire industry, so prepare to arrive exceptionally early if flying between the hours of 11:00 AM and 1:00 PM to avoid missing your flight. Cape Air, Yellow Air Taxi, and Gulfstream Air all provide regular flights between Key West and Fort Myers, Naples, and Miami/Fort Lauderdale, for a nominal fee.

FROM THE AIRPORT

The three most practical ways to get to your destination from Florida's airports are via rental car, taxi, or shuttle. The majority of visitors will pick up their rental car after baggage claim and head to their respective destinations. Given the shortage of taxis across Florida and the prices they dictate, rides to destinations far from the airport become excessive. The 20-minute taxi ride from MIA to South Beach runs approximately $35. If you already have hotel reservations, check with your hotel to see if they provide a complimentary shuttle to and from the hotel. Those flying into Miami and Tampa Bay also have the option of the SuperShuttle (SUPERSHUTTLE.COM), available curbside near baggage claim. SuperShuttle is a cheaper option for long distances if you're not renting a car, or when traveling alone. Tri-Rail (South Florida's unfortunate rail system (TRI-RAIL.COM)) is a final option for the brave and patient (not recommended). Destination points are ill-placed and will usually require a farther taxi ride after disembarking.

YOUR OWN CAR

With the rising cost of fuel, it is highly unlikely you will be entering Florida on a good old-fashioned road trip. Driving the extreme length of Florida from Pensacola to the Keys requires a solid 13 hours over 500 miles, the same amount of time and distance to reach Chicago from Pensacola! Luckily the distances between the major cities of Central and South Florida are more reasonable, and in a matter of 3.5 hours you can exchange the Atlantic beaches of South Florida for the beauty of the Gulf of Mexico in St. Petersburg. Note that almost all major roadways in Florida will be chock full of tolls (the turnpike trip from Miami to Orlando will cost you $15). It is recommended for trips greater than a weekend that you invest in a Sunpass toll gizmo (which can be purchased for $25 at any grocery store or drugstore like CVS or Walgreens) and top it up before your trip. This will save you 25% on tolls and scrounging for change under the car seat while allowing you to drive right through the Sunpass/E-Z Pass lanes.

PUBLIC TRANSPORTATION

As a rule of thumb, do not rely on public transportation throughout Florida. This is for travel between cities and also intra-city. Personally, I am a huge fan of public transportation. But even the most well-developed public transportation infrastructures in Florida are erratic, sporadic, noncomprehensive, and scarier than the Orange Line on the "T" in Boston. Short distances across Miami Beach are feasible but require patience (MIAMIDADE.GOV/TRANSIT/MIAMI BCH.ASP).

RENTAL CAR OR NOT?

Unless friends are escorting you around, renting a car is a must in Fort Lauderdale, the Palm Beaches, Tampa Bay, and Orlando. Time spent in South Beach and Key West does not require a rental car, especially in South Beach where a car is more of a hindrance and a ghastly daily parking expense (around $30/day). If you plan on visiting more than one city in Florida (as I suggest you do), then ditch the rental car for your days in South Beach and Key West and enjoy the sights, sounds, and tastes by foot. The perimeters of other major downtowns are pedestrian friendly, but do not necessarily house all the tourist attractions and sights on your list.

UNDERSTANDING YOUR SECTIONS

LODGING

With more than 370,000 hotel rooms across the state, Florida caters to all types of travelers. All hotels listed under their respective cities are considered at a minimum gay friendly and TAG approved. Where lodging is divided between LGBT and Mainstream, the distinction is made between exclusively gay hotels and others. I personally visited all hotels listed in the book—a duty that required sacrificing over 150+ nights of check-in and checkout. I tried to include a variety of lodging types—from gay guesthouses to traditional B and B's to reward-point powerhouses for the corporate gay. Each has its own advantage. Gay guesthouses are an unparalleled investment in social capital. Traditional B and B's make you feel at home. Corporate standards never fail to impress. The final lists included are intentionally selective.

TO DO AND SEE

This section highlights the most appealing sights for the LGBT traveler both on and off the beaten path. I have taken the life-changing experiences from this section and placed them at the end of this chapter under "Forgotten Florida: Treasures Off the Beaten Path."

DINING

Sampling a sufficient quantity of ethnic and American eateries while maintaining a 31-inch waist spelled long hours of cardio and grapefruit lunches. Though I had developed a number of personal favorites over the years, I wanted to include flavors to please all palates. I began with shameless solicitation of recommendations from locals, colleagues, friends, and family, supplemented by long hours with Zagat and sifting through local reviews. Over the course of my research I posited questions to thousands of individuals through interviews, dialogue, and online—requesting details of

FIGURES AND FACTS

NICKNAME: The Sunshine State
STATE ANIMAL: Florida panther
STATE FRUIT: Orange
STATE PIE: Key lime pie
STATE GEM: Moonstone
MILES OF SAND BEACHES: 1,200
MILES OF COASTLINE: 1,800
FLORIDA POPULATION (2007): 18,251,243 (4th in U.S.)
NUMBER OF VISITORS ANNUALLY (2007): 84.5 million
ECONOMIC IMPACT OF TOURISM (2007): $65.5 billion
TOP ORIGIN STATE: NY (11.6% of domestic visitors)
LEISURE-BASED TRAVEL: 81.5%
TOP INTERNATIONAL MARKETS: Canada and UK

a "last supper" or a meal that outshines any sexual experience. I paid close attention to body language and passionate descriptions, knowing I hit the jackpot when I saw people break a near sweat describing a meal, mouth wide open, eyes rolled back, foaming and salivating in tandem—in the process of a true food orgasm. On this lead, I personally verified the flavor exorcisms to create an intentionally nonexhaustive list that cherry picks the best of the best. In most instances I avoided putting in chain restaurants or places where I recognized preservative-laden Sysco products. Nevertheless, in Orlando I featured some of the best restaurant imperialists and still recommend a gluttonous trip to the Cheesecake Factory (CHEESECAKEFACTORY.COM), especially for Europeans arriving in America for the first time.

NIGHTLIFE

From a quick glance at my official "coming out" guide, Spartacus 2000–2001, I notice over 90% of the listings under bars and dance clubs in Florida cease to exist. Even in the months of writing and editing this guide, two dozen nightclubs came and went across the state! A scary thought, especially for somebody writing a gay guide that includes numerous such listings! For the nightlife section, therefore, I tried to focus mostly on what I call gay anchors, establishments very likely to remain for years, and the most fabulous nights in town. In some instances, I have also included some suggestions for alternative nightlife, away from the bar and club scene. As a general rule, Sundays and Fridays are the biggest party nights in South Florida, followed by Thursdays and Saturdays.

In the nightlife maps at the end of the book, I still provided the addresses of bars and clubs beyond those described in detail to give readers more options and to get a better sense of the widespread nightlife scene. Since new clubs often replace old ones in the locations of former establishments, this tool should be useful. Given the nature of the nightclub industry, I suggest scene queens check out the latest information from Florida's nightlife authorities, the *411 Magazine* (THE411MAG.COM) and JUMPONMARKSLIST.COM (both free). These two resources will tell you what's new and hot in Florida's scene, serving as the perfect complement to this guidebook.

A WORD ON PRICES

Since lodging prices tend to change often (and in the case of lodging can vary greatly at the same property depending on how you book), I've chosen to simply put each listing in a basic cost category: Inexpensive (below $125 per night), Moderate ($125–$250), Expensive ($250–$350), and Very Expensive (>$350). Moreover, I have avoided putting cost categories for dining since I was effectively able to find cheap dishes at the poshest restaurants and expensive dishes at supposed cheap eats!

FLORIDA'S CITIES IN A NUTSHELL

MIAMI: Hetero hot, trendy, international
FORT LAUDERDALE: Homolicious, self-indulgent, waterbound
PALM BEACHES: Powerful, formal, botoxed
KEY WEST: Relaxing, serene, welcoming
ST. PETERSBURG: Cultural, charming, surprising
TAMPA: Young, urban, growing
ORLANDO: Consumerist, brat laden, globally appealing

LGBT EVENTS BIG AND SMALL

These events are described in more detail in their appropriate chapters. Note that registering for event updates from the specific event promoters (via event Web sites) makes you privy to early invitation emails translating into deep discounts for different events. For example, the fall before Gay Days, eight months prior, tickets go on sale for one week at a discount of roughly 40%. Likewise, White Party in Miami offers a virtual 2-for-1 for the first 100 tickets sold to Florida residents (giving tickets to both the Vizcaya Party and Muscle Beach for the price of one ticket). Discounts vary by year and reward advanced purchase.

BIG (INTERNATIONAL AND NATIONAL APPEAL)

FEB–MAR	Winter Party (WINTERPARTY.ORG)	*Miami*
APRIL	Stampede Rodeo (FGRA.ORG)	*Fort Lauderdale*
MAY	Aqua Girl (AQUAGIRL.ORG)	*Miami*
MAY	Pensacola (MEMORIALWEEKENDPENSACOLA.COM)	*Pensacola*
JUNE	Gay Days (GAYDAYS.COM) One Mighty Weekend (ONEMIGHTYWEEKEND.COM) Girls at Gay Days (GIRLSATGAYDAYS.COM) Girls in Wonderland (GIRLSINWONDERLAND.COM)	*Orlando*
JUNE	St. Petersburg Pride (STPETEPRIDE.COM)	*St. Petersburg*

SEPT	Womenfest (WOMENFEST.COM) *Key West*
OCTOBER	Fantasyfest (FANTASYFEST.NET) *Key West*
OCTOBER	Tampa International Gay & Lesbian Film Festival (TIGLFF.COM) *Tampa*
NOVEMBER	White Party (WHITEPARTY.ORG) *Miami*

SMALL (LOCAL APPEAL)

MARCH	Pridefest (PRIDESOUTHFLORIDA.ORG) *Fort Lauderdale*
MARCH	Pride of the Palm Beaches (COMPASSGLCC.COM) *Palm Beach*
APRIL–MAY	Miami Gay and Lesbian Film Festival (MGLFF.COM), followed by Fort Lauderdale Counterpart (MGLFF.COM/FLGLFF.COM)
MAY	Sizzle (SIZZLEMIAMI.COM) *Miami*
JUNE	The Stonewall Street Festival (STONEWALLSTREETFESTIVAL.COM) *Fort Lauderdale*
OCTOBER	Orlando Gay Pride (COMEOUTWITHPRIDE.ORG) *Orlando*
OCTOBER	Wicked Manors (WICKEDMANORS.COM), Halloween *Fort Lauderdale*
OCTOBER	Gay Days Tampa Bay (GAYDAYSTAMPABAY.COM) *Tampa*

OTHER GAY POPULAR EVENTS

| JANUARY | Gasparilla (GASPARILLAPIRATEFEST.COM) *Tampa* |
| FEBRUARY | Palm Beach Jewelry, Art and Antique Show (PALMBEACHSHOW.COM) *Palm Beach* |

MARCH	Calle 8 (CALLE8.COM) *Miami*
MARCH	Winter Music Conference (WINTERMUSICCONFERENCE.COM) *Miami*
OCTOBER	Boat Show (SHOWMANAGEMENT.COM) *Fort Lauderdale*
OCTOBER	Halloween Horror Nights (HALLOWEENHORRORNIGHTS.COM) *Orlando*
DECEMBER	Art Basel (ARTBASEL.COM) *Miami*
DECEMBER	Boat Parade (WINTERFESTPARADE.COM) *Fort Lauderdale*
DECEMBER	New Years Shoe Drop (GAYKEYWESTFL.COM) *Key West*

AIDS WALKS AND EVENTS

APRIL	AIDS Walk Fort Lauderdale (FLORIDAAIDSWALK.ORG)
APRIL	AIDS Walk Miami (AIDSWALKMIAMI.COM)
APRIL	AIDS Walk Orlando (AIDSWALKORLANDO.ORG)
SEPTEMBER	AIDS Walk St. Petersburg (AIDSWALKSTPETE.ORG)

In addition, around late April hundreds of restaurants participate in Dining Out For Life (DININGOUTFORLIFE.COM) across South Florida and the Tampa Bay Area. Participants give 25% of the total register tally as a charitable donation to AIDS service organizations. Key West also hosts "A Taste of Key West" on the Truman Waterfront in April, uniting 50 fine restaurants in an exchange of food and wines samples for charitable donations to benefit AIDS Help Inc.

FOOD EVENTS

One of the best parts of peak rainy season and the tourist low season is the opportunity to eat well in myriad restaurants, sometimes unattainable to the average Joe Six-Pack. During August and September, for example, Miami's top restaurants offer three-course meals (lunch $23, dinner $36) featuring signature dishes created by world-renowned chefs.

Similarly, from October 1 through November 14, Fort Lauderdale's top restaurants and chefs offer specially created, three-course menus at a $35 fixed price.

DINE OUT LAUDERDALE
SUNNY.ORG/STATIC/INDEX.CFM?CONTENTID=507
MIAMI SPICE
ILOVEMIAMISPICE.COM
SOUTH BEACH WINE & FOOD FESTIVAL
SOBEWINEANDFOODFEST.COM
LAS OLAS WINE AND FOOD FESTIVAL
LASOLASWINEANDFOOD.COM

GAY PUBLICATIONS AND WEB SITES

These are your one-stop scene queen and nightlife shops! Be wary of glossy ads. Trust my advice in the respective nightlife sections or local word of mouth.

SCENE MAGAZINES

THE 411 MAGAZINE Central Florida edition (THE411 MAG.COM)
GIR(L) (GIRL-MAGAZINE.COM)

THE 411 MAGAZINE South Florida edition
(THE411MAG.COM)
LATINO BOYS MAGAZINE (LATINOBOYSMAGAZINE.COM)
SHE, THE SOURCE FOR WOMEN (SHEMAG.COM)
HOTSPOTS (HOTSPOTSMAGAZINE.COM)
THE GAY RAG KEY WEST (KEYWESTGAYRAG.COM)

411 and *Hotspots* are printed weekly and distributed on Thursdays.

IMPORTANT WEB SITES

FLORIDA VISITFLORIDA.COM
FLORIDA'S LESBIAN SCENE PANDORAEVENTS.COM
FLORIDA'S NIGHTLIFE JUMPONMARKSLIST.COM features the latest and greatest information on nightlife venues and the South and Central Florida social scenes; updated daily.
FORT LAUDERDALE GAYFORTLAUDERDALE.COM; SUNNY.ORG
KEYS GAYKEYWESTFL.COM; FLA-KEYS.COM
MIAMI MIAMIANDBEACHES.COM; GOGAYMIAMI.COM; SOBEGAYINFO.COM; SOBESOCIALCLUB.COM
ORLANDO ORLANDOINFO.COM; GAYORLANDO.COM
PALM BEACH PALMBEACHES.COM; GAYPALMBEACHES.COM
TAMPA VISITTAMPABAY.COM; GAYTAMPA.COM; MYSPACE.COM/GAYBOR
ST. PETERSBURG FLORIDASBEACH.COM; STPETE.ORG

GAY PAPERS

CENTRAL FLORIDA *Watermark* (WATERMARKONLINE.COM); *Gazette Tampa Bay* (GAZETTETAMPABAY.COM)
KEY WEST *Conch Colors* (CONCHCOLOR.COM)

MIAMI *The Wire*
SOUTH FLORIDA *The South Florida Blade* (SOUTHFLORIDABLADE.COM)
TREASURE AND SPACE COAST *Out on the Coast* (OOTCMAG.COM)

RELIGIOUS ORGANIZATIONS

Numerous temples and churches throughout Florida are welcoming of gays and gay couples without specifically catering to the LGBT community. However, the religious organizations listed below openly welcome the LGBT community and provide sanctuaries of worship.

METROPOLITAN COMMUNITY CHURCHES provide an open and inclusive place of Christian worship for gays, lesbians, bisexual, and transgender people. As worship times vary by location and season, please call ahead.

FORT LAUDERDALE Sunshine Cathedral MCC, 1480 S.W. 9th Avenue, (954) 462-2004, SUNSHINECATHEDRAL.ORG

KEY WEST MCC Key West, 1215 Petronia Street (1 block northeast of White Street), (305) 294-8912, MCCKEYWEST.COM

MIAMI BEACH Circle of Light MCC Miami Beach, Meeting location: 2100 Washington Avenue, (305) 535-2287

ORLANDO Joy MCC, 2351 S. Ferncreek Avenue, (407) 894-1081, JOYMCC.COM

ST. PETERSBURG King of Peace MCC, 3150 5th Avenue N., (727) 323-5857, KINGOFPEACEMCC.COM

TAMPA MCC of Tampa, 408 E. Cayuga Street, (813) 239-1951, MCCTAMPA.COM

WEST PALM BEACH MCC of the Palm Beaches,
4857 Northlake Boulevard, (561) 775-5900,
MCCPALMBEACH.ORG

UNITARIAN UNIVERSALISM churches (UU churches) can be found throughout Florida. Consult UUA.ORG for congregation information to experience "a caring, open–minded religious community that encourages you to seek your own spiritual path that ordains openly bisexual, gay, lesbian, and transgender people."

JEWISH CONGREGATIONS listed on LGBTJEWS.ORG provide a place of worship for the LGBT Jewish community. In South Florida, Congregation Etz Chaim fulfills a mission to "provide a nurturing environment for gay and lesbian Jews, inclusive of bisexual, transgender, and heterosexuals." (954) 564-9232, 1881 N.E. 26th Street, ETZCHAIMFL.ORG

GYMS

Keeping the body beautiful is a must for avid gym rats. The following establishments across Florida offer memberships or day passes.

BALLY TOTAL FITNESS 951–965 E. Commercial Boulevard,
Fort Lauderdale, (954) 491-9196, BALLYFITNESS.COM

CRUNCH 1676 Alton Road, Miami Beach, (305) 531-4743,
259 Washington Avenue, Miami Beach, (305) 674-8222,
CRUNCH.COM

EQUINOX 520 Collins Avenue, Miami Beach (305) 673-1172,
EQUINOXFITNESS.COM

THE FIRM 928 N. Federal Highway, Fort Lauderdale, (954)
767-6277, FIRMFITNESSCENTER.COM

FORT LAUDERDALE L.A. FITNESS 3825 N. Federal Highway,
Oakland Park, (954) 567-2727, LAFITNESS.COM

THE ISLAND HOUSE FOR MEN 1129 Fleming Street, Key West, (800) 890-6284, ISLANDHOUSEKEYWEST.COM

MIAMI DAVID BARTON GYM 2377 Collins Avenue, Miami Beach, (305) 604-1000, DAVIDBARTONGYM.COM

ORLANDO BALLY TOTAL FITNESS 6385 W. Colonial Drive, Orlando, (407) 296-4231, BALLYFITNESS.COM

PALM BEACHES BALLY TOTAL FITNESS 501 Village Boulevard, West Palm Beach, (561) 683-5800, BALLYFITNESS.COM

PROPER FORM: PERSONAL FITNESS TRAINING 1935 West Avenue, Suite 298, (305) 531-8818, PROPERFORM.COM

TAMPA BAY LIFESTYLES FAMILY FITNESS 1510 W. Swann Avenue, Tampa, (813) 258-0500, LFF.COM

X-TREME FITNESS 936 S. Howard Avenue, Tampa, (813) 258-2639, XTREMEFIT.ORG

PAMPERING: FLORIDA'S TOP SPAS

Let's face it: Going to the spa is not cheap. But the potential release of compacted stress sometimes is the only thing that saves us from internal combustion. And even more so, we all love to be pampered. Rain or shine, a trip to the spa is always rewarding.

Living in developing nations for extended periods of time, I have been undoubtedly spoiled for years with insanely cheap spa treatments. As economics dictates the price of goods and services in different corners of the world, a typical 60-minute massage in Malaysia, for example, runs around $12. (Even more interesting is the fact that the massage industry is dominated by blind men and women who are trained through cooperatives to work through the sense of touch.) A hundred massages later, I am a harsh and parsimonious critic who succumbs to Western prices for only the best services (as listed below). These spas are the *crème de la crème* of Florida's oversaturated spa industry.

MIAMI: THE STANDARD SPA The Standard Spa recognizes that your body is a shrine and should be treated accordingly. In a hypermodern setting of body, soul, and Miami Beach, the Standard promotes holistic indulgence and encourages communal, shared rituals of traditional bathhouses with an outdoor hydrotherapy playground. The creative spa menu focuses on interdisciplinary treatments that customize traditional and innovative techniques to your body's needs. 40 Island Avenue, Miami Beach, (305) 673-1717, STANDARDHOTELS.COM/MIAMI/SPA-WELLBEING

MIAMI: THE RITZ-CARLTON SPA The Ritz-Carlton Spa, South Beach showcases an elite menu of La Maison de Beauté Carita treatments as well as the novel Astro Balance massage, a unique 80-minute massage treatment based on your birth date and astrological sign and element. The Spa recently added an entire section dedicated to men, which features a Juniper Muscle Soothing Treatment, A Beach Body massage, Gentleman's Refiner Facial, and Back Facial. The Ritz-Carlton, South Beach, One Lincoln Road, Miami Beach, (786) 276-4000, RITZCARLTON.COM

FORT LAUDERDALE: THE GRAND SPA The Grand Spa was aptly ranked one of the top 10s *in the country* in the spring 2008 issue of *Out Traveler*. Small and intimate, tucked into the back of a gay guesthouse, the Grand offers traditional spa services and more innovative ones such as Jack Black body wraps and some of the most indulgent massages ever. Masseuses exhibit firm and utter command of their extreme strength. Professional and personable staff caters to personalized needs. 539 N. Birch Road, Fort Lauderdale, (954) 630-3000, GRANDRESORT.NET/SPASERVICE

FORT LAUDERDALE: DESSANGE PARIS Dessange Paris presents the complete array of deluxe spa services that made the brand famous among French bourgeoisie in the last decade. Their signature facial, Les Soins Precieux combines the use of precious metals, minerals, oils, and clays based on skin type, to strengthen and protect the skin. My sister always raves about the Detox Facial and claims it is her secret to still looking 25 at age 34 (and after two kids)! 1845 Cordova Road, Fort Lauderdale, (954) 524-9424, DESSANGEFORTLAUDERDALE.COM

PALM BEACHES: ANUSHKA DAY SPA A top spa in the Palm Beaches has to work extra hard. Intense competition and high expectations mandate a level of excellency on par with Beverly Hills. Anushka Day Spa outperforms upscale counterparts with first-rate services and medical treatments completed by true industry professionals. The 12,000-square foot pampering palladium houses an endless realm of self-indulgence. A facial by the Croatian goddess Katia is a must and a quick chat with the world famous Anushka herself is an added bonus! City Place, 701 S. Romemary Avenue, Suite 200, West Palm Beach, (561) 820-0500 ANUSHKASPA.COM

KEY WEST: PRANA SPA Has your shrink ever made you feel uncomfortable by glancing at the clock while you bawl your eyes out? Have you ever experienced a spa treatment where the specialist longed for the treatment to finish before you started? At Prana Spa you are the center of attention, not the clock. A one-hour massage lasts a full hour, not 50 minutes, as in other spas. There is no rush, with 30 minutes between appointment times. Staff are genuinely interested in customer satisfaction and commitment to quality, void of useless time-fillers like questionnaires. Jon Harper at gay-owned and operated Prana Spa promises "sacred tropical tranquility for mind, body, and soul," and delivers. A true gem. 625 Whitehead Street, Key West, (305) 295-0100, PRANASPAKEYWEST.COM

ORLANDO: RITZ-CARLTON SPA, ORLANDO, GRANDE LAKES The 40,000-square-foot Ritz-Carlton (Mega) Spa, Orlando, Grande Lakes features the talents of 75 different massage therapists (including out hunk Paul Anderson from television's *The Janice Dickinson Modeling Agency*). The Spa takes great pride in catering to the LGBT community. 4012 Central Florida Parkway, Orlando, (407) 393-4200, RITZCARLTON.COM

FLORIDA'S BEST MAINSTREAM SHOPPING

It's every traveler's worse nightmare—arriving in the Sunshine State to thunderstorms and torrential downpours. It's the tropics, so it's bound to happen to some. Fret not; these days are prime opportunities for retail therapy.

SOUTH FLORIDA

AVENTURA MALL The flagship triple-story mall of South Florida houses many global top performers such as the most lucrative Abercrombie in the United States, a massive Crate & Barrel, the latest and greatest Nordstroms, and 248 other shops that help create the fifth largest mall in the United States. 19501 Biscayne Boulevard, Aventura, (305) 935-1110, AVENTURAMALL.COM

GALLERIA MALL Reworked and remixed with marble floors and fine dining options, Galleria now has more to offer than its anchor department stores such as Macys and Dillards. It is conveniently located near Fort Lauderdale beach and accessible by water taxi. 2414 E. Sunrise Boulevard, Fort Lauderdale, (954) 564-1015, GALLERIAMALL-FL.COM

IKEA The long-awaited Swedish furniture powerhouse made its debut in South Florida in 2007 to long lines for affordable home furnishings and good old Swedish (meat)balls. The buzz hasn't died since. 151 N.W. 136th Avenue, Sunrise, (954) 838-9292, IKEA.COM

SAWGRASS MILLS OUTLET MALL Sawgrass claims to be the second most-touristed attraction in Florida after Disney World. Once the largest outlet mall in the world in the shape of an alligator, the 2-mile outlet stretch of 300 retail shops boasts a reputation that reaches the far ends of Latin America and Europe. For locals it's mostly a headache or a guaranteed anxiety attack. 12801 W. Sunrise Boulevard, Sunrise, (954) 846-2350, SAWGRASSMILLS.COM

CENTRAL FLORIDA

THE MALL AT MILLENIA, ORLANDO AND INTERNATIONAL PLAZA, TAMPA Two of the hottest and freshest malls in America, Millenia and Plaza are both contemporary two-level upscale shopping malls, with all your corporate favorites and big department stores. Millenia wows with grandiose high ceilings and state-of-the-art screens and projectors, and an IKEA adjacent. Plaza boasts the adjoining Bay Street outdoor mall section with fabulous restaurants and more upscale shopping. 4200 Conroy Road, Orlando, (407) 363-3555, MALLATMILLENIA.COM, 2223 N. West Shore Boulevard, Tampa, (813) 342-3790, SHOPINTERNATIONALPLAZA.COM

PRIME OUTLETS MALL, ORLANDO Finally, an outlet mall that has clothes from recent seasons and in sizes other than XXL! Prime Outlets offers top stores such as Armani, Diesel, Coach, and Armani Exchange in a fashionable outdoor setting. 4953 International Drive, Orlando, (407) 354-9881, PRIMEOUTLETS.COM

FLORIDA'S BEACHES

Florida's palm-fringed, sun-drenched beaches are a huge draw for the LGBT community. Collecting documents old and new over the past 10 years, I set out to confirm or deny listings of numerous gay and gay-friendly beaches scattered throughout the peninsula. I combed the beaches, climbed mosquito-infested sand dunes, and even followed sounds of rustling bushes—only to find mating birds, a few teens getting it on, and a few topless Europeans. While Florida surprisingly only boasts four major gay beaches, a number of other deep blues on and off the beaten path lure curious visitors; beaches that have been consistently ranked in the top 10 of "America's top beaches" by Dr. Beach and the Travel Channel. Indeed, most of Florida's beaches are unique, pristine, and paradisiacal. The Atlantic's waters are bluer and calmer. The Gulf Coast boasts some of the world's finest sand. Barrier islands on the west coast and keys off the south provide seclusion and mental isolation.

LGBT BEACHES

- **12TH STREET** South Beach, Miami
- **HALOUVER BEACH** North Miami
- **SEBASTIAN BEACH** Fort Lauderdale
- **SUNSET BEACH** St. Petersburg

BEACHES TO VISIT FOR BEAUTY

- **CALADESI ISLAND STATE PARK** Dunedin/Clearwater
- **CAPE FLORIDA STATE PARK** Key Biscayne
- **DRY TORTUGAS NATIONAL PARK** Key West
- **CAYO COSTA** Fort Meyers
- **FORT DESOTO PARK** St. Petersburg
- **SANDSPUR BEACH** Bahia Honda Key
- **SIESTA BEACH** Sarasota

FORGOTTEN FLORIDA: TREASURES OFF THE BEATEN PATH

Digital photography and Photoshop have revolutionized the travel industry. Tree tops are greener; skies and oceans bluer. It seems that every day the divide between appearance and reality grows larger. The ubiquitous use of Getty images and image alteration by savvy Web designers has catalyzed a competition among businesses to offer glossy and flossy Web sites to lure the unbeknownst traveler to destinations unknown.

Discovering raw beauty may grow increasingly difficult, but the state of Florida flaunts a natural splendor that needs no visual enhancement. Indeed, the Florida that I know and love is far beyond the world of amusement parks and chain restaurants. I encourage those who love to live and feel to become inspired through this section and to discover or rediscover a land of inspiration and mystique. These are eight forgotten treasures to uncover in your lifetime.

DRY TORTUGAS NATIONAL PARK North America's most inaccessible and least-visited national park, 68 nautical miles due west of Key West, began as a 30-year construction project called Fort Jefferson. Construction commenced in 1846 to control navigation and trade but was never completed. Smack in the middle of nowhere, the fort served as a military prison during the Civil War, even housing Dr. Samuel Mudd, notorious for his assassination plot of Abraham Lincoln. After the army abandoned the fort in 1874, it progressed from a wildlife refuge to a national monument to a national park.

Dry Tortugas National Park is comprised of seven small islands, a remote and removed sanctuary for magnificent frigate birds and vast marine life, a living piece of American history, and a pocket of utter seclusion and isolation. The turquoise and lucid waters flow in synchronicity over the downy sands. All coral types can be found around the west moat wall, and the pilings near the entrance of the fort offer supreme snorkeling (complete with sea turtles and sea horses) for advanced water enthusiasts.

Day trips and overnight trips are both available, but arrival is possible only by seaplane or by boat, and overnight excursions require your own equipment and advance reservations with the park service. Though not cheap, a seaplane to the Dry Tortugas is a once in a lifetime experience, gliding at 500 feet across a vast expanse of lapus lazuli and rainbows of blue, first over shallow flats followed by underwater dessert with rolling sand dunes, spotting sea turtles, ship wrecks, and often schools of sharks along the way. A cheaper and less recommended alternative is the daily Yankee Freedom ferry or a private boat. For those who choose to camp overnight, prepare yourself for the ultimate star gazing experience and the beautiful sounds of nesting sooty terns on adjacent Bush Key come 5 AM. All visitors should arrive with adequate supplies and take note that the island lacks any running water, hence the description "dry." With limited shade and ultra-intense heat, heavy duty sunscreen, bottled water, snacks, and towels are a necessity.

TO MAKE THIS A REALITY:

Dry Tortugas National Park, Key West, (305) 242-7700, NPS.GOV/DRTP

Seaplanes of Key West: Departure at 10 AM, return 2 PM. Check-in 9:30 at the Island City Flying Service, to the left of the Key West International Airport. 3471 S. Roosevelt Boulevard, Key West, (305) 294-0709, SEAPLANESOFKEYWEST.COM

Dry Tortugas National Park Ferry: If you have already done a few boat trips, the 2.5 hour journey each way can be a bit long! 240 Margaret Street, Key West, (305) 294-7009, YANKEEFREEDOM.COM

AN AERIAL VIEW OF DRY TORTUGAS NATIONAL PARK

FALL IN LOVE WITH THE MANATEES According to the National Wildlife Refuge Service, every winter the pristine rivers of Citrus County, Florida are home to approximately 400 endangered West Indian manatees. Evolutionary biology suggests these gentle giants evolved from four-legged land mammals over 60 million years ago, with the closest living relatives being *Proboscidea* (elephants). Often referred to as sea cows, manatees grow to an average length of 10 feet and an average weight of 1,000 pounds. An adult manatee consumes approximately 9% of its body weight per day (and remember, what goes in, must come out!).

Between November and March, large congregations of these colossal beasts of docility and magnificence patiently glide through the serene waters of the Crystal, Homosassa, and Chassawohitzka rivers north of Tampa. Outfitters have established small excursions to the Crystal River Wildlife Refuge to experience the splendor and grace of the manatee, alongside and amongst the creatures themselves. During the winter months, around the two main springs, Three Sisters and King Spring, a hundred manatees may be spotted at once. Entering the world of the manatee is an animal lover's dream come to life. They are sweet and gregarious, curious and humble. They will actively approach you for contact and channel some spiritual energy your way.

The experience of swimming with the manatees provides an unparalleled bonding experience with nature. Crystal River is the only place in the world that it is legal to swim with the endangered manatee. The growing popularity of this activity, however, has attracted the presence of more and more tour companies. It's still far from the mainstream tour-packaged whale-watching trips of Maui, but it's only a matter of time.

An hour north of Orlando, Blue Spring State Park also offers the chance to witness manatees frolicking in the warm waters of the St. John's River. Manatees congregate here during the winter months, but sightings are not guaranteed. Colder winters draw more manatees to the area. Park rangers venture to the river at sunrise to count the number of individuals and to advise tourists whether or not to make the ride from Orlando. However, park visitors may not enter the water with manatees present. Call ahead to avoid disappointment. (386) 775-3663

TO MAKE THIS A REALITY:

Crystal Lodge Dive Center: 525 N.W. 7th Avenue, (352) 795-6798, MANATEE-CENTRAL.COM

Native Vacations, Inc: 547F W. Fort Island Trail, (866) 466-2848, NATIVEVACATIONS.COM

Aardvark Kayak Company: a hands-*off* approach, you will kayak with the manatees. 640 N. Citrus Avenue, Crystal River (352) 795-5650, FLORIDAKAYAKCOMPANY.COM

THREE FRIENDLY MANATEES

LITTLE PALM ISLAND A piece of heaven awaits visitors at mile marker 29.5 off Little Torch Key. The 15-minute journey to Little Palm Island transplants passengers to a foreign world of isolation and beauty on par with Bora Bora and Micronesian gems. An exclusive island oasis of palms, orchids, thatched roofs, and Key deer, this luxurious and private resort commands a minimum of $1,000 per night, but a visit to the island for a celebratory lunch or dinner is within the reach of all budgets.

The journey to Little Palm Island begins with a glass of welcome champagne and a scenic boat ride on a Jackie O–style luxury boat. Greeted at the boat ramp, you are escorted to the Dining Room or your secluded oceanfront bungalow. Key deer take refuge in the lush vegetation of the island. Baby hammerheads glide across the sand bars. The palms sway with the zephyrs. In a few short minutes, you have reached an arena of total escapism, void of television, wireless, and cellular telephones. Little Palm Island boasts the luxury of the Palm Beaches but the humbleness of the Keys.

The island caters to couples, providing the ideal setting for romance, solitude, and relaxation. Those staying the night will be treated to a world of outdoor showers, Zen gardens, king-sized beds draped in butterfly netting, and Polynesian-style furnishings under a thatched roof. It's no surprise that Little Palm Island has been listed as one of the top 100 fine hotels in the world.

Those arriving to sample the "Floribbean cuisine" of the Dining Room often begin with one of the signature drinks such as the Gumby Slumber (coconut rum, spiced rum, tropical juices, finished with fresh coconut soaked in 151 rum) or the Jolly Mamma Margarita (fresh-squeezed Key lime and lemon margarita). Next, homemade foccacia bread arrives with a trio of homemade dipping sauces (oil and balsamic, hummus, and artichoke and roasted pepper dip) followed by your personal gastronomic journey into the eclectic Carribean fusion of local, island, and European flavors. My culinary sojourn began with avocado ceviche, followed by a Key West shrimp quesadilla, and finished with a key lime pie in a cashew crust complemented with sugar-torched fruit. An extraordinary and unforgettable experience. No children allowed.

TO MAKE THIS A REALITY:

Little Palm Island: 28500 Overseas Highway, Little Torch Key, (800) 343-8567, LITTLEPALMISLAND.COM

ENTER THE MIND OF SALVADOR DALÍ Even most Spanish tourists and art history majors are dumbfounded to find out that the largest concentration of Dalí's works reside in sunny Florida. In fact, the Dalí museum in St. Petersburg showcases his largest and most comprehensive collection in the world. The first-class Euro-

THE ELUSIVE KEY DEER

museum experience allows patrons to enjoy the lunacy and genius of Salvador Dalí, leaving inspired and fascinated by the multifaceted and contentious artist most noted for surrealism. Even an entire bottle of absinthe and space cake barely provides a personal breakthrough to Dalí's mental brilliance.

Dalí's sinister and dark works exude sexual anxiety and moribund creativity through easily recognized flagship pieces such as the *Persistence of Memory* (1931) and the lobster phone, as well as lesser-known splendor such as the *Metamorphosis of Narcissus, Hallucinogenic Toreador, Involuptate Mors,* and *Spellbound,* arguably outshining its counterpart in Figueres, Spain.

So why St. Petersburg? Dalí's works arrived in the Tampa Bay area in 1982 as a permanent home for the private collection of industrialist A. Reynolds Morse and Eleanor Reese. Morse and Reese were friends of Dalí and his wife, Gala, and the greatest collectors of Dalí's work. Beginning in 1943 with the purchase of *Daddy Longlegs of the Evening—Hope!,* Morse and Reynolds amassed a collection over 40 years, larger than the Teatre-Museu Dalí in Spain. Twenty-five years strong, the Dalí is the only museum in Florida unable to close on Mondays due to high demand. Current plans will expand the size of the museum threefold.

TO MAKE THIS A REALITY:

Visit the Salvador Dalí Museum: 1000 Third Street S., St. Petersburg, (727) 823-3767, SALVADORDALIMUSEUM.ORG

THE EVERGLADES A vast expanse of roughly 1.5 million acres spanning the width of Florida, Everglades National Park is the largest subtropical wilderness in the United States and the largest national park in the United States. Rich in wildlife, these mysterious wetlands are a photographer's dream, brimming with opportunity for personal interaction with wading birds, charismatic alligators, frivolous otters, lounging turtles, and for those lucky enough, the Florida panther, the American crocodile, and West Indian manatee. Season and serendipity dictate wildlife sightings but as a general rule migratory birds frequent during winter and gators are more visible as the dry season ensues. From December to April the Everglades grow increasingly drier. During this time, wildlife congregates closer to watering holes, sometimes culminating in scenes of alligators piled one on top of the other. The wet season from June to October means more mosquitoes, lusher vegetation, and more accessible habitat area and hence less wildlife viewing.

Access to nature's wonderland begins at one of four visitor centers throughout the park. The most frequented, the Ernest Coe Visitor Center in Homestead, is an easy day trip from anywhere in South Florida. The short and easy Anhinga Trail reveals living images from the pages of *National Geographic* magazine—eight gators mark their territories, a baby gator ventures into the receding water, a double-breasted cormorant flies overhead, an anhinga swallows a fresh catch, a blue heron lands alongside. The scenes change constantly. The most vivid pages come to life mid-March.

My favorite access point, Shark Valley Visitor Center, provides an extraordinary opportunity to bike through 9 miles of the Everglades, immersed in shallow wilderness. With rental bikes plentiful at the center, visitors need only remember to bring water, snacks, and sunscreen. In many instances you will have to get off your bike to shoo alligators off the bike path. This is half the excitement! Views from the water tower after 5 miles provide rare and precious aerial views of the Everglades. Between February and March, rangers lead rather frightening but exhilarating night trips on the path to observe nocturnal behavior. All access points are open 365 days a year.

TO MAKE THIS A REALITY:

Visit the government's Web site for the Everglades National Park: NPS.GOV/EVER

Shark Valley Visitor Center: 36000 S.W. 8th Street, Miami

Ernest Coe Visitor Center: 40001 State Road 9336, Homestead, (305) 242-7700

UNEARTH A MEGALODON

One of Florida's best kept secrets, the Peace River of Central Florida hosts numerous fossils dating back tens of millions of years to the times of mastodons and megalodons. Paleontological excursions offered through FOSSILEXPEDITIONS.COM span over 25 different sites across the Peace River, led by owner, Mark Renz, who works closely with the Florida Fossil Museum in Gainesville. Following a crash course in paleontology and a quick kayak ride to prime digging territory, it's shovel and sifters in hand for a hearty afternoon of

AN ALLIGATOR LAYS IN WAIT

digging, identification, and possible discovery. Renz provides a brief historical background for your expedition and rapid identification of your fossils—ranging from 15 species of shark (some alive, some extinct), mammoth, hornless rhino, humpless camel, giant sloths (four stories tall), giant deer, horse, tortoise, crocodile, and alligator. Every excursion brings a new discovery.

The excursion is truly fascinating and very much off the beaten path, so much so that more than half the group in my trip were repeat customers—some inspired by the rich natural history of the river and others in search of the "gold"—an intact megalodon tooth—worth up to $20,000 (the Peace River was once a nursery for the 10-foot shark babies.) On my excursion I walked away with a pocketful of gorgeous shark teeth representing five different species, dugong bone marrow, stingray bite plates, and the find

SIFTING FOR MEGALODONS

of the day—part of the gum and tooth of an 8-million-year-old bear! Mark actively encourages the gay community to take part in his excursions.

Departure points vary at rotating locations in Arcadia and Wauchula. Exact location details given upon reservation. Excursions usually depart at 10 AM and last 4–7 hours.

TO MAKE THIS A REALITY:
Book at (239) 368-3252, FOSSILEXPEDITIONS.COM

DOLPHIN ENCOUNTERS People travel far and wide for personal encounters with dolphins. Sadly, the interface with these mystical creatures often transpires in contrived settings such as glorified fish tanks and man-made ponds. Even worse, in countries such as Mexico and even certain states in the United States, dolphins stand unprotected, subject to captivity as tourist ornaments. Though some sound operators utilize the swimming with the dolphins experience as an educational tool, the most rewarding dolphin encounter requires you to enter *their* world—a world of grace, charm, and advanced social behavior. The shallow waters surrounding Key West are optimal for up-close yet noninvasive interactions with the numerous resident pods of the Atlantic bottlenose dolphin. Sightings are never guaranteed on wildlife excursions; however, resident groups in the Florida Keys National Marine Sanctuary and Tampa Bay are commonly witnessed engaging in natural behaviors such as playing, sleeping, eating, and mating. A few lucky onlookers may even get a glimpse at newborn calves or gay dolphin porn (male bull in the pod engaging in sex with the younger male calf as a form of domination). Rather than joining the masses on uncomfortable, impersonal large fleets, opt for an intimate experience on a small boat to traverse the shallow waters and get a closer look. Dolphin tours in the Tampa Bay area are second best to those in the Keys, but readily available (though the dolphin racing boats that encourage dolphins to jump in the wake of the boat near the propellers are very controversial and not personally recommended).

TO MAKE THIS A REALITY:

Dolphin Safari Charters—Leaves from the Banana Bay Resort, Key West. Trips at 8:30, 12:30, and 4:00. Captain Gary exudes genuine enthusiasm with each sighting and promotes responsible viewing of wild dolphins through the Dolphin SMART program. The trip is complemented by snorkeling off a local sandbar renowned for large populations of gentle sea giants such as sting rays, turtles, and nurse sharks. 2319 N. Roosevelt Boulevard, Key West, (305) 296-4691, SAFARICHARTERS.COM

Dolphin Encounters at Florida Aquarium—On any given day, a bottlenose dolphin or manatee spotting is common on the Tampa Bay. Through the Florida Aquarium, a trip on *The Bay Spirit* guarantees wildlife spotting and educates its guests on the importance of this magnificent bay and the species that call it home. 701 Channelside Drive, Tampa, (813) 273-4000, FLAAQUARIUM.ORG

WITNESS ONE OF THE FINAL SPACE SHUTTLE LAUNCHES
Following the launch of moon-bound *Apollo 11* in July 1969, space travel fascinated the world throughout the 1970s and 1980s and promoted an unhealthy obsession with finding extraterrestrial life on Mars, outshining the Soviet Union's technological gains, transcending the thermosphere, and gorging on Neapolitan space ice cream. While space travel is not the topical issue it was during the late 20th century, experiencing a shuttle launch at the Kennedy Space Center in Cape Canaveral proves a spectacular feat of mind, body, and technology. The experience can be an emotional one for some and just awe-inspiring for others.

NASA has planned approximately eight more shuttle flights in total for Destiny's Space Child (*Discovery*, *Atlantis*, and *Endeavor*) before the Space Shuttle program ends in 2010. NASA's Constellation Program is building the next generation of spacecraft for human exploration, expected to be ready by 2014. According to NASA, "Constellation will return humans to the moon by 2020 to set up a lunar outpost in preparation for journeys to Mars."

TO MAKE THIS A REALITY:

Check NASA's latest launch schedule and plan ahead to watch the launch at the closest possible location, the Kennedy's Visitor Complex. These tickets are limited and must be purchased in advance from the complex (KENNEDYSPACECENTER.COM/LAUNCHES/SCHEDULESTATUS.ASPNUMBER).

Alternatively, a number of off-site viewing locations are ideal vantage points. The most popular are along the Indian River on U.S. Highway 1, especially in Titusville; the Beach Line Expressway (SR 528), especially over the Indian River (the Bennett Causeway) and the Banana River; off State Road A1A along the Atlantic Ocean in Cocoa Beach; and Jetty Park ((321) 783-7111) at Port Canaveral, on the Atlantic Ocean just south of the Cape Canaveral Air Force Station border. (321) 867-5000, NASA.GOV/CENTERS/KENNEDY/HOME/INDEX.HTML

MIAMI

4

OUT TRAVELER RATINGS GUIDE

GAY-FRIENDLY: ▼▼▼
GAY SCENE: ▼▼▼▼
LESBIAN SCENE: ▼▼
PRO-GAY LAWS: ▼▼▼▼▼
HIV RESOURCES: ▼▼▼▼

BIENVENIDOS A MIAMI

The mystique of Miami has hypnotized the world since the art deco movement made its way to the subtropics in the 1930s. A paragon of fashion, glamour, and evolving avant-garde, Miami presented a worldly style unknown to most parts of the United States in tandem with a fledgling progressive beach culture. Beginning with the hype of Streamline Moderne and transcending to the trends of present day, the Miami the world has grown to endear and laud in fact stands as a two-square mile section of a small island known as Miami Beach, encompassed by the ocean and bay, engulfed by tourists, contemporary architecture, and archetypal trends. In this case, pigeon-holing the diverse cultures of a colossal city to a solitary focus of a petite area known as "South Beach" has generated an unprecedented marketing tool; the world at large believes that the crown jewel of Miami is, in fact, the city itself.

Today, the revived art deco of the 1950s still dominates the landscape of South Beach, prevailing as the world's foremost example of this extraordinary style. The legacy of immigration waves from the 1970s onward endures omnipresent with Spanish and Creole

THE ROYAL PALM, ONE OF MANY EXAMPLES OF MIAMI'S ART DECO STRUCTURES

spoken more often than English. A shadow of the nightlife rage and period of gay celebrity circa 1990s persists with a few gay strongholds holding resolute in defense of their territory. The LGBT community fades into the South Beach landscape as an integrated entity. Lincoln Road surpasses Ocean Drive as the prime spot for endless people-watching and fine dining.

Regardless of cultural evolution and occasional stagnation, South Beach has never compromised the fashion novelty that placed it on the map more than half a century ago. The legend of beautiful people, fashionistas, and hipsters has generated a self-fulfilling prophecy, as stunning men and women from around the world come to South Beach to outshine one another. The less fortunate endure painstaking efforts to camouflage through equally discerning outfits and accessories. No doubt the streets of Lincoln Road, Ocean Drive, and Washington and Collins Avenues are lined with living models of next season's Gucci, D & G, Vivienne Westwood, and John Galliano. Whereas trendy equates to the latest A & F muscle tee in Fort Lauderdale and Tampa, its designer jeans, chunky glasses, exclusive T-shirts, and posh trimmings that envelope the tasteful on South Beach. Nonetheless, those with simple tastes (such as me) will not be shunned for sporting Hollister and Havaianas!

Outside of looking fabulous in the silhouette of art deco neons, scores of people venture to South Beach for world-famous hotels, renowned restaurants, and gregarious beaches rammed with diesel bodies, chic sunglasses, and fierce Speedos. The deserved reputation of South Beach's finest accommodations and boutique hotels attracts foreigners to sample custom-designed pools, intricately furnished space maximizers, decked-out rooftops, meticulously chosen color schemes, and the individualistic themes that define each hotel. Moreover, the originality and stout flavors of dining options on the Beach make each meal an experience to anticipate;

this holds especially true at eateries that offer true one-of-a-kinds, such as the succulence of Joe's Stone Crabs or the bedazzlement of Barton G's. And lest we forget, the very splendor that first made Miami Beach famous—the calm, wet shades of blue and endless expanses of powdery sand. Despite the battle of the gay beach across the United States, Miami still retains the superlative it has held for nearly two decades as the hottest and flashiest of locales.

Interestingly, most tourists fall short of venturing beyond the borders of Alton Road and Ocean Drive, and fail to enter the world of the real Miami: a dichotomy of suburbs and cities torn between arrogance and opulence (Bal Harbour, Key Biscayne, Aventura, Coral Gables, Coconut Grove) and desperate, envious wannabees (Kendall, South Miami, Miami Lakes, Hialeah) with a displaced downtown still searching for an identity. The convoluted yin and yang that comprises both of these categories makes one no better or worse than the other; however, the clashing cultures, uncouth individuals, perilous drivers, and suburban ghettos of the real Miami are a well-kept secret from the visiting public.

West and south of Miami Beach, smack-talking, sharpy lip-lined "chongas" (think Bon Qui Qui from Mad TV) and pseudo-gangsta "papos" roam the streets of suburban Miami with a sense of ownership and anger. They pollute public spaces with mismatched Rave, Wet Seal, and Hot Topic clothing two sizes too small, riotous antics (including hackneyed yo' mama jokes), and nasty attitudes, rejecting the very country that provided asylum to them or their parents at some point in time. While their demand has kept R & D at Dep SuperGel busy developing their strongest formulas to date, they thrive and multiply in areas where this social behavior is acceptable and in fact common. Meanwhile, residents of other beachfront cities and prestigious suburbs live a privileged life in a virtual bubble of fancy houses, glorious shopping facilities, and ubiquitous wealth.

ESSENTIAL MIAMI IPOD PLAYLIST

WELCOME TO MIAMI Will Smith
TAKE YOU THERE Sean Kingston
MAMI EL NEGRO DJ Laz
MIAMI VICE THEME Jan Hammer
LA VIDA ES CARNAVAL Celia Cruz
DOCTOR PRESSURE Gloria Estefan and Mylo
WHEN I HEAR MUSIC Debby Deb
BAILAMOS Enrique Iglesias
ME SO HORNY 2 Live Crew
COME GO WITH ME Exposé

Perhaps the complexity of this dichotomy has prevented major tourism from launching outside of Miami Beach; even still, day trips to cultural clusters such as charismatic Little Havana and pristine Key Biscayne are essential for those planning to rent a car and venture outside of the beach.

Long before Miami reigned as the melting pot of all Latin American cultures, politically ostracized Cubans formed a stronghold along Southwest 8th Street (Calle Ocho) retaining traditions in cooking, coffee, celebration, and favorite pastimes such as dominos; don't miss an afternoon of delicious Cuban food, cortaditos, pastelitos, and old-school charm. Across the bay from South Beach, Key Biscayne has maintained its serenity and marine sanctity mainly through its status as a protected park. A combination of nature and gentle development, Key Biscayne promises beauty and elegance, most thoroughly enjoyed through an excursion around Crandon Park or a luscious bayside meal at the Ritz-Carlton Key Biscayne.

Despite the growth of neighboring Fort Lauderdale and the long-standing reputation of the Keys, Miami maintains status as the main anchor of South Florida. This may not hold as true in the gay community as it did a decade ago, but Miami will always reign as the global icon of Florida and will continue to host the *crème de la crème* of both the gay and straight world. The hype, high fashion, and unique style that form present day "Miami" stand poised as an indestructible cultural and social force, advancing to the next level with each approaching season.

THE HOLLYWOOD OF LATIN AMERICA

Thanks to its unique location between North and South America and the relative political instability of Latin America in the 1980s through 1990s, Miami effectively took over the world of Spanish-speaking media for a solid decade. The world's major record companies established their Latin market headquarters in Miami while the two largest Spanish-speaking television networks for the Latin American market, Telemundo and Univisión, began to call South Florida home. These Latin media empires soon found this strong centralized location a means for expanding their work to the fast-growing Latino market in the United States while simultaneously consolidating their power in Latin America. The new Miami-based shows such as *Sábado Gigante, El Gordo y La Flaca,* and *El Show de Cristina* and countless *telenovelas* revolutionized the television industry for Spanish-speaking audiences all around the world.

Economic growth and power in Mexico, Colombia, and Venezuela have translated to increased production budgets and decentralization of the television industry away from the Miami axis. However, Miami irrefutably remains the Hollywood of Latin America. Home to who's who in Latin American celebrity, a Latin

INTERESTING, RANDOM, AND USELESS FACTS

- On March 13, 1988, the world's largest conga line, comprised of 119,986 people, formed on the street of Calle Ocho and earned an entry in the *Guinness Book of World Records*.
- According to *Women's Wear Daily*, Bal Harbour Shops in Miami Beach earns more revenue per square foot than any other mall in the United States, nearing $2,000 per square foot compared to the national average of $300 per square foot.
- Long before the Rodney King scandal, riots broke out in Liberty City in 1980 after five white police officers were acquitted for the fatal beating of Arthur McDuffie. The riots resulted in 18 deaths and 850 arrests.
- Winter Music Conference in March is the world's largest showcase of music.
- The famous flamingo scenes from the opening sequence of TV's *Miami Vice* were filmed at Parrot Jungle.
- Though photographic evidence fails to exist, according to eye witnesses (including my Aunt Bonnie) an exceptionally inebriated Jim Morrison did indeed pull out his meat during the 1969 Doors concert at the Dinner Key auditorium in Coconut Grove. Apparently, nobody in the audience was too fazed, but Bible thumpers were outraged; and Morrison was later convicted of two misdemeanors including indecent exposure.

walk of fame, a Latin Grammy Academy, and some of the relevant award ceremonies in the industry (including the Latin MTV Music Awards, Latin Grammys, and Premios Lo Nuestro), the Hispanic capital continues to dictate the Latin American entertainment world. Some long-running television favorites are described below.

SÁBADO GIGANTE More than 20 years without a single rerun, this Spanish-language Saturday variety/game show has hosted the gamut of who's who in Latin America, along with an exaggerated cast of presenters and models sporting excessive makeup, disproportionate breasts, and gleaming veneers. Filmed weekly in Miami, *Gigante* manages to keep Latinos all over the world glued to their screens every Saturday for the latest Hispanoantics. Setting standards for infinite television shows in Latin America, host Don Francisco and his sidekicks have become a part of Latin TV royalty.

EL GORDO Y LA FLACA After a successful career as the Vanna White of *Sábado Gigante,* Latino showbiz blue-blood Lilly Estefan (Emilio's and Gloria's niece) left Don Francisco in 1998 to join Raúl de Molina in a gossip television show that inspired all those Perez Hilton–type gossip bloggers in the preblogosphere days. This daily show lets anyone willing to watch know what is going on with celebs in the Latin entertainment world.

EL SHOW DE CRISTINA Another member of the Miami-based entertainment elite of Latin America, Cristina Saraleghi is also known as "Spanish Oprah" thanks to the border-breaking success of her talk show. Since the '90s she has extended her empire, like Oprah, to a self-entitled magazine, various books, a home decoration line inspired by her own Miami home, and by simply being the undisputed queen of Hispanic talk shows. To complete the Latin-

American television dream, Spanish Oprah's "Gayle" is none other than Gloria Estefan, and her "Stedman" is Marcos Ávila, a former member of the Miami Sound Machine.

POCKET GUIDE TO FLORIDA SPANGLISH

Visitors to Florida will quickly realize that in many of the state's neighborhoods the dominant language is not English. Nor is it Spanish. Somewhere in the middle evolved an informal language called Spanglish—a jocular combination of English and Spanish.

This is a brief, rough, and informal guide to my native tongue.

PRONUNCIATIONS

ADD AN "E" TO ALL WORDS THAT BEGIN WITH AN "S" OR A "T." The famed '80s singer Bonnie Tyler would be "Bonnie Etyler." The muscle-builder steroids would be "esteroids" (sounding like asteroids).

PRONOUNCE "CH" LIKE "SH." Ordering a quarter chicken at a restaurant would be "quarter shicken."

WITH WORDS THAT END IN "TE" LEAVE THE "TE" SILENT. The popular soft drink, Sprite, would be pronounced "es-pr-eye."

SWAP "J"S AND "Y"S AND SOMETIMES "G"S. Jello gelatin would be "yellow yelatin." The color yellow would be pronounced "jello." "You" would be pronounced "jew" such as in "jew know."

Replace the unfortunate English transitional and pause words "you know," "like," and "um" with "O sea" or "pues" between statements.

EVENTS (LGBT)

WINTER PARTY (FEBRUARY/MARCH) The Miami circuit scene toasts the winter sun through this annual nonprofit event for the National Gay and Lesbian Task Force, which gathers over 10,000 international hotties for a weekend of homo mayhem and celebration. Several rotating local venues downtown and on the beach transform ordinary spaces into party palladiums for Winter Party; however, the host hotel pool party on Saturday (previously the Surfcomber) and the Beach Party on Sunday prevail as the two paramount events. Tickets are cheaper in advance and tax deductible! WINTERPARTY.COM

AQUA GIRL (MAY) A loose female equivalent to the shallowness and superficiality of male circuit parties, the largest charity women's weekend in the country each May unites thousands of beautiful women across the streets and oceans of Miami Beach for a wild and steamy weekend. Truth be told, Aqua Girl is still more inclusive than its male counterparts, offering comedy events, art exhibits, concerts, and a jazz brunch in addition to the dance parties, the chaotic pool party, and the token mega beach party. One hundred percent of the net proceeds from the weekend benefit the Aqua Foundation for Women, a not-for-profit foundation whose primary mission is to promote the equality, strength, health, and visibility of gay, lesbian, bisexual, and transgender women. AQUAGIRL.ORG

SIZZLE (MAY) On the down-low or loud and proud, this Memorial Day Weekend event combines hip-hop and homosexuality in what is billed as Florida's "most anticipated black gay event." With rotating host hotels downtown (previously including the

Hyatt Regency Miami, Marriott Courtyard, and Hilton Biscayne Bay Hotel) and five days of events including fierce parties, booze cruises, and beach dance-offs, Sizzle Miami and Sizzle Her (female version) unite the African-American community and their admirers for nonstop madness. SIZZLEMIAMI.COM; SIZZLEHER.COM

WHITE PARTY (NOVEMBER) White Party began in 1985 as a pioneering fundraiser to raise money for research and awareness on a new disease called AIDS. Twenty-five years later, the Party remains true to its roots as a primary income source for Care-Resource, a nonprofit, multicultural, community-based AIDS service organization, which provides education, prevention, research, care and treatment, and support services. Surrounded by an entire weekend of events, Saturday's actual "white party" at the Vizcaya mansion casts thousands of gay men and women dressed in white into a fairy tale setting of 16th-century Italian Renaissance-style grandeur with parties throughout the mansion and gardens. World-famous DJs and recording artists perform under the stars. Sunday's Muscle Beach Party recruits over 5,000 muscle boys for an afternoon of barefoot dancing, dripping sweat, and inebriation. Tickets are cheaper in advance and tax deductible! Previous host hotels include the Surfcomber and the Eden Roc. WHITEPARTY.ORG

EVENTS (NON-LGBT)

CALLE 8 (CARNIVAL WEEKEND) The pinnacle of Carnival Miami celebrations, this extraordinary street festival in the heart of Little Havana is a tribute to everything Latin America and everything party time! The vibe on the street embodies the merriment and charisma of the late Celia Cruz, who danced her way down Eighth

GREAT SOUTH BEACH READING

Strip Tease by Carl Hiaasen
Diary of a South Beach Party Girl by Gwen Cooper
The Everglades: River of Grass by Marjory Stoneman Douglas
The Exile: Cuba in the Heart of Miami by David Rieff
South Beach: The Novel by Brian Antoni
The Out Traveler: South Florida by Paul Rubio
The South Beach Diet by Arthur Agatston
Going to Miami—Exiles, Tourists and Refugees in the New America by David Rieff
Miami by Pat Booth
Miami by Joan Didion
Dave Barry's Complete Guide to Guys by Dave Barry

Street well into her eighties. Thirty years strong, the festival takes place between 27th Avenue and 4th Avenue along Southwest 8th Street with over 30 stages of live music, DJs, and dancing spread over nearly a million people. CALLE8.COM

WINTER MUSIC CONFERENCE (MARCH) A wonderland for the old rave crowds and cutting-edge music enthusiasts, Winter Music Conference draws together 40,000 partygoers, amateurs, and professionals for the largest DJ showcase in the world. Worshipping the sounds and beats of drum 'n' bass, techno, and house, WMC is a rare event where boundaries of gay and straight blend. Crowds stand united by their favorite DJs and artists as they preview new tracks and mixes while industry executives and press converge on the business end. WMC transforms the energy of South Beach each March as the international be-all and end-all of music industry parties. Hotels all across South Beach host 250-plus intimate parties while the Ultra Music Fest held on Saturday in Bicentennial Park marks the single largest electronic music concert in the United States, with 200 DJs spinning for 14 hours. WINTERMUSICCONFERENCE.COM

MIAMI URBAN BEACH WEEK (MAY) African-Americans from around the country congregate in Miami Beach on Memorial Day weekend for Urban Beach Week, or unofficially titled "Hip Hop Weekend." What began as an urban fashion weekend in 2000 has now become an intensely jam-packed hetero party and unfortunately an unwelcoming arena for the gay community. Most of the LGBT community heads north to Fort Lauderdale during this weekend; alternatively, the development of a gay hip-hop weekend called Sizzle lures revelers downtown to enjoy Urban Beach Week in a welcoming environment.

ART BASEL (DECEMBER) Following the footsteps of its Swiss counterpart, Art Basel Miami stands arguably as the most prestigious art show in the United States since its inception in 2002. Held six months after the show in Basel, the global congregation of top designers, architects, 200+ gallery owners, and 2,000 artists from all continents provides a complementary outlet for the world's premiere art show. During this short weekend in December, South Beach shines as the international model of art, culture, and fashion with special exhibitions, over-the-top parties, and crossover events featuring music, film, and architecture. DESIGNARTBASELMIAMIBEACH.COM

TO DO AND SEE

IN SOUTH BEACH

PEOPLE-WATCHING ON SOUTH BEACH Day or night, people-watching indisputably constitutes the most popular activity on South Beach. Whether sipping mojitos on Ocean Drive, strolling down the ocean side in your Speedo, or sipping a cappuccino on Lincoln Road, the beautiful and eccentric, fashionable and distasteful provide endless hours of entertainment.

TAKING IN THE RAYS The gay beach between 11th and 12th Streets, parallel to A1A, sports diesel bodies and an erotic homo playground for hundreds of gay men and women on a daily basis. The beach is situated down the sand directly in front of the Palace Bar, marked by the boundaries of gay flags and lifeguards. Alternatively, nudists and those looking for a more thorough bronzing

THE PLACE TO BE FOR BABE WATCHING, SOUTH BEACH

experience can head up 11 miles north to **HALOUVER BEACH**. The northernmost "naturist beach" of Halouver is where you will find the vast half-mile clothing-optional area. The farther north you walk the more gay it becomes (until you hit the fence). Using a rental car is easiest (park in the northernmost parking lot); a taxi ride is very expensive (get dropped off at the northernmost lot); and Bus 108 (Route H) on Miami-Dade public bus service from South Beach is a viable alternative. Use main entrance 10800 Collins Avenue if programming to GPS for bearings; then look for Halouver Park North Lot (which has no official address).

ART DECO PHOTO SAFARI Most visitors forget to snap photos of the very element that globally distinguishes South Beach—the foremost examples of the art deco design movement. In fact, both the interiors and exteriors of the Beach's buildings, namely the hotels, maintain the love affair of everything art deco and house an iconoclastic decorative ambience that has become synonymous with South Beach. Found all along Ocean Drive, Collins Avenue, and Washington Avenue, the architecture impresses by day contrasted against blue skies and by night illuminated by fluorescents and neons.

BOUTIQUE AND OUTDOOR SHOPPING No trip to Miami is complete without a few new designer threads to strut down A1A and then show off in your home city. The best boutique and outdoor shopping is found along **LINCOLN ROAD MALL** and 8 miles north in **BAL HARBOUR SHOPS,** the most exclusive shopping area in Florida outside of Worth Avenue in Palm Beach. Bal Harbour is a designer open-aired powerhouse of shops, fountains, and gardens and an essential visit for fashion and label whores. 9700 Collins Avenue, Miami Beach, BALHARBOURSHOPS.COM

EXPLORE THE SOUTH BEACH GALLERIES Contemporary art galleries tucked into far corners of Lincoln Road, Collins Avenue, and Ocean Drive inspire and liberate the artistic and creative. Most notably, the infamous **ROMERO BRITTO GALLERY** showcases the artist's distinctive portraits, sculptures, and prints along Lincoln Road, which have become a virtual trademark of South Beach and Miami (818 Lincoln Road, BRITTO.COM, (888) R-BRITTO). Also of notable interest, the **WORLD EROTIC ART MUSEUM,** houses a vast collection of everything erotica, including homosexual-themed art, sculpture, tapestries, and artifacts. Collection includes neoclassical pieces, 20th-century American art, and 17th- through 20th-century European art. (305) 532-9336, WEAM.COM

BEYOND THE BORDERS OF SOUTH BEACH

FREEDOM TOWER The Ellis Island of Miami, the Freedom Tower was used by the federal government to process and document Cuban immigrants between the late 1950s and 1960s and provide medical and dental services for the immigrants. Originally a printing facility and later abandoned, the Freedom Tower has now been restored and converted into a monument for the refugees who once fled Cuba and passed through the very doors of the establishment nearly 50 years ago. Inside it houses occasional art exhibitions. 600 Biscayne Boulevard, Downtown Miami

VIZCAYA MUSEUM AND GARDENS A 16th-century Italian Renaissance-style villa, Vizcaya is well recognized in the LGBT community for hosting the White Party every November. A daytime trip through the 10 spectacular acres of gardens, fountains, and museum of James Deering's former winter residence allows you to fully appreciate the beauty and opulence of the bayfront estate. 3251 S. Miami Avenue, Miami, (305) 250-9133, VIZCAYA-MUSEUM.ORG

PARROTT JUNGLE ISLAND Since moving from its former dilapidated location to an exclusive island of serenity, Parrott Jungle has learned that making cockatoos ride mini tricycles is downright idiotic and that education and awareness of these beautiful creatures and their friends overpowers pseudo-circus tricks. A Florida mainstay since 1936 that once attracted the likes of Winston Churchill, Parrot Jungle Island is the top kids attraction in South Florida with

AVOID RENTING A CAR IN SOUTH BEACH

If you are solely planning to visit South Beach on your vacation, a car will quickly become a hindrance due to limited parking and exorbitant valet rates. Most hotels charge in the range of $25–$35 per night for valet parking. The parking garages charge $15 for 24 hours; however, these hours must be consecutive. You will pay each time you enter and leave the parking garage. And, in general, street parking is a hot mess.

South Beach is best enjoyed by foot. It is one of the few places in Florida where residents can live without a vehicle, so take advantage! A taxi from Miami International Airport to your South Beach hotel totals roughly $35.

entertaining shows, water activities, and exotic animals such as a 900-pound "liger" (a cross between a lion and a tiger), a 2,000-pound, 20-foot crocodile, and of course the hyper-trained parrots. 111 Parrot Jungle Trail, (305) 400-7000, PARROTJUNGLE.COM

CORAL CASTLE Imagine the life of a 5-foot, 100-pound Latvian twink left stranded the day before his wedding by his 16-year-old bride-to-be. Apparently, Edward Leedskalnin took solace in hand-building a monument to his lost love over 28 long years in Florida City (1932–1951). Eleven hundred tons of coral rock later, the amazing feat of this nonconformist had been completed single handedly with the use of only hand tools. Dancing on a fine line between romance and lunacy, Leedskalnin's cathartic Coral Castle is a sight to behold and admire. 28655 S. Dixie Highway, (305) 248-6344, CORALCASTLE.COM

UNIVERSITY OF MIAMI Some college campuses wow and woo with architecture, history, and design; the University of Miami tends to be more famous for its football team and hot boys than the actual college campus. Unlike the mildly charming campuses of FSU and UF, UM's college campus does not merit a visit unless you randomly end up there from having a one-night stand.

MIAMI SPANISH MONASTERY The Miami Spanish Monastery (functioning as St. Bernard de Clairvaux Church) is the oldest building in the Western Hemisphere—nearly 900 years old. The Monastery was an active part of church life in Segovia, Spain, for centuries until it was disassembled and shipped to America and then reassembled in Miami Beach in the 1950s. The Monastery now doubles as a tourist attraction and one of the most popular wedding venues in Florida. Call before visiting as grounds often close for private events. 16711 W. Dixie Highway, North Miami Beach, (305) 945-1461, SPANISHMONASTERY.COM

FAIRCHILD TROPICAL GARDENS A 33-hectare (83-acre) verdant paradise, Fairchild Tropical Gardens is Florida's finest and most pristine botanic garden, worth the drive for those willing to drive (and spend $20) to indulge and enjoy collections of extensively diverse and well-presented rare tropical trees and plants against a lush Florida background. 10901 Old Cutler Road, Coral Gables, (305) 667-1651, FGT.ORG

THE EVERGLADES No trip to South Florida is complete without a journey to the widest and slowest-moving river in America. The magnificence of the Everglades can be experienced in many ways, as described in the section "Forgotten Florida: Treasures Off the Beaten Path." Note that public transportation does not go to and from the Everglades. NPS.GOV/EVER

EXPLORING "THE GROVE"...OR NOT? Coconut Grove was the "it" girl in the early 1990s with fancy hotels such as the Mayfair, the new outdoor mall concept called Cocowalk, funky novelty stores such as Condom USA (did anyone really ever buy anything there?), and Florida's first Cheesecake Factory (when the cheesecakes were actually made in-house). During this time, the trendy "Grove" was worth the risky drive down Grand Avenue (when approaching from the suburbs), where unsavory residents would often throw glass bottles at passersby. Though all the original establishments of

Coconut Grove remain, the lure and appeal of the "Grove" has faded as a tourist destination and has been replaced with a more residential feel. COCONUTGROVE.COM

PERUSING DOWNTOWN MIAMI AND NEIGHBORING AREAS... OR NOT? Now synonymous with the word "foreclosure," Downtown Miami was never given a proper chance for complete economic turnaround and has been particularly devastated by the credit crunch and dwindling state of national economic affairs. The undeniable potential for a complete and utter revitalization of Miami's depressing downtown attracted global and local investors to pour hundreds upon hundreds of millions into making the rebirth possible. However, a modern-day "gold rush" in tandem with national stagflation has left downtown "half-done," a juxtaposition of unoccupied modern high-rises and neighboring ghettos peppered with a few trendy restaurants. Pockets of life still emerge among the Dawn on the Foreclosed, such as **MARY BRICKELL VILLAGE** (901 South Miami Avenue, (305) 381-6130, MARYBRICKELLVILLAGE.COM), an enclave of fine dining, shopping, live entertainment, and cultural attractions adjacent to the luxury hotels of Brickell, including the Four Seasons, the Conrad Hilton, the Mandarin Oriental, and the JW Marriott. There was a huge buzz about a residential revitalization of the **DESIGN DISTRICT** and **WYNWOOD** circa 2007, which presently house more than 70 art galleries, showrooms, and stores. While the dramatic contrasts between industrial wasteland/poverty/Little San Juan and trendy galleries/hypermodern lofts are personally fascinating and artistically inspirational, the area hardly merits a touristic visit beyond the specific purpose of visiting an esoteric gallery. In general, those expecting the amenities and excitement of a major downtown city will be grossly disappointed with Miami. Aimless wanders with the iPod are better accomplished in the 2 square miles of South Beach.

LODGING

Unless business or family dictates your visit, there is no reason to stay in parts of Miami other than Miami Beach. Lodging in Miami Beach is hardly segregated between gay and nongay; most hotels listed are crammed with gays and lesbians year round. In general, the character of your lodgings will largely define your South Beach experience. The fabulous hotels scattered along Washington, Collins, and Ocean boast scrupulous individualism, showcasing feats of design and architectural ingenuity. No doubt friends will ask where you stayed in South Beach since most notable hotels have global reputations. For those still preferring an exclusively gay hotel, South Beach has two options: the **EUROPEAN GUESTHOUSE** (721 Michigan Avenue, (305) 673-6665 EUROPEANGUESTHOUSE.COM) and the **ISLAND HOUSE** (1428 Collins Avenue, (305) 864-2422. ISLANDHOUSESOUTHBEACH.COM)

THE ANGLER'S BOUTIQUE RESORT The archetype of luxury boutique hotels, the Anglers combines the styles of old Florida with South Beach neo-art deco revival to produce a four-building enclave of casual elegance. A delicate merger of new construction and 1930s renovations, the suites are a perfect starting point for immersion in the South Beach lifestyle, with contemporary designs, rooftop terraces, a sleek pool, private gardens, and private Jacuzzis. The superior level of service stands on par with 5-star beachfront hotels. (305) 534-9600, 660 Washington Avenue, THEANGLERSRESORT.COM **EXPENSIVE**

THE CATALINA HOTEL AND BEACH CLUB A budget, mildly glam option on South Beach without going totally cucaracha, the Catalina is conveniently located on hotel row Collins Avenue and offers rooms for less than $100 per night outside of major party weekends (as low as $58/night during off-season 2008). The crowd here is young, hip, and generally hetero, though Catalina heavily markets to the gay community. The quintessential art deco lobby and verdant gardens/pool area complement the vintage rooms and host gregarious nightly happy hours though rooms are generally in desperate need of refurbishments (and the harsh, sandpaperish toilet paper reminiscent of the kind from grade school is a detraction). 1732-1756 Collins Avenue, (305) 674-1160, CATALINAHOTEL.COM **INEXPENSIVE**

DELANO HOTEL A South Beach institution and favorite of the "rich and famous," the Delano celebrates the apex of Miami glamour on a daily basis. A-listers grace the halls of Philip Stark's grandiose indoor/outdoor lobby, seeking refuge in the purity and elegance of their stark white guestrooms or the chic, expansive lap pool. 1685 Collins Avenue, (305) 672-2000, DELANO-HOTEL.COM **VERY EXPENSIVE**

THE DOUBLETREE SURFCOMBER Former host to the major LGBT events throughout the year, including White Party, Winter Party, and Aqua Girl, this art deco beachfront landmark consistently provides a welcoming arena and hip backdrop for brilliant pool parties and after-party shenanigans. The common areas exude South Beach style, most notably the pool area that spills out onto the sands of Miami Beach. The 186 rooms are rather uninteresting, standard Doubletree fare. 1717 Collins Avenue, (305) 532-7715, SURFCOMBER.COM **EXPENSIVE**

GANSEVOORT SOUTH The Gansevoort South "brings the pulse of New York to the heart of South Beach." Well bring it on! The paragon of envy has risen as the latest bastion of evolving South Beach style. The 334 oversized, hypermodern guestrooms peer over the fervor of South Beach and the city skyline, interrupted only by the tranquility of the ocean and bay. Three oceanfront pools grace the contemporary enclave, including a 110-foot rooftop pool, an expansive infinity-edge pool on the plaza level, and a family-friendly south pool. 2377 Collins Avenue, (305) 604-1000, GANSEVOORTSOUTH.COM **EXPENSIVE**

THE RITZ-CARLTON, SOUTH BEACH Flawless and fabulous, the Ritz-Carlton, South Beach combines the elegance and precision of the Ritz-Carlton name with iconoclastic SoBe style and ambience (translation: it's cool and casual). Housed in the former, historic DiLido Hotel, the Ritz unveils a modern twist of quintessential Streamline Modern Art Deco cast over prime oceanfront. The influence of renowned architect Morris Lapidus and the inspiration of a deluxe luxury liner dictate the cohesive synthesis of luxury, comfort, and Ocean Drive. The Ritz South Beach is also home to the ultimate in poolside pampering with the world's only Tanning Butler who keeps you lubed and protected (from the sun) all day long by the pool. One Lincoln Road, (786) 276-4000, RITZCARLTON.COM **EXPENSIVE**

THE SETAI The fusion of art deco preservation and Asian persuasion, the Setai jets 40 stories high as 360 degrees of glass and opulence with unparalleled bird's-eye views. The daddy mack of South Beach hotels, the Setai has been aptly recognized for a new level of sheer sophistication and magnificence. The impeccable details of the spacious rooms and enchanting courtyards leave

4 ESCAPE THE WORLD IN KEY BISCAYNE

Couples looking for a secluded, romantic retreat should look no further than a weekend getaway to the island of Key Biscayne. The only hotel standing on the island, **THE RITZ-CARLTON KEY BISCAYNE,** offers all the relaxation and vacation utopia of the Bahamas' Atlantis and the Caribbean's top resorts, just across the bay from Miami Beach yet miles away from the crowds. Tradition meets modernity in perhaps the most approachable and relaxed Ritz-Carlton in operation, Miami's only AAA 5 diamond property. The self-contained destination emerges as a leader in Florida's hotel industry, the perfect blend of serenity, comfort, superior service, and exceptional fine and casual dining. Escapism truly becomes reality on this island oasis. For a day, a weekend, or a week, the Ritz-Carlton Key Biscayne grants guests a mental retreat often only achieved by a long-haul plane flight to seclusion. 455 Grand Bay Drive, Key Biscayne, (305) 365-4500, RITZCARLTON.COM **VERY EXPENSIVE**

---

guests spellbound and stimulated. 2001 Collins Avenue, (305) 520-6000, SETAI.COM **VERY EXPENSIVE**

THE TIDES The pearl of South Beach avant-garde, the Tides Hotel unveiled a $112-million facelift to its flagship hotel in late 2007. The eye-opening transformation reduced 110 rooms to 40 luxurious suites *each* equipped with breathtaking views of oceanic paradise. The structural readjustment and renovations have been overshadowed by the interior transformation conceived by world-famous designer Kelly Wearstler. The curiously fascinating fruits of her labor prevail as a sinister Salvador Dalí earth tone amalgamation fantasy. 1220 Ocean Drive, (305) 604-5070, THETIDESHOTEL.COM **VERY EXPENSIVE**

TOWNHOUSE HOTEL Completely affordable and highly respectable, the Townhouse Hotel combines boutique style with cost consciousness through its 69-room, five-story trendsetter. The juxtaposition of red and white across minimalist furnishings and kitschy accessories fruitfully fosters the intended vibe of freshness and simplicity. In place of a swimming pool, Townhouse features a hip, innovative rooftop terrace—a succession of eight bright-red king-size waterbeds paired with over-the-top umbrellas positioned under the sun and stars, rising as a contemporary art playground for sunbathing, drinking, and socializing. Rates include breakfast in vogue each morning at the "pantry." 150 20th Street, (305) 534-3800, TOWNHOUSEHOTEL.COM **MODERATE**

DINING

BARTON G It's Cirque de Palate at the most bedazzling and fantastical gastronomic circus known to man. Each dish and drink offered at Barton G is uniquely delivered in a theatrical display of grandeur—from the swinging pendulum of Voodoo Shrimp to the slithering, flashing electronic fish accompanying the Flash Dance Grouper to the swordfish on a sword to the cotton candy dessert that resembles the wig of Marie-Antoinette. The ornate presentation stimulates all five senses in tandem, wowing audiences for this over-the-top dining experience. Gimmicks aside, the food itself merits attention for its robustness and innovative flavor sensations.

The drink menu escalates mixology to a new level of imagination with the use of genuine vodka popsicles as alcoholic diffusers. Unlike anything you have ever experienced; be sure to bring a camera and a huge appetite. 1427 West Avenue, (305) 672-8881, BARTONG.COM

BIG PINK Get your mind out of the gutter! An old-school diner South Beach style, the Big Pink feeds into cheesy Florida stereotypes with its pink Flamingo décor and its grease pit label, serving up gargantuan portions of a few hundred varied dishes. With plates big enough to share, Pink aims to please with classic American favorites as well as funky deviations from traditional choices, like sweet potato fries, a barbeque chicken wrap layered in smashed red bliss potatoes, and arugula. A local favorite and cheap. 157 Collins Avenue, (305) 532-4700, BIGPINKRESTURANT.COM

BOND STREET South Beach's top sushi hot spot, this intimate restaurant tucked into the basement of the Townhouse hotel serves up the most tender and luscious sashimi in town. Famed for its sister location in New York City and popularity on *Sex and the City*, the SoBe outpost uses only the freshest and finest ingredients to produce mouth-watering rolls and delectable Japanese classics. 150 20th Street, (305) 398-1806, TOWNHOUSEHOTEL.COM

DILIDO BEACH CLUB The *only* oceanfront restaurant in South Beach, DiLido Beach Club is a true gem. Gently situated on the border of the beach, DiLido serves an array of healthy and organic dishes complemented by signature über-refreshing drinks such as the watermelon and peach sangrias (a must try!). The so-called sun cuisine, inspired by beach towns along the southern Mediterranean and North African coasts, shines as perfect, light beach fare that does not leave you bloated and puffy; you can still lay out after lunch here without feeling 5 pounds heavier! The restaurant boasts a relaxed, sensual environment which is a perfect stop after a day at the beach or for a casual lunch or early evening cocktails (closes by 9 PM seven days/week during the Fall and Spring. 6 PM weekdays during the Summer and until 9 PM on weekends). One Lincoln Road, (786) 276-4000, RITZCARLTON.COM

DUNE/CIOPPINO/CANTINA BEACH (THE KEY BISCAYNE TRIAD) It's rare for a single restaurant to get all the ingredients right for the ideal blend of ambiance, taste, and presentation; well imagine three of South Florida's most decadent and fabulous restaurants under a single roof. The Dune Oceanfront Burger Lounge, Cioppino, and Cantina Beach at the Ritz-Carlton Key Biscayne dish up exemplary American, Italian, and Mexican cuisine in a fairy tale bayfront setting. Dune's beachfront elegance stands reminiscent of Nikki Beach's heyday with white couches nestled into the sand, gentle light ocean breezes, and trendy cocktail lists, including the best sangria in South Florida; the burgers are also noted as some of the best in town. Cioppino brings a piece of Tuscany to South Florida in the literal sense, with ingredients flown in twice weekly from Italy, including fresh cheese, spices, olive oils, and aged balsamic vinegars. The more informal Cantina Beach showcases the best Mexican food in Miami including fresh guacamole made tableside, the country's only tequilier, and spectacular coastal Mexican seafood dishes. 455 Grand Bay Drive, Key Biscayne, (305) 365-4500, RITZCARLTON.COM

FRONT PORCH Everyone's favorite oceanfront brunch spot, this is the place to see and be seen gorging on your hangover food and mimosas. The Breakfast Bonanza special of eggs, mushrooms, and cheese with home fries is the best remedy for your throbbing headache or spotting your trick from last night with his unbeknownst boyfriend. 1418 Ocean Drive, (305) 531-8300, FRONTPORCHCAFE.COM

ICE BOX It's not often that I support Oprah's brainwashing tactics, but the media mogul's claim that Ice Box Café fed her the "greatest cakes in America" has given much deserved attention to the latest gem of Lincoln Road. Truth be told, the cakes are not really the highlight of Ice Box; everything is delicious. The ever-changing menu of breakfast, lunch, and dinner brings daily variety to the global pan-American fusion. The warmth of a diner, the structure of a mini-cafeteria, and the sophistication of a contemporary restaurant unite over healthy and hearty dishes. Interestingly, the affordability and quality of the unpretentious Ice Box draws an A-list South Beach crowd of Muscle Marys, fashionistas, and trendsetters. 1657 Michigan Avenue, (305) 538-8448, ICEBOXCAFE.COM

JOE'S STONE CRABS It's hard to find a restaurant that has received more publicity than Joe's Stone Crabs. The pioneer of serving up the Florida endemics, Joe's has grown to become a global institution, noted by Patricia Shultz as "One of the 1,000 places to see before you die!" Joe's is getting props for delivering the world's most sustainable food to the plate, leaving the crabs to regenerate their limbs after removing one claw. However, for the 15 years I have accompanied my mother to Joe's for her birthday dinners I have found myself less than impressed with the alternative entrees, and the restaurant a tad bit overhyped for dishes beyond the crabs themselves and the decadent key lime pie. Point being—go for the crabs! 11 Washington Avenue, (800) 780-CRAB, JOESSTONECRAB.COM

RAPHAEL: FOOD AND MORE Following the fame of cosmos on *Sex and the City,* cocktail addicts constantly search for the latest advances in "mixology." Situated in the heart of Lincoln Road, Raphael fills the niche of innovative drink concoctions through its champagne specialties such as the Champagne Mojito (champagne with fresh mint, lime, brown sugar) or Champs Lime (champagne with lime sorbet), or the Mango Color (champagne with mango nectarine). Raphael doubles as a Mediterranean bistro with an outstanding breakfast, lunch, and dinner menu combining the best of light Mediterranean cuisine with lowfat options. Happy Hour 5–7. 530 Lincoln Road, Suite 100.

SUSHI SAMBA DROMO The crossing of Peruvian and Japanese cultures spawned two major events in history: the Peruvian presidency of Alberto Ken'ya Fujimori from July 28, 1990 to November 17, 2000 and the conception of Sushi Samba, an exquisite taste explosion of East-meets-South. The "sashimi seviches" blend the tanginess and zest of Peruvian flavors with the tenderness of top-grade sushi, most notably through the "Yellowtail Sashimi Seviche" bathed in ginger, garlic, and soy and the "Lobster Sashimi Seviche" infused with mango and lime. Regardless of the countless sushi options, the highlight of any trip to Sushi Samba is still the exceptional "chicharron de calamar"—cornmeal-crusted calamari with tamarind sauce, tomato salsa, and plantain. The innovative drink menu focuses heavily on the sweet and fruity. 600 Lincoln Road, (305) 673-5337, SUSHISAMBA.COM

TABLE 8 Cast over the entire first floor expanse of the De Soleil South Beach hotel, Table 8 offers gourmet cuisine in a stylish lounge environment. Design is a protagonist in this refined dining space, with an oblong section located under the pool deck of the

CUBAN FOOD IN LITTLE HAVANA

If time permits, a quick trip to the center of the Cuban exile community, Little Havana, makes for a rewarding cultural and gastronomic excursion. While the streets of Little Havana are not exactly pedestrian friendly (due to poor city planning), a drive down the famous Calle Ocho and cross streets brings you to a united neighborhood of current and former immigrants, where English is rarely spoken. Strolling the aisles of local grocery stores or peering over a group of men playing dominos, it's a great way to pick up some new Spanish words, especially Miami-Cuban slang. The best part of visiting Little Havana is gorging on delicious Cuban food, best enjoyed at the famous **VERSAILLES RESTAURANT.** Versailles is the quintessential Cuban experience, from its perfect location smack in the center of Little Havana to its traditional preparation of entrees such as ropa vieja (pulled pork), arroz con pollo (chicken and rice), and bistec palomilla (flank steak with onions) with all the authentic trimmings such as yucca, beans and rice, and fried plantains. Though it's hotly debated whether Versailles or La Carretta (across the street) is the restaurant of choice for Cubans across South Miami, they both provide authentic food at reasonable prices. You need a car to get around! 3555 Southwest 8th Street, Miami, (305) 444-0240.

hotel. The fare is standard South Beach upscale—refreshing salads, flavorful fish dishes, tender cuts of meat, and the occasional signature dishes, such as the lamb sausage stuffed olives. 1458 Ocean Drive, (305) 695-4114, TABLE8LA.COM

NIGHTLIFE

HALO LOUNGE The snow-white powerhouse has brought a much-awaited upscale lounge to Miami Beach. An intimate room of stark white and sensational lighting, Halo has helped revive the South Beach scene with long queues on weekends as well as steady crowds Sunday through Thursday. Halo's bartenders are some of the hardest workers in the business; the specialty cocktail list packed with muddled fruits, infusions, and countless ingredients requires intense labor best done by local hotties. Fridays and Saturdays are packed! 1625 Michigan Avenue, (305) 534-8181, HALOLOUNGE-MIAMI.COM

SCORE/CRÈME LOUNGE Score was the hottest thing to hit South Beach in the late 1990s as a high-end lounge *and* dance club, an innovative concept for its time. The Armani motif has since been replaced more than once, to adequately change with the times and remain on top of the South Beach game. Popular nights have come and gone but for the past few years Planeta Macho Tuesdays has reigned as the hottest Latin party in Miami Beach; late Thursdays upstairs at the Crème Lounge are part of the South Beach Thursday ritual; Evolution Fridays are hit or miss; Siren at Crème Lounge on Saturdays stands popular with the lipstick and glam lesbians. 727 Lincoln Road and Meridian Avenue, (305) 535-1111, CREMELOUNGE.NET, SCOREBAR.NET

BUCK 15 LOUNGE Now a Thursday night tradition, Buck 15 began "The Simple Life" Thursdays in 2005 and has not looked back since. With door whore Chyna and DJ Daisy Dead Petals it's a no-frills, fun-in-the-frat-party atmosphere above Miss Yip's Chinese Café. 707 Lincoln Lane, (305) 534-5488, BUCK15.COM

SOUTH BEACH REMEMBERED BY TARA SOLOMON

The South Beach of the late 1980s to late 1990s was quite a different world, one in which gay culture was not only prevalent, but groundbreaking. And I was fortunate enough to be at the epicenter of history in the making, documenting the hypercreative, self-amused scene for various publications, including my "Queen of the Night" column in the *Miami Herald*.

So what was so different? In a word, everything. With cost-effective rents and a steady stream of visiting avant-garde New Yorkers to fuel the frenzy, a community of gay and gay-friendly artists, designers, writers, and bohemians du jour emerged. It was a 24-hour party where you could come as you are, although many of us preferred to reinvent ourselves.

TARA SOLOMON, CIRCA 1989

TWIST A palladium of debauchery, seduction, and drunk men, Twist is a massive enclave of five virtually separate gay parties. From the eye-opening strip bar in the back to the dark room dance floor upstairs to the casual bars downstairs to the hip-hop room or the outdoor patio, Twist is a certain late night meeting point for locals and tourists, open until 5 A M. Most end up here late at night both

SOUTH BEACH REMEMBERED BY TARA SOLOMON

Drag cabaret was a well-practiced art form, with insanely fun local talent such as Daisy Deadpetals (as a menacing Pippi Longstocking on a tricycle), Damian Deevine (ever in Sweet Baby Jane mode), and Kitty Meow, the Beach's beloved version of RuPaul. And who can forget Adora—one of the few gender illusionists still performing in the area—in her Aqua Net-ed, glitter-lipped glory, lip-synching 1950s-era Peruvian soprano Yma Sumac?

And it's not just my martini talking, either. Other South Beach "pioneers," as we are termed, miss the good old days when eccentricity was the norm and creativity trumped commerce. There may now be a Starbucks in the space where Elton John once bought platform heels one New Year's Eve more than a decade ago, but at least we have our memories. And they're damn good ones.

—TARA SOLOMON

Tara Solomon is a writer and the coprincipal of TARA, Ink., a public relations firm specializing in modern culture.

drunk and horny. Enough said. 1057 Washington Avenue, (305) 538-9478, TWISTSOBE.COM

PALACE BAR Situated smack-dab directly in front of the entrance to the gay beach on 12th and Ocean, South Florida's only oceanfront gay bar is also the most relaxed of all Sobe's venues, where you can sip cocktails and people-watch in your Speedos and tank-top. The vibe is more Fort Lauderdale than South Beach, meaning this is one local bar where it's more about the fun and the drinks than standing and posing. Evening performances by drag queens are true show stoppers. Using passing cars and Ocean Drive as a stage, these queens command the attention of all passersby, stopping oncoming traffic with street-side splits and hood-top straddles. Sunday tea dance is a must! Breakfast, lunch, and dinner also served. 1200 and Ocean Drive, (305) 531- 7234, PALACESOUTHBEACH.COM

VLADA LOUNGE MIAMI With yet another A-list magnet opening this past winter, Miami appears posed to reincarnate the gay spirit of the '90s. The South Florida outpost of New York's hottest gay bar transports the ambience, the clientele, and the signature design of the hell's Kitchen institution, including the "Ice Bar," a custom-designed bar counter composed of frosted ice that maintains drinks at optimum temperatures. Situated in the trendy Design District, SoBe scene queens finally have an excuse (besides a hurricane) to leave Miami Beach and head west. Choose from the infamous infused vodka drinks, with 17 unique flavors, including pear and pineapple, or create your own mixology fantasy. 3215 NE 2nd Avenue, Miami Design District, VLADBAR.COM

ROOFTOP AT THE TOWNHOUSE HOTEL About one Saturday every month, the Townhouse Hotel infuses life to South Beach with its evening social on its renowned rooftop. The party under the stars over the famed series of red waterbeds is what South Beach is all about—the boys, the style, the weather, and the drinks. Dates change monthly so it's best to ask a local or check out the

Wire newspaper on South Beach. 150 20th Street, (305) 534-3800, TOWNHOUSEHOTEL.COM

MARTINI TUESDAYS AND ART DECO PUB CRAWL The lobbies and bars of South Beach's renowned art deco hotels are sights to behold. On Tuesday nights Edison Farrow hosts his Martini Tuesdays at rotating venues, which include the Victor Hotel, the Delano, the National, and the Setai. Crowds swell or shrink depending on the location of the week, but the aforementioned are some of the most popular (check out SOBESOCIALCLUB.COM for the current week's venue). Even outside of Martini Tuesdays, a pub crawl through a selection of SoBe's hottest hotels is an essential evening for Miami newbies.

DISCOTEKKA AT METROPOLIS An entire dancehall dedicated to A-list gay Latinos, Diskotekka is South Florida's biggest party on Saturday nights. Located in downtown Miami, the party reigns as a high energy mix of dance, Latin, raggaeton, and house, packed with hot guys from the beach and the burbs. Be prepared to pay $20 for parking downtown and to dodge sketchy characters from nearby venues. 950 N.E. 2nd Avenue, (305) 371-3773, DISCOTEKKA.COM

FORT LAUDERDALE

5

OUT TRAVELER RATINGS GUIDE

GAY-FRIENDLY: ▼▼▼▼▼
GAY SCENE: ▼▼▼▼
LESBIAN SCENE: ▼▼
PRO-GAY LAWS: ▼▼▼▼▼
HIV RESOURCES: ▼▼▼▼▼

LIVING YOUR DEADLY SINS IN FORT LAUDERDALE

Fort Lauderdale shined in the '80s as a spring break haven for Generation X, the ultimate palladium of wet T-shirt contests, Sun-In, and carcinogenic tan lines. *Miami Vice* met the trailer park during the decade of excess and Reaganism as this once-small town became a world-renowned mecca of sardine-packed motel rooms and Pabst Blue Ribbon–strewn beaches.

Spring breakers were literally kicked out in 1986 when the

mayor booted MTV and appeared on *Good Morning America* to uninvite college students. By the following year Fort Lauderdale had begun to lose its identity.

Fearing paradise lost, the city soon undertook what would become a $2 billion face-lift to clean up the Aquanet oil slick and promote urban economic development. With a new mayor in '92, a revitalization strategy, and a tourism marketing blitzkrieg, by the mid-'90s Fort Lauderdale was promoting gay tourism and recruiting upscale clientele to visit.

Capitalizing on the beauty of the labyrinthine intracoastal waterways, Fort Lauderdale was rechristened the "Venice of America," a home for the world's fastest-growing yachting community, with turquoise beaches that rival the Caribbean and a progressive, gay-friendly atmosphere on par with San Francisco. It seems that Fort Lauderdale went into hiding for a good 10 years, through a painful process of nip and tuck, until its slogans matched reality. Unveiled in the mid-2000s, the removal of the final bandages revealed a new Fort Lauderdale—a growing metropolis in the early stages of a social and cultural renaissance.

Chic, urban high-rises now line the Atlantic Ocean and the intricate waterways of the Intracoastal. Trendy bars and clubs link Himmarshee Street. Strips of boutique shops and lofts along Las Olas Boulevard house Fort Lauderdale's new bourgeoisie. At the dawn of 2010, most of the beach-side dumps have been bulldozed and replaced with pimped-out hotels, including the eye-catching W Towers, a world-class resort even by W standards. The influx of luxury hotels incorporated into Fort Lauderdale's new chic line has been accompanied by a slew of upscale ethnic eateries that match the taste and style of big city casual sophistication.

While the Fort Lauderdale "swan" has indeed emerged, the urban growth has not compromised the small-town feel that has historically defined the city. It is still very much a beach town where it is socially acceptable to wear shorts, tank tops, and flip-flops to restaurants and bars. A hedonistic mentality of "spring break forever" remains, namely in the gay community. Men well into their forties and fifties need not live vicariously through a younger generation. They live a life well-engrossed in sex, drugs, alcohol, and dance remixes. It's almost as if the nonbaby-making baby boomers are making up for lost time and embracing the freedoms that have come only in recent decades.

The truth of the matter is that most people venture to Fort Lauderdale simply for sun, sex, and booze. Gays were a $1.24 billion force in the Fort Lauderdale economy in 2007. With such specialized tourism converging in one destination, the city has landed a star location on the gay global map.

FORT LAUDERDALE IN THE SPOTLIGHT

With over 150 gay guesthouses, bars, clubs, and stores and 4,000+ restaurants, Greater Fort Lauderdale is an ever-changing scene relentlessly trying to outshine Miami. There's always talk of what's in and what's out these days, Miami or Fort Laud. Regardless of trendsetter rhetoric, Fort Lauderdale proudly maintains the title Fort Liquordale for the greatest amount of booze consumed per capita in the United States. It's an unparalleled arena for indulging in leisure and ignoring Surgeon General warnings. With this in mind, this chapter places a heavy and detailed emphasis on accommodations, restaurants, and nightlife.

Greater Fort Lauderdale or, more generally, Broward County, is divided into more than 30 cities and towns, populated with an eclectic mix of nearly 2 million inhabitants. The actual city of Fort Lauderdale is the county seat of Broward, with approximately 10% of the greater area's population and the epicenter of the famed

> ## INTERESTING, RANDOM, AND USELESS FACTS
>
> - The sole tunnel in Florida cuts under the New River in downtown Fort Lauderdale.
> - Fort Lauderdale became known as "Fort Liqourdale" due to its distinction as the highest alcohol consumption locale per square foot in the United States.
> - Fort Lauderdale boasts more yachts than anywhere else in the world.
> - The New River in Fort Lauderdale is the shortest, deepest, and narrowest river in the world.
> - Boats have right of way over pedestrians and cars in Fort Lauderdale.
> - Fort Lauderdale is known as the "Venice of America" due to its 185 miles of local waterways.

waterways, the best beaches, and a growing city center. Heading away from downtown and the beach, the Fort Lauderdale sheds all remnants of its more urban counterparts, approaching the suburban gayborhoods of Wilton Manors and Oakland Park.

Fort Lauderdale's gay heart and soul, Wilton Manors, shines as a queer utopia for 35-plus couples and retirees, complete with bars, restaurants, gyms, novelty stores, realtors, and travel agents that specifically cater to the gay community. With stores affectionately named Bottoms and Tops and Gay Mart, Wilton Manors is the core of Fort Lauderdale's gay life. A textbook tale of gays cleaning up the ghetto, Wilton Manors was a crack-infested neighborhood just

20 years ago, ripe for gentrification. Flash forward to 2009 and it's now one of the few places in Florida where same-sex couples can comfortably display affection.

With the hard economic times that began in 2007, Fort Lauderdale took an extraordinary hit in the real estate market. Following the post-millennium economic boom when housing prices seemed to skyrocket daily, foreclosures beleaguered the real estate landscape and tales of financial hardships became commonplace. Housing prices may have dropped, but the life of leisure continues.

Aspects of Fort Lauderdale still stand as a nostalgic reminder of everything 1984 and sometimes the décor matches outdated MC Hammer pants. But tireless efforts to change the face of the Fort Lauderdale have truly paid off, and the city is on everyone's gaydar. The city has evolved as a unique rotation of new and old, urban and residential, the trendy and distasteful.

EVENTS (LGBT)

Until recently Fort Lauderdale preferred to host national events like the rotating Gay Softball World Series and the Sunshine Stampede Rodeo rather than monster circuit parties or massive gay prides. To most, it always seemed strange that an area so populous lacked a major pride headliner. In light of this pressure, event coordinators have upped the stakes to produce more mainstream pride events throughout the city.

PRIDEFEST FORT LAUDERDALE (MARCH/APRIL) A celebration and tribute to the LGBT community and its unique culture, Pridefest is held annually in early spring. It attracts a very local crowd and is best described on par with a small-town pride event—tragic but fun. PRIDESOUTHFLORIDA.ORG

STONEWALL STREET FESTIVAL (JUNE) Since rescheduling the event from Father's Day to the weekend following the paternal celebration, the Stonewall Street Festival has exploded into a weekend of parties and pride mayhem, including the token parade, street parties, a host hotel (the Hilton), D-list gay acts (like Crystal Waters in 2008), and top-tier DJ favorites (like Tracy Young). STONEWALL-STREETFESTIVAL.COM

SUNSHINE STAMPEDE RODEO (APRIL) First the world was shocked to find out about black cowboys. Then *Brokeback Mountain* cast the spotlight on gay cowboys. While typically void of Jake Gyllenhaals and Heath Ledgers, the annual Sunshine Stampede Rodeo held at the Bergeron Arena in Davie features all the traditional rodeo favorites for both men and women—bareback bronco riding, steer riding, barrel racing, macho bull riding, and calf roping—and new

A BIKER BABE AT THE STONEWALL STREET FESTIVAL

favorites such as goat dressing (a team trying to get a pair of undies onto a goat). FGRA.ORG

WICKED MANORS (OCTOBER) Trick or treat, give me something good to eat! It's a celebration of hard candy at this Wilton Manors Halloween street party, and not the Madonna kind! Most of the pumpkins have been swapped for alcohol in greater Fort Lauderdale's premiere opportunity to celebrate the holiday that made Jamie Lee Curtis famous. Patrons dress up in the full range of Party Supermarket's tacky costumes while some showcase creative homemade ingenuity. WICKEDMANORS.COM

EVENTS (NON-LGBT)

FORT LAUDERDALE INTERNATIONAL BOAT SHOW (OCTOBER) In late October Fort Lauderdale hosts the world's largest boat show, the be-all and end-all of marine envy, with more than $2 billion worth of boats, yachts, superyachts, electronics, engines, and thousands of accessories from every major marine manufacturer and builder worldwide. FLIBS.NET

WINTERFEST BOAT PARADE (DECEMBER) The largest one-day spectator event in Florida draws a crowd of 1 million onlookers each December as a stampede of 1,500 pimped-out, jaw-dropping yachts cruise 10 miles of Fort Lauderdale's waterways, complete with original themes and decorations. While traditional viewing along bridges and costly platforms is an option, the best way to experience the spectacle involves food and drink in hand at one of the many lavish boat parade parties taking place in backyards and hotel and condo balconies across the New River. The International Festival and Events Association has ranked Winterfest #20 out of 50,000 parades in the United States. WINTERFESTPARADE.COM

TO DO AND SEE

SEBASTIAN BEACH Greater Fort Lauderdale's strongest attraction is arguably the 23 miles of powdery sand and palm-fringed, lucid waters that line the coastline from Hallandale to Deerfield Beach. Ready for action or relaxation, gay men swarm a small section of this Atlantic bliss known as Sebastian Beach (directly south of the lifeguard stand on Sebastian Street, north of the Ritz-Carlton formerly Saint Regis Hotel, A1A). Frolicking on nature's playground, roasting in the fiery sun, the scantily clad expose both the latest and the outdated. As opposed to SoBe's "Muscle Beach" reputation, Sebastian finds itself the *Cheers* of South Florida's beaches—gregarious

CATCH SOME RAYS AT SEBASTIAN BEACH

and relaxed, stripped and raw, with all ages and sizes, from Latino twinks and porn stars to leather daddies and oversized bears.

HOLLYWOOD BEACH If time permits, a day stroll and tanning session along the quieter Hollywood Beach is popular with couples. The subtle remnants of Hollywood's 1950s glamour and the newly refurbished boardwalk make this beach ideal for a romantic wander.

HALOUVER BEACH Another favorite for those reveling in Fort Lauderdale's delights: a quick 20-minute trip down to South Florida's only nude beach, Halouver Beach (see "To Do and See" in Miami chapter). Other notable beaches in Broward include Deerfield and Dania, but don't expect a large gay presence. What you can expect is some of the cleanest, safest, and most user-friendly beaches in the country, all certified as "Blue Wave beaches" for responsible beach management, all ideal for night-time star gazing.

FORT LAUDERDALE'S AQUA BACK LOT A boat trip through the "Venice of America" is an essential but often overlooked experience for visitors. Traveling the streets and grotesquely grand highway of I-95, the Venetian analogy puzzles most first-time visitors. However, a quick glance at the car GPS reveals a wondrous water-bound world, appreciated only by boat. While a number of tour outfitters offer this opportunity to journey behind the scenes of Fort Lauderdale, the best way to experience the aqua back lot of multimillion-dollar homes, hotels, and seafood restaurants is via Fort Lauderdale's public **WATER TAXI** ((954) 467-6677, WATERTAXI.COM/FORTLAUDERDALE). For an $11 unlimited day pass, the taxi serves as both a tour and a means of transportation between Fort Lauderdale's most renowned sights.

AIRBOATS AND KAYAKS Though the best way to see the Everglades is a trip deep into Everglades National Park, a quick 30 minutes away, visitors can gain instant eco-gratification gliding over the sawgrass on an exhilarating airboat ride. Three main outfitters offer service east of US 27. The airboats at **SAWGRASS RECREATION PARK** ((888) 424-7262, EVERGLADESTOURS.COM) are spacious and uncovered but the distant view of gargantuan telephone poles prevents the feeling of total environmental immersion. Visitors desperate to see an alligator may be disappointed with this trip since they are one of the few companies who follow the rules and have not habituated any gators. The overwhelmingly popular **EVERGLADES HOLIDAY PARK** ((954) 434-8111, EVERGLADESHOLIDAYPARK.COM) caters to larger crowds and cruise ships with cattle-packed megaweatherproof airboats. This trip is about providing the tourist with great photos and gator sightings at all costs—illegally habituating and actively feeding several local gators that will swim right up to the boat during the tour. **BILLY'S SWAMP SAFARI** ((863) 983-6101, SEMINOLETRIBE.COM/SAFARI) integrates the airboat ride into the full Everglades "safari" experience.

GET WET Wreck sites teeming with marine life off the coast of Fort Lauderdale remain one of the city's most inaccessible points and best-kept secrets. However, the inland reef damage sustained from dredging and boat activity is no secret in Broward County. With restoration efforts underway, some excursions still present decent snorkeling opportunities. The **SEA EXPERIENCE SNORKEL CRUISE** ((954) 627-4631, SEAXP.COM) takes visitors to a reef parallel to Sebastian Beach on a glass bottom for a two-hour opportunity to explore the world of damsel fish, with snacks, beers, and sodas all for sale on board. Parking costs $5 in a lot off Bahia Mar, with cheaper parking in the public lot across the street.

STROLL DOWN LAS OLAS BOULEVARD What Lincoln Road is to South Beach, Las Olas Boulevard is to Fort Lauderdale. The terrestrial heart and soul of Broward County, Las Olas is the premiere street for restaurants, art galleries, shopping, and people watching. From west to east the landscape of Las Olas transforms from modern downtown high-rises to original boutiques and ethnic eateries, spilling onto the beautiful mansions and traditional Floridian homes that line the intracoastal and define Fort Lauderdale. The streets of Las Olas connect to the pedestrian friendly Riverwalk, which continues to the edge of the New River on Avenue of the Arts. LASOLASBOULEVARD.COM

MUSEUM OF ART The regular collection holds few interesting pieces; however, rotating world-class exhibits such as King Tut and the Bodies Exhibit warrant a visit. The permanent collection consists of Dalí, Picasso, Calder, Warhol, and many other notable artists' works. More exciting than the pieces inside is the structure itself, an architectural work of art. One E. Las Olas Boulevard, (954) 525-5500, MOAFL.ORG

BONNET HOUSE Located beachfront, this subtropical manor serves as a monument to old Fort Lauderdale. A nice visit for history buffs and those who caught a glimpse of the beautiful structure on the *Amazing Race* a few seasons back. 900 North Birch Road, (954) 563-5393, BONNETHOUSE.ORG

INTERNATIONAL SWIMMING HALL OF FAME MUSEUM AND AQUATIC COMPLEX This is a one-of-a-kind tribute to underwater achievements and home to many important international aquatic competitions. Both of the 50-meter, 10-lane pools are open to the public on all days outside of competitions, attracting a very cute crowd of aspiring swimmers. One Hall of Fame Drive, (954) 462-6536, ISHOF.ORG

RUMMAGING THROUGH THE TRASH: SWAPSHOP FLEA MARKET Billed as the world's largest of its kind, the "Swap Shop" no doubt puts the flea back in flea market. One can find the odd collectible here and there along with melted Colgate toothpaste and the previous month's ExtraCare specials from CVS. The streets surrounding the Swap Shop were once a hotbed of controversy as animal rights activists protested the abysmal and cruel circus that once took place in the center of the food court (including a bear in a tutu on a tricycle). Thankfully, the circus was shut down but the food court remains. The best part of the Swap Shop is the fruit and vegetable market outside, where you can get fresh sugar cane juice, a Cuban tradition, pressed by hand through an old-school hand press. The Swap Shop also boasts the world's largest drive-in movie theater, but this is usually plagued by unsavory characters. 3291 W. Sunrise Boulevard, (954) 791-7927, FLORIDASWAPSHOP.COM

LODGING (LGBT)

With nearly 30 gay guesthouses located within walking distance of Sebastian Beach, survival of the fittest will surely claim the lives of the weak in the coming years. Due to the competition of chic, fresh hotels, the 1950s duplexes have been forced to up the stakes—goading guest service to dizzying extremes, refurbishing with new amenities, sometimes advertising with chiseled men who bear no resemblance to the clientele, and promoting specials in a weak economy. However, these singular B and B's will always offer a personal touch absent from most corporate establishments and a relaxed social forum for productive networking and good conversation. And lest we forget the advantage of letting it all hang out, day and night, poolside, roomside, or even at the breakfast table. The five below are the best in Fort Lauderdale and worth keeping the B and B alive!

FLAMINGO INN AMONGST THE FLOWERS Locals often outnumber snowbirds at Fort Lauderdale's therapeutic floral beach oasis, a sheltered tranquility from the drama and craziness of the gay world. Flowers is the Ritz of gay guesthouses minus the pretension, a welcomed retreat for the upper-middle echelons of gay society. 2727 Terramar Street, (954) 561-4658, THEFLAMINGORESORT.COM **EXPENSIVE**

THE GRAND RESORT AND SPA The Grand is simple and fantastically social, consistently busy and active, arguably flaunting a younger mean age than all of the other guest houses (meaning 35). The front building centers on the sizable pool with rooms radiating outward a la Melrose Place-style. The clean symmetric design welcomes domestic and international guests to 33 guestrooms and suites with contemporary walk-in showers, minimalist cappuccino furniture, and flat-screen televisions. First-rate staff is on the premises 24-7, catering to all needs and possible demands. Late (and even *very* late) checkout is not a problem or an additional charge. The full-service spa is featured as one of the best in Florida. 539 N. Birch Road, (954) 630-3000, GRANDRESORT.NET **MODERATE**

PINEAPPLE POINT A little less than a mile from the beach and closer to downtown, Pineapple Point boasts a nearly extinct breed of genuine service that would easily outshine *Desperate Housewives* diva Bree Van de Camp. A maze of tropical cottages and dense foliage, the treasure map leads to four hot tubs and swimming pools (including a sleek lap pool), hammocks, a gymnasium, and gardens, all touched with luxury and class. It comes as no surprise that Pineapple Point sports the symbol for the service industry. 315 N.E. 16th Terrace, (954) 527-0094, PINEAPPLEPOINT.COM **EXPENSIVE**

ROYAL PALMS Not only has the Royal Palms received a 5-star Planet Out rating between 1991 and 2009, but it was the winner of Planet Out's "Best Gay Resort" in both 2007 and 2008. Twelve sumptuously appointed rooms, a heated pool, and a 10-man spa in a garden of orchids cultivate an intimate setting of tranquility. 2901 Terramar Street, (954) 564-6444, ROYALPALMS.COM **MODERATE**

WORTHINGTON GUESTHOUSE/ALCAZAR RESORT This B and B tag team attracts sizable crowds, entering the market at a very affordable and reasonable price point without compromising quality. A pathway between the two allows guests to choose from two pools and room types, though I always pick the Worthington side hands down. The fresh-squeezed OJ in the morning is pure citrus bliss! 543-555 N. Birch Road, (954) 563-6819, THEWORTHINGTON.COM; ALCAZARRESORT.COM **INEXPENSIVE**

LODGING (MAINSTREAM)

For those who prefer the contemporary hotel experience, Starwood has staked a major claim on the Fort Lauderdale oceanfront with four hotels over one mile and elevated A1A to a new level of opulence and sophistication. The latest additions, the W Hotel and the Atlantic Hotel shine as flagship properties for their respective collections, while the Hilton and Ritz-Carlton complement the list of contemporary beach elegance.

THE ATLANTIC The pioneer of Fort Lauderdale's luxury hotel collection, the Atlantic took roots on A1A when it was still a playground of rundown motels. The investment has now paid off and its new neighbors strive to compete with the chic vibe and elegance it has cast over the beach for six solid years. 601 N. Fort Lauderdale Beach Boulevard, (954) 567-8020, THEATLANTICHOTELFORT LAUDERDALE.COM **EXPENSIVE**

HILTON FORT LAUDERDALE BEACH RESORT In my experiences, Hiltons are hit or miss (be sure to miss the ones in Antananarivo, Madagascar, Sydney, Australia, and near the Eiffel Tower, Paris!). In the case of Fort Lauderdale, peer pressure has produced one of Hilton's finest and most spectacular structures to date. The impressive white tower stands poised among a myriad of luxury hotels, offering an advantageous price point and all the comforts associated with a famed top-category Hilton plus amazing views of the Atlantic Ocean. A supporter of the LGBT community, the establishment was the official sponsor and host hotel for Stonewall Street Festival. 505 N. Fort Lauderdale Beach Boulevard, (954) 414-2222 **EXPENSIVE**

THE W The crown jewels of Fort Lauderdale beach, the W twin towers are the talk of the town. The freshness and innovation associated with the W brand bring a hip, young outlook to Fort Lauderdale beach with cutting-edge modernity and style. 401 N. Fort Lauderdale Beach Boulevard, (954) 414-8200, STAR WOODHOTELS.COM **EXPENSIVE**

DINING

ANTHONY'S COAL FIRE The coal-fired oven is the center of attention and the only means of cooking the two hot dishes offered at Anthony's—pizza and wings. Keeping it simple has paid off with fame for the succulent, mouth-watering wings drenched in roasted onions, and several signature pizzas, most notably the Eggplant Marino (cheeseless) and the peppers and onions. Salad is also great. 2203 S. Federal Highway, (954) 462-5555, ANTHONYSCOALFIREDPIZZA.COM

BLUE MOON FISH CO. Hands down Blue Moon Fish Co. is the best seafood restaurant in South Florida, noted for incomparable freshness and quality. It's also the best deal in town with a 2-for-1 word-of-mouth lunch special, which makes 5-star dining affordable at prices lower than Red Lobster (no joke). Start with whole roasted garlic and bread and continue on to the langostino salad or snapper. 4405 West Tradewinds Avenue, (954) 267-9888, BLUEMOONFISHCO.COM

CAFÉ EMUNAH Totally off the beaten path, Café Emunah offers a true one-of-a-kind cuisine—kosher and organic sushi. Japanese favorites are prepared with a Jewish flair and daring taste combinations cast in a contemporary setting. 3558 N. Ocean Boulevard, (954) 561-6411, MYEMUNAH.COM

CANYON Southwestern fusion in an intimate setting, Canyon's cooking is truly unlike any other I have experienced elsewhere in the world. With starters such as comal-grilled red chili chicken tostada (with goat cheese crumbles, caramelized Bermuda onion, baby arugula-and-avocado serrano chili with white truffle crema) or the tequila-and-jalapeno smoked salmon tostada (with goat cheese, capers, grilled scallions, pepper confetti-and-scotch bonnet tartar sauce), it's hard to sample a dish that will leave you in anything but a state of ecstasy. The chocolate bread pudding ranks as one of my favorite desserts in the entire world! This is my first stop when I come home to Fort Lauderdale. 1818 E. Sunrise Boulevard, (954) 765-1950, CANYONFL.COM

CHINA GRILL The mammoth design masterpiece houses a new element of contemporary dining in Fort Lauderdale and mitigates the endless waiting list of its Miami counterpart. The restaurant's concept of Asian fusion draws inspiration from Marco Polo and his descriptions of the Far East and its riches. Grill delivers this inspiration through meticulous presentation, aromatic entrees, and refreshing taste sensations. (Adjacent to Grand Hotel) 1881 S.E. 17th Street, (954) 759-9950, CHINAGRILLMGT.COM

THE FOUR RIVERS The Four Rivers combines tradition and ingenuity, catalyzing a new dimension of Thai cooking. Rivers excites the senses through showpieces of flavor and presentation while remaining distinctly Thai, with a focus on quality, the organic, macrobiotic, and seasonal. Cast in a setting of chic elegance, the chefs prepare all items from scratch, meticulously combining complementary ingredients to avoid bastardizing the intended tastes. 1201 N. Federal Highway, (954) 616-1152

GALANGA RESTAURANT A local favorite for its prime location on the gay strip in Wilton Manors and sophisticated ambience, Galanga offers the likes of both Thai and Japanese cooking. It is the place to see and be seen in the Fort Lauderdale gay community. My personal favorites are the Victor roll and the calamari appetizer. 2389 Wilton Drive, (954) 202-0000, GALANGARESTAURANT.COM

FOOD AND DRINK ORGASMS

AHI TUNA CEVICHE AT FOUR RIVERS succulent and smooth ahi tuna saturated in fresh Chinese grapefruit, shallots, and roasted coconut topped with a coconut-lime dressing.

WOK BRAISED MONK FISH AT FOUR RIVERS Japanese eggplant, fresh heart of palm, holy basil, and wild ginger garnish sweet and succulent monk fish doused with green curry.

CRACKLING CALAMARI SALAD AT CHINA GRILL taste explosion of zest with crispy lettuce, calamari, citrus, and lime in lime-miso dressing.

SHANGHAI LOBSTER AT CHINA GRILL a 2.5-pound female lobster, unbelievably soft and tender, drenched in ginger and curry and accompanied by crispy spinach. Best with wasabi mashed potatoes.

STOLI DOLI AT CAPITAL GRILLE Stoli vodka marinated in a tub of fresh-cut pineapples for two weeks and then drained. Slides down like liquid pineapple rock candy.

GRILLED SHRIMP AND SCALLOP BURRITO AT CANYON delectable seafood burrito overstuffed with tender shrimp and scallops, grilled peppers and onions, and creamy melted mozzarella cheese, served with a toasted cumin corn salsa and chipotle cream sauce.

FOOD AND DRINK ORGASMS

PRICKLY PEAR MARGARITA AT CANYON fresh sour mix and strained prickly pears, Canyon's signature margarita is the best and most sought-after in town.

GREEN AND CHAI TEA SEARED TUNA AT EMUNAH mouthwatering fillet of tuna marinated in green and chai tea, accompanied by sweet mango and cucumber spaghetti salad topped with avocado, crispy plantains, and an eel glaze.

MARINATED GRILLED OCTOPUS AT TRINA marinated grilled octopus seasoned with oregano and sherry vinaigrette.

MEATBALL AND RICOTTA PIZZA AT ANTHONY'S COAL FIRED PIZZA crispy thin crust pizza smothered in rich ricotta cheese and a fresh tomato sauce, topped with many petite yet hearty meatballs.

GRILLED EGGPLANT PANINI AT GRAN FORNO grilled panini filled with sliced grilled eggplant, fresh tomatoes and lettuce, divine roasted peppers, and mild provolone cheese.

LANGOSTINO SALAD AT BLUE MOON FISH CO. appetizing blackened langostinos served over a bed of crisp baby spinach leaves, topped with succulent caramelized onions and fiery pecan-goat cheese, tossed in walnut oil vinaigrette.

GRAN FORNO A piece of northern Italy situated on Las Olas Boulevard offering six different fresh homemade sandwiches and mountains of ever-changing baked goods made on the premises before your very eyes. Lunch only. Closed Mondays. 1235 E. Las Olas Boulevard, (954) 467-2244, GRANFORNO.COM

J. ALEXANDERS A standard of corporate excellence, the location in Fort Lauderdale deserves press for its popularity in the gay community, probably the number one first date spot in all of Broward County. Classic American food prepared in vast quantities without compromising taste and the best veggie burgers I have ever tried! 2415 N. Federal Highway, (954) 563-9077, JALEXANDERS.COM

LE TUB After the fame this establishment gained on Oprah as the country's greatest hamburger joint, the famous 13-ounce bloody sirloin slab satisfies but fails to impress. The funky décor of decorated bathtubs and toilets used as plant potters feels more original. Bottom line is that this was probably Oprah's first stop when breaking her latest diet. 1100 N. Ocean Drive, (954) 921-9425, THELETUB.COM

ROSIE'S BAR & GRILL The food may be a slight cut above T.G.I. Fridays prepackaged potato skins, but no other restaurant in Fort Lauderdale is consistently as busy, as fun, or as lively as Rosie's—the former Hamburger Mary's that has become an institution in South Florida. The theme here is alcohol, bar food, friends, and cruising. Popular Sunday brunch. 2449 Wilton Drive, (954) 567-1320, ROSIESBARANDGRILL.COM

SUBLIME Its vegan rhapsody as South Florida's most popular vegetarian restaurant cuts the by-products and even the dairy to show the world how vegan eating does not compromise flavor or taste.

Cast in an eco-Zen setting of greens, whites, and falling water, this restaurant is a favorite for even many carnivores and of course animal rights activists such as Pamela Anderson. 1431 N. Federal Highway, (954) 539-9000, SUBLIMEVEG.COM

TAVERNA OPA Best experienced with a large group on weekends, it's Eurovision come to life *à lá* Greek party mayhem—loud music, dancing on the tables, overweight belly dancers, and most importantly, amazing and authentic Greek food. Be prepared to eat well, sweat, and leave smelling like grilled octopus. The original location is always the best—410 N. Ocean Drive, Hollywood, (954) 929-4010—but the more conveniently located one is also fun. 3051 N.E. 32nd Avenue, (954) 567-1630, TAVERNAOPARESTAURANT.COM

TRINA After a slew of bad press shortly after opening, the nicest waterfront restaurant in the city has revamped the menu, changed chefs, and put itself on par with Fort Lauderdale's most savory and memorable dining experiences. Since good news travels slowly, Trina remains a well-kept secret, fighting off its previously tarnished image. Popular Sunday brunch spot. 601 N. Fort Lauderdale Beach Boulevard, (954) 567-8070, TRINARESTAURANT.COM

ZONA FRESCA Natural and original, Zona leads the healthy Mexican fast-food revolution with the best chips, salsas, and burritos in town. Their exceptionally affordable cuisine outshines all chain competitors. 1635 N. Federal Highway, (954) 566-1777, ZONAFRESCA.COM

BEST 24-HOUR FIXES AND COFFEE SHOPS

DOWNTOWN PIZZERIA Open until 4 A M. Downtown Pizzeria has swapped the smell of sewage lingering outside the dim, pale yellow building for a fresh, new location. Inside is your best and cheapest late-night slice of pizza in town. A jumbo slice and soda is $2.25. 1590 S. Andrews Avenue, (954) 463-4801, DOWNTOWNPIZZA.NET

FLORIDIAN The Floridian was the gay diner hot spot for 20 years during the reign of the Cathode Ray dynasty. It was a regular spot for Ray's crowds and became a Las Olas staple. It remains popular with the gay community as the quintessential Floridian diner. 1410 E. Las Olas Boulevard, (954) 463-4041

JAVA BOYS The crusiest coffeehouse in Fort Lauderdale, Java Boys is known more for its wandering eyes than its cup of joe. 2230 Wilton Drive, (954) 563-1454

PETER PAN A traditional Greek diner with gay flavor, Peter Pan is an essential 4 AM stop for hangover prevention and my Uncle Mike's favorite restaurant for over 20 years. In addition to affordable diner favorites, Peter Pan features homemade Greek specialties, homemade salad dressings, kabobs, amazing omelets (like the Athenian omelet—with spinach and feta cheese), and the pièce de résistance—emerald-eyed hottie and Greek owner Billie! 1216 E. Oakland Park Boulevard, (954) 565-7177

STARBUCKS WILTON MANORS It's comforting to know that there is still one Starbucks that espouses the original ethos of the company, where it is "cool" to be a barista and people enjoy Alanis Morrisette acoustic. A real coffeehouse feel, this Starbucks draws in the crowds day and night. 1015 N.E. 26th Street, (954) 566-1304, STARBUCKS.COM

STORKS A sweet and cozy coffee shop with ample indoor and outdoor seating, Storks remains a java stronghold of Wilton Manors even with competition from encroaching Starbucks. The white chocolate pistachio cheesecake, fabulous customer service and flavored drip brews outshine the insipid espresso. 2505 N.E. 15th Avenue, (954) 567-3220, STORKSCAFE.COM

NIGHTLIFE

In general, Fort Lauderdale caters to a 35-plus crowd; however, a mini-urban revolution has spilled into downtown, catalyzing a younger "glam" scene, with nights that vie with neighboring South Beach. Nevertheless, the renaissance that has touched the city center has yet to reach all of Wilton Manor and Oakland Park's nightlife venues. Sporadically tawdry and tacky but irrefutably casual and inexpensive, Wilton Manors and Oakland Park's nightlife consists of bars and clubs housed in strip malls and shopping centers, requesting no cover charge and requiring no formal dress codes. Shorts, flip-flops, tank tops, and even Daisy Dukes are allowed.

WILTON MANORS AND OAKLAND PARK

BILL'S FILLING STATION A relocation and significant size expansion, Wilton Drive welcomes its newest and biggest watering hole. Very popular for people in the biz and bears, the station does not fill as quickly as Alibi or Sidelines, but its adjacent location makes it worth a visit. 2209 Wilton Drive, (954) 567-5978, BILLSFILLINGSTATION.COM

BOARDWALK Fort Lauderdale's most popular strip bar with different themes nightly, Boardwalk showcases scantily clad recent imports from the Americas hosted by Florida's favorite tactless drag queens. Boardwalk brings in the big stars such as Bel Ami superstar Lukas Ridgestone for holiday weekends. Open every night of the week. 1721 N. Andrews Avenue, (954) 463-6969, BOARDWALKBAR.COM

BOOM Dark and hazy with smoke, Boom is often the last stop on the Wilton Manors strip for a short boogie; a noble attempt to work off the drunken stupor to remixes of diva classics. Nobody really sets out to go to Boom, they just end up there. Karaoke Mondays are hit or miss. 2232 Wilton Drive, (954) 630-3556, MYSPACE.COM/CLUBBOOM

GEORGIE'S ALIBI A historic anchor for the Wilton Manors community, Alibi remains the ultimate neighborhood bar, with nightly drink specials and consistent crowds, notorious for its $3 Long Island Ice Tea Thursdays and a no-frills, laid-back appeal. Come as you are. 2266 Wilton Drive, (954) 565-2526, GEORGIESALIBI.COM

NEW MOON Fort Lauderdale's only and hence premiere lesbian bar, Moon is a crowd pleaser for all ranges of butches and femmes. The outdoor patio is relaxed and gregarious. 2440 Wilton Drive, (954) 563-7660, NEWMOONBAR.COM

RAMROD Shirts off and clippers unplugged, Fort Lauderdale's leather and bear communities "represent" at South Florida's most popular a Levi/leather/uniform bar. Open nightly. Saturdays are superpacked. Attendants will guide you to parking. 1508 N.E. 4th Avenue, (954) 763-8219, RAMRODBAR.COM

ROSIE'S Rosie's takes over where Hamburger Mary's left off, with seven popular all-nights-of-the-week drink specials and mayhem (like Thursday $2 Miller Lites after 7 PM, and Saturday $10 Bacardi buckets all day). 2449 Wilton Drive, (954) 567-1320, ROSIESBARANDGRILL.COM

SCANDALS SALOON "It's all about the cowboys at the Saloon." Novices can feed into the clichéd *Brokeback Mountain* fantasy in an attitude-free environment that features good old-fashioned country western and line dancing. In my opinion, the most welcoming bar in Fort Lauderdale. Free line-dancing lessons on Monday and Tuesday at 7 PM (replaced Manhattan South) and two-step and shadow on Thursdays at 7 PM. Three bars, two pool tables, and no cover. 3073 N.E. 6th Avenue, (954) 567-2432

SIDELINES Sidelines is a spacious but smoky sports bar that taps into the butch side of gay culture. Pop tunes from the electro jukebox dominate the sounds at night but the main appeal rests in the handsome crowds and continuous congregations for watching sports events on the abundant flat screens. The bar boasts a number of accolades as "Best Gay Bar in South Florida." Their biggest night is Friday, but all nights draw crowds both young and old with nightly drink specials. Open daily at 2 PM; Saturday and Sundays at noon. Also popular with women. 2031 Wilton Drive, (954) 563-8001, SIDELINESSPORTS.COM

TRANNIE PALACE After testing and trying an unadulterated drag extravaganza across various venues and nights in South Florida, powerhouse performer, Misty Eyez, has finally found a permanent home for Trannie Palace on Sunday nights at Bill's Filling Station. Misty leads a cast of all-star trannies and drag queens with shows at 10 PM and 11:30 PM. 2209 Wilton Drive, (954) 567-5978, BILLS-FILLINGSTATION.COM

DOWNTOWN

SUNDAY T-DANCE Referred to as "church" by South Florida locals, come 5 PM, Sunday's T-dance marks an intoxicating, hedonistic commencement to the week. Enticed by cheap premium drinks most of the evening, there's no excuse to stay sober till Monday morning. Held in Voodoo Lounge between 5:00 and 11:00, this weekly debauchery also takes place at Sea Monster Nightclub, though the two keep competing for the same market! 111 S.W. 2nd Avenue, 2 Southern River Drive W., SEAMONSTERBAR.COM

HALO NIGHT CLUB FORT LAUDERDALE Following its success on South Beach, Halo brings the magic to Fort Lauderdale in a space filled with the spirit of Cathode Ray, while offering the sophistication, ambiance, and superior quality that has become synonymous with the brand. HALOLOUNGEMIAMI.COM

LIVING ROOM NIGHTCLUB Reigniting a glory once attained by the legendary China White, the Living Room Nightclub has redefined the South Florida nightclub experience through a much needed infusion of sophistication, modernity, and style to the Fort Lauderdale scene. Friday nights shine as a sensual juxtaposition of sounds, sights, lights, and beauty flows across an expanse of five esoteric lounges and chic dance rooms, drawing Florida's finest glam crowd. 300 S.W. 1st Avenue, Upper Level Las Olas Riverfront, (888) 992-7555, LIVINGROOMNIGHTCLUB.COM

JOHNNY'S BOYS Former Boardwalk founder Sean David recently acquired Fort Lauderdale's twinky, barely legal strip bar and turned it into a classier venue. 1116 W. Broward Boulevard, (954) 522-5931, JOHNNYSBARFL.COM

LIFE'S A DRAG AT VOODOO LOUNGE SUNDAYS Fort Lauderdale's longest running (and best!) drag show, hosted by the fabulous and hilarious Daisy Deadpetals, Fort Lauderdale's A-list parties late into the night with the only official gay/straight mixer in town (11 PM–4 AM). Holiday weekends translate to major events at Voodoo when doors open between adjacent and adjoining clubs to produce some of Florida's largest gay parties on the scale of 3,500+ attendees! 111 S.W. 2nd Avenue, (954) 522-0733, VOODOOLOUNGEFLORIDA.COM

TORPEDO Can't get enough come 2 AM or dying to get your rocks off? Head due west on Broward Boulevard, enter the ghetto, and venture to Torpedo to "dance, drink, cruise, and shoot" as the party starts extra late and goes way beyond sunrise. Don't forget to lock your doors before driving into the area to avoid the embarrassing loud lock "click" when locals approach your car at red lights. More popular on Tuesdays and weekends. 2829 W. Broward Boulevard, (954) 587-2500, TORPEDOBAR.COM

ALTERNATIVE NIGHTLIFE

PLAYING IT STRAIGHT

Traveling with your best girlfriend or your sister and it's her turn for a night out? A few straight places where you still may get lucky include **PANGEA AT HARD ROCK** (5707 Seminole Way, (954) 581-5454, PANGAEA-LOUNGE.COM), Wednesdays nights at **VOODOO LOUNGE** (111 SW 2nd Avenue, (954) 522-0733, VOODOOLOUNGEFLORIDA.COM), and **AUTOMATIC SLIMS** (15 W. Las Olas Boulevard, (954) 522-8585, AUTOMATIC-SLIMS.COM).

WINE TASTING AND LIGHT COCKTAILS

Sit back and relax at the **NAKED GRAPE** (2039 Wilton Drive,

(954) 563-5631, NAKEDGRAPEWINECO.COM), a small and cozy wine bar tucked into the gay strip on Wilton Manors that provides an intimate experience for friends looking to socialize away from the scene. Often filled with only a handful of people and the owners, the comfortable chairs and the wooden winery provide a warm backdrop for good conversation. Another good alternative, especially for women, is a light drink at the bar at **FOOD AMONGST THE FLOWERS** (2345 Wilton Drive, (866) 377-2985, FLOWERS2345.COM).

BOWLING

Knock some pins down and play with balls at **MANOR LANES** (1517 N.E. 26th Street, (954) 566-7457, MANORLANESFL.COM). Half the fun is interacting with the staff—real-life teddy bears.

DRAG DINING

Living in the shadow of its New York and San Diego counterparts, the latest installment of the hit restaurant and show bar **LIPS** (1421 E. Oakland Park Boulevard, (954) 567-0987) FLORIDALIPS.COM) has struggled to gain a strong Fort Lauderdale following. Tarnished by the unfortunate location off Oakland Park Boulevard in the 1401 eyesore, the blend of homo kitch, pop art, and black walls strives to foster a vibe of fun and fabulousness. Some of the shows are undoubtedly entertaining, seemingly most enjoyed by straight women seeing their first drag show or older gay male couples who relish in these productions (or my friends Will and Mark who are obsessed with Lips Sunday Gospel brunch and rarely miss the only "church" service with unlimited champagne).

THE PALM BEACHES

6

OUT TRAVELER RATINGS GUIDE

GAY-FRIENDLY: ▼▼▼▼
GAY SCENE: ▼▼
LESBIAN SCENE: ▼▼
PRO-GAY LAWS: ▼▼▼▼▼
HIV RESOURCES: ▼▼▼▼▼

THE POWER OF THE PALM BEACHES

The lifestyle contrasts in Palm Beach County are remarkable. In economics terms, economists would rank the Gini coefficient (measure of inequality of income distribution) on par with that of the two most income disparate countries in the world, Sierra Leone and Bolivia. Palm Beach County is by no means a developing nation, yet it is the largest county east of Mississippi; and while the island of Palm Beach houses one-third of the entire wealth of the United States between January and March every year, the sequence of red-headed stepsisters across the Treasure and Gold Coasts struggle to compete for attention and an average income.

Tourist destinations and gay life in the Palm Beaches center principally on the cities of West Palm Beach and Palm Beach. Preservation plays a very big role here compared to the general "bulldoze it" Florida philosophy; and the Palm Beaches boast the highest concentration of historically designated areas in Florida. While Palm Beach has steadfastly remained America's money vault, West Palm has seen significant upswings and downturns, most recently a rebirth largely spearheaded by gay community members. Bungalows from the 'teens and '20s and Spanish Mission–style and Spanish Mediterranean–style homes have resurfaced—reworked and revisited with a touch of homo sophistication. The crack dens have returned to their original states of grace, and gay couples dominate the neighborhood associations. West Palm's latest downtown revival focuses

CITY PLACE AT NIGHT

on the Clematis Street district and the chain-laden City Place, both chic and modern with notable restaurants, bars, spas, and shopping.

The late night scene remains quiet, and the singles scene a bit lacking. The Palm Beaches are more couples oriented. Saturday nights are less about cruising and clubbing, more about private dinner parties, theater, and entertaining. Sundays are about brunch and gardening in penny loafers and polos.

Driving over to Palm Beach Island from West Palm Beach, the landscape transforms into what appears to be the set of *Honey, I Blew Up the House*. Tales of opulence and extravagance date back to the city's founding as the first resort town in the United States and the birthplace of Florida tourism circa 1894. The legacy of grandeur instituted by Henry Flagler and John D. Rockefeller remains in this former tropical jungle and Florida's first coconut grove. The legacy of Mediterranean revival architecture established by Addison Mizner shines on Billionaire's Row (yes billionaire!). Ranging from 30,000 to 80,000-square feet, the palatial old-money estates dotting the 11-by-1-mile island host winter homes for some of the most famous names in American high society—Rockefeller, Kennedy, Post, Vanderbilt, Kellogg, and the ex-wife of comb-over extraordinaire, Donald Trump (who is usually on the balcony smoking cigarettes, hair naturally bouffant). With überexclusive high society clubs, it's a competition of who can outshine whom, the quintessence of big pimpin' and bling bling.

EVENTS

PALM BEACH JEWELRY, ART, AND ANTIQUE SHOW (FEBRUARY) Held annually over Presidents' Day weekend, over 200 international vendors showcase the vastly impressive collections of art, jewelry, and antiques at the Palm Beach Convention Center. PALMBEACHSHOW.COM

PRIDEFEST OF THE PALM BEACHES (MARCH) A growing pride with nearly 15,000 in 2008, the Palm Beaches' annual Pridefest draws a local crowd for a day celebration of everything gay in Palm Beach County. COMPASSGLCC.COM

TO DO AND SEE

PALM BEACH CRIBS The highlight of any trip to the Palm Beaches entails a car stroll of envy and amazement around and about Palm Beach Island to view homes that even top celebrities could never afford. Stacked one after the next, the lavish and prolific cribs astonish and bewilder the mere commoner. Given that Palm Beach is much more seasonal than other Florida destinations, this excursion is best enjoyed outside of the summertime when homes are sealed with hurricane shutters (and when residents have moved on to the Hamptons).

DO SOME WINDOW SHOPPING DOWN WORTH AVENUE

INTERESTING, RANDOM, AND USELESS FACTS

- Palm Beach has the highest per capita police protection in the country, with a camera on each corner and light.
- The *Palm Beach Daily News* is printed on special high-quality paper to avoid smudging of any shape or form and has earned the nickname the Shiny Sheet.
- In August 2008 Donald Trump sold his villa in Palm Beach for $95 million to Russian billionaire Dmitry Rybolovlev, boasting the highest amount paid for a single-family home in the United States. Trump had paid a mere $41 million for the home in 2004.
- According to the Glenmary Research Center and information from the Association of Religion Data Archives, Palm Beach County has the most Jewish residents of any Florida county (roughly 15%).

WORTH AVENUE Before Julia Roberts's infamous *Pretty Woman* shopping snub on Rodeo Drive, store attendants from the even posher Worth Avenue in Palm Beach were damaging the self-esteem and confidence of millions. The series of beautifully appointed boutiques and designer stores housed in Moorish architecture exude exclusivity and originality. Even the Ralph Lauren store on Worth showcases a special line found only in Palm Beach. Come dressed to kill. WORTHAVENUE.COM

ANTIQUING 1100–3300 Dixie Highway boasts the finest antiquing in Florida and arguably some of the best in the country (Hudson,

New York comes in a close second). Over 40 antique and home design stores cover three blocks where both novices and amateurs can browse through rare and fascinating pieces and collections. The local presence of Mediterranean architecture dictates demand for antique decoration, but collectors come far and wide to discover the gems of Antique Row. A favorite among the LGBT community is James & Jeffrey Antiques, 3619 S. Dixie Highway, West Palm Beach, (561) 832-8818, WESTPALMBEACHANTIQUE.COM

BIKING THE PALM BEACH BEACHES The Palm Beaches were clearly designed with leisure in mind, offering over 20 miles of bike paths along the waterfront and the pristine Palm Beach Lake Trail.

HENRY FLAGLER MUSEUM While the architectural, cultural, and historical gifts of Henry Flagler can be found scattered throughout the state, the Whitehall mansion in Palm Beach houses a rich and concise history of the man whose name is now synonymous with Florida. The museum offers fascinating insight into the life and achievements of Flagler and his legacy of solid infrastructure and luxury tourism. Revered as one of the greatest gilded age mansions in the world, Florida's first museum is the best in South Florida. One Whitehall Way, Palm Beach, (561) 655 2833, FLAGLERMUSEUM.US

MORIKAMI GARDENS At the onset, the idea of Japanese gardens conjures up images of bonsais and lush waterfalls. But while the one-mile trail of gardens is indeed serene and peaceful, do not expect the richness and beauty of botanical gardens. The café is award-winning by the Food Network and reasonably priced for lunch. 4000 Morikami Park Road, Delray Beach, (561) 495-0233, MORIKAMI.ORG

LODGING

THE BREAKERS Consistently awarded every accolade as Florida's finest and most luxurious resort, the Breakers is a blue blood paradise, rich in Gilded Age opulence, Italian Renaissance style, and the legacy of Henry Flagler's personal drama. Unattainable for the majority of the upper-middle class, most visit the Breakers for an overpriced $15 drink at the bar or an $8 cappuccino to feel privileged enough to have stepped foot in Henry Flagler's historical hotel (don't forget the $20 valet parking!). Compared to the ornate 200-foot long lobby and arched ceilings, some rooms are simple and bleak. Others staunchly house the richness and elegance that originally made the Breakers so famous. Most are wheelchair accessible for the elderly and the disabled, whose heirs patiently wait for their timely demise. 1 S. County Road, Palm Beach, (888) 273-2537, THEBREAKERS.COM **VERY EXPENSIVE**

GRANDVIEW GARDENS BED AND BREAKFAST After 16 years in Germany, power couple Rick and Peter opened their doors in 2003 to Florida's premiere B and B, with aesthetic prowess and service excellence on par with Palm Beach's finest hotels. Located in the residential Gardenview Heights historic neighborhood, Rick and Peter take immense pride in the fruits of their labor and investments in this historic 1924 home, diligently restored to its original Spanish Mediterranean architectural roots (with the addition of a fabulous pool). A good blend of gay and straight, homines and class, Grandview Gardens is *the* place to stay for an overnight venture in the Palm Beaches. 1608 Lake Palm Avenue, West Palm Beach, (561) 833-9023, GRANDVIEW-GARDENS.COM **MODERATE**

DINING

BELLE AND MAXWELL'S Hidden among the antique stores, this quaint teahouse and luncheonette would gladly host the Mad Hatter's tea party. The desperate housewives of the Palm Beaches wear their cutest *Alice in Wonderland* party dresses for delectable lunches heavy on the caramelized onions but light on the pocketbook. Alternatively, Belle and Maxwell's doubles as a lively coffee shop famous for homemade desserts (including the $10 sampler platter which gives you four different treats). 3700 S. Dixie Highway, West Palm Beach, (561) 832-4449

FORTE DI ASPIRINO The youngest contestant and now *Top Chef* regular, Stephen Aspirino, demonstrates the cuisine and flair that brought him within four shows of being America's "top chef." An innovative experience of contemporary Italian cuisine in a modern chic setting, Forte provides a reprieve from the traditional and often stuffy backdrop of the Palm Beaches. The 3,500-bottle wine cellar is the starting point for Forte's extensive drink list and dabbling in mixology, combining culinary-driven cocktails with succulent delights such as butter-poached Maine lobster complemented with roasted Russian banana fingerlings. 225 Clematis Street, West Palm Beach, (561) 833-3936, FORTEPALMBEACH.COM

LES BEANS A tried and true coffeehouse, Les Beans is a dying breed. With activities, game nights, movie nights, open mic nights, and even live music, it offers the lot of a local, artsy college coffeehouse while catering to both gays and straights, but mainly les beans (lesbians). Check the most up-to-date calendar. Located near West Palm Beach. 410 2nd Ave N., Lake Worth, (877) 262-2384, MYSPACE.COM/LESBEANSCOFFEE

RHYTHM CAFÉ Relaxed, funky, and eclectic the former drugstore-cum-restaurant features an ever-changing menu to supplement customer favorites including the lemon-doused saganaki (flaming cheese) or the graham cracker-crusted chicken in key lime sauce. The red table cloth, terrazzo floors, original chandeliers, and kitsch tchotckes (including a feathered pink flamingo) give the restaurant distinction and flavor. The dessert menu features rotating flavors of homemade ice creams. 3800 S. Dixie Highway, West Palm Beach, (561) 833-3406, RHYTHMCAFE.COM

NIGHTLIFE

THE LOUNGE Smack-dab in the middle of downtown Clematis, the Lounge restaurant doubles as West Palm's principal gay lounge Thursdays through Saturday nights, with varying themes and events, most notably Saturdays with DJ Daisy D. Open 9 PM–4 AM. 517 Clematis Street, Downtown West Palm Beach, (561) 655-9747, MYSPACE.COM/LOUNGETHURSDAYS

A MARINA IN WEST PALM BEACH

THURSDAYS AT THE COLONY HOTEL The unofficial gay night at the world-famous Colony Hotel every Thursday (7–8:30 PM) provides a rare opportunity to experience true Palm Beach elitism and homo-networking. The silver daddy power forum mandates proper dress code (blazer required year-round, dress pants in winter), maintaining the exclusivity of both the hotel and Palm Beach. A must-do in Palm Beach! 155 Hammon Avenue, Palm Beach, (561) 655-5430, THECOLONYPALMBEACH.COM

H. G. ROOSTERS *The* neighborhood bar of the Palm Beaches, Roosters is reliably busy and comfortable with nightly drink specials and the occasional stripper. Given the name, the bar is aptly decorated with cocks of all shapes and sizes. 823 Belvedere Road, West Palm Beach, (561) 832-9119, HGROOSTERS.COM

7

THE KEYS

OUT TRAVELER RATINGS GUIDE

GAY-FRIENDLY: ▼▼▼▼▼
GAY SCENE: ▼▼▼
LESBIAN SCENE: ▼▼▼
PRO-GAY LAWS: ▼▼▼▼▼
HIV RESOURCES: ▼▼▼▼▼

CRACKED CONCH REPUBLIC

We Just Ain't Right Here!

—*Stephen Smith, longtime Keys resident*

Mile marker 130, Florida City. Shadows of the Wal-Mart Supercenter fade in the distance; suburban sprawl gives way to mangroves and ocean. The massive eight-lane turnpike condenses into two-lane bridges, rising as vehicular islands bordered by the Gulf of

Mexico to the west and the Atlantic Ocean to the east. The landscape change commences a 180-mile journey over 42 bridges and through countless barrier islands, ending 3 hours later in the crown jewel of Florida—Key West.

Despite being connected to the mainland in 1938 through an extension of US Highway 1, the progressive and intoxicating culture of Key West has evolved in isolation, virtually untouched and unaffected by the outside world. The distinctive lifestyle, topography, and geography that define the island merit a claim of independence as an entirely separate entity from the United States, the iconoclastic "Conch Republic." The concept of "One Human Family" governs everyday life in the Conch Republic, where everyone "around the world is entitled to equal rights, dignity, and respect." It's this unique and utopian philosophy that has always attracted the brave and the eccentric, the persecuted and the liberal.

In a sanctuary where transvestites stroll the aisles of Publix without snickers and glares, Key West poses no social sanctions on those who deviate from supposed societal norms. While this has fostered a welcoming atmosphere for hairy, overweight men (and

IN KEY WEST, EVERYONE IS PART OF ONE BIG FAMILY

women) in leather thongs, it's the very cheetah prints, fluorescents, and bad highlights that lend an unparalleled charm to America's only Caribbean island. Beauty or the Beast, you are welcome in Key West. It's rare and special, welcoming and irresistible.

Long famous for outrageous parties with hedonistic overtones, Key West was a homosexual playground in the 1970s and 1980s, an oasis of acceptance in a vastly prejudiced world. Native conchs and transplants will gladly indulge you in erotica from the age of the Copa, the Monster, Lighthouse Court, and Atlantic Shores; they will tell you that Key West was never a land of fashionistas or pretension. Attention-grabbing antics and styles are still futile endeavors. Key West has much less in common with Ibiza, much more in common with Brighton (U.K.), Provincetown, and San Francisco. The theme is and always has been unadulterated fun. And while there is currently no gay nightlife anchor as large as the Copa, the shenanigans of the Keys live on with rowdy happy hours at the Island House for Men, skinny-dipping cruises, random show-and-tell sessions, gratuitous self-exposure at the Sunday La Te Da Tea Dance, and escapist events such as Fantasy Fest.

The 2-by-4-mile stretch of verdant paradise was an endless source of inspiration for Tennessee Williams and Ernest Hemingway. Gingerbread houses, coconut palms, ubiquitous bougainvillea, and lucid waters generated literary genius and embedded a sense of literary dignity throughout the island. The Key West that Williams and Hemingway adored remains frozen in time as "Old Key West," preserved structurally by law and culturally by community.

Beyond architecture and timeless rapture, Key West has matured as a destination over the past decade. Soaring real estate prices and investments have raised the stakes, and the Conch Republic has veered toward an upscale market. Guest houses have been renovated and bars stocked with Grey Goose, broadening the appeal to the upper-middle classes but inadvertently pricing out the younger market. Nightlife and life in general appear more integrated and people now come to the Keys for adventure travel, water sports, and nature as well as relaxation and a bit of debauchery. There are more "invisible gays" in Key West than before—those who prefer to stay at home, garden, and cook; but the island is still considered a refuge for its 35% LGBT community and a magnet for artists and the eccentric.

Over 100,000 gay and lesbian visitors grace the island on an annual basis. Year-round Key West offers sunshine, calm waters, excellent boating, arts, and culture at your disposal, including opera, symphony orchestra, live theater, and cabarets. Undoubtedly you will come back with your own stories and long for a return visit.

THE DRIVE UP FROM (AND DOWN TO) THE KEYS

The approximate three-hour journey from Florida City to Key West provides ample time to shed city stress and marvel at the 360 degrees of blue and green rainbows. Embrace this scenery and note mile markers where you may want to stop on your return drive. Impatiently tailgating the slow truck in front of you will only delay your arrival into a relaxing and patient Keys state of mind.

If you're a curious traveler, you'll find yourself wanting to turn onto side roads, longing to discover hidden coves off the beaten path. But for the drive down, I recommend leisurely car gazing but arriving in Key West as early as possible to enjoy the day. The drive back, on the other hand, should be made into a day trip.

As you begin your journey back, hopefully you are tanned, well rested, and well sexed, but not quite ready to end your vacation. You have checked out of your hotel, have made new friends, and taken with you special memories of Key West. Unless you're feeling tremendous separation anxiety from the Keys, I would suggest heading out around 11 AM to enjoy a day of extraordinary food and a bonding session with nature.

FOOD OPTIONS

Ideally you will stop at mile marker 21 to eat lunch at the rustic **SQUARE GROUPER BAR & GRILL** (22518 La Fitte Drive, Cudjoe Key, (305) 745-8880) the "best-kept secret in the entire Keys" according to many locals and home of my favorite conch fritters in the Keys. If you just had a big breakfast at your B and B, a second good choice for lunch arrives 1.5 hours later at the original **ISLAMORADA FISH COMPANY** (81532 Overseas Highway, Islamorada, (305) 664-9271, FISHCOMPANY.COM). Albeit mildly touristy, the resident groups of sharks, tarpons, and pelicans are guaranteed crowd pleasers and make for fantastic photo opportunities. Approaching Key Largo, the **KEY LARGO CONCH HOUSE** (100211 Overseas Highway, (305) 453-4844, KEYLARGOCOFFEEHOUSE.COM) at mile marker 100.2 features a dessert now made famous on the Food Channel, Blueberry Pecan Crunch Fruit Tart, to complement the fabulous coffees and lunches.

NATURE OPTIONS

Dolphin lovers and couples with kids may want to stop on Grassy Key at the **DOLPHIN RESEARCH CENTER** (58901 Overseas Highway, Grassy Key, (305) 289-0002, DOLPHINS.ORG), a not-for-profit organization with goals to promote peaceful coexistence, cooperation, and communication between marine mammals, humans, and the environment. The main draw at the DRC entails personal encounters with rehabilitated dolphins in a safe, welcoming, and healthy environment for swimming with these magical creatures. Due to high demand, reservations are a must.

Beach lovers and water sports enthusiasts will want to spend the afternoon at **BAHIA HONDA STATE PARK** (36850 Overseas Highway, Big Pine Key, (305) 872-3210, BAHIAHONDASTATEPARK.COM). The powdery sand of Bahia Honda at mile marker 37 once earned the title of the "Best Beach in America" from *Condé Naste Traveler*. The island boasts both secluded and more trafficked spots for sunbathing, as well as rustic cabins for overnight visitors. They also offer fishing, kayaking, and snorkeling at very reasonable prices. The waters are spectacular and the largest intact section of Henry Flagler's historic overseas railroad is an eye-catcher.

If you did not get your fill of snorkeling in Key West or fancy a bit of diving, **JOHN PENNEKAMP STATE PARK** (102601 Overseas Highway, Key Largo, (305) 451-1202, PENNEKAMPPARK.COM)

DOLPHINS SWIM BY, WAITING FOR COMPANY

showcases living, shallow-water coral reefs of the Florida Keys National Marine Sanctuary, vibrant with color and activity. The PADI 5-Star Gold Palm facility at the park offers two-location, two-tank dives twice daily, at 9:30 and 1:30.

If you have not already visited the wetlands wonderland known as the Everglades, **EVERGLADES NATIONAL PARK** (40001 State Road 9336, Homestead, (305) 242-7700, NPS.GOV/EVER) is a quick 10-minute drive before you enter the turnpike. The short Anhinga Trail is fantastically gratifying, teeming with the glades' most famous wildlife. A stop at **ROBERT IS HERE** (19200 Southwest 344 Street, Homestead, (305) 246-1592, ROBERTISHERE.COM) is an essential if choosing this option. Robert whips up the best milkshakes I have ever had in my life (my favorite being key lime). See chapter 3's "Forgotten Florida" section for more details.

EVENTS

NEW YEAR'S SHOE DROP (JANUARY 1) As seen on CNN, watch the world-famous drag queen, Sushi, drop inside a ginormous red high-heeled shoe in tandem with Times Square's apple, as the clock strikes midnight. The best New Year's event in Florida. December 31. GAYKEYWESTFL.COM

PRIDEFEST (JUNE) One of the more low-key events on the island, Pridefest is a celebratory week of everything gay Key West. Produced by the GLCC, events change annually, but always include the Pride parade along Duval Street and parties before and after the parade. On its 25th anniversary in 2007 Pridefest celebrated with a sea-to-sea rainbow flag. PRIDEFESTKEYWEST.COM

TROPICAL HEAT (AUGUST) An ode to old Key West debauchery, this is typical Keys: clothing optional, raunchy mayhem in its purest form. It's an entire weekend of adult-themed parties including a feisty fetish bash. Be prepared for lengthy sessions of "show and tell." TROPICALHEATKW.COM

WOMENFEST (SEPTEMBER) This annual event of Labor Day weekend draws over 4,000 women from around the world, with reserved cultural events for the conservative crowd and raucous parties for the more liberal, such as clothing-optional pool parties and sexy bull riding competitions with gregarious and forthcoming crowds. WOMENFEST.COM

FANTASY FEST (OCTOBER) Talk about squeezing something large into a small space! The population of Key West swells more than threefold to 87,000 people during its most popular event of the year—Fantasy Fest! An entire week of eccentric activities, costume parties, and special events around the time of Halloween, including the Pet Masquerade (where people parade their pets in the most hilarious costumes) and the centerpiece of the week—the Headdress Ball (FANTASYFEST.NET; KEYSTIX.COM for ticketed events). Proceeds from Fantasy Fest benefit AIDS Help, Inc. to the tune of nearly half a million dollars annually. FANTASYFEST.NET

TO DO AND SEE

Any trip to the Keys should include a combination of land and sea activities. Don't fall into the trap of hotel reclusion; the Keys are too beautiful to miss! By land, skip all the touristy, cruise ship passenger crap near the port, and focus on the suggestions I provide. By sea, a minimum of two separate boat excursions are recommended, one for leisure and one for nature. The Florida Keys National Marine Sanctuary encompasses 2,900 square nautical miles between Dry Tortugas and Miami, housing the beautiful Florida Reef with over

INTERESTING, RANDOM, AND USELESS FACTS

- Key West has the highest average temperature in the United States.
- Key West's title as the southernmost point is valid only in the continental United States as points in Hawaii stem farther south.
- The Southernmost Point is no longer the southernmost point of the continental United States since surrounding land was dredged to expand Key West by over one-third its size and now reclaimed lands sits to the south.
- A pioneer in marine conservation, Key Largo designated the nation's first undersea preserve, John Pennekamp Coral Reef State Park, in 1960.
- In April 1982, Mayor Dennis Wardlaw announced that Key West had seceded from the union as "the Conch Republic," as retaliation against blockades from the Mariel Boatlift.
- Islamorada is billed as the sport fishing capital of the world.
- The Key West Business Guild Office is the oldest gay chamber-of-commerce-type organization in the United States.

311 species of tropical fish. Do not expect snorkeling or diving on par with Australia's Great Barrier Reef; however, the waters are clear, crisp, refreshing, and inviting. Options are available that combine snorkeling with water sports or the LGBT favorite—skinny

dipping! Be sure to read about the **DRY TORTUGAS NATIONAL PARK, DOLPHIN ENCOUNTERS,** and **LITTLE PALM ISLAND** in chapter 3, "Forgotten Florida"; these are three life-changing experiences available in the Keys.

BY SEA

BLU Q DAY TRIP Year-round, Key West's only all-gay sailing catamaran offers a rewarding half-day snorkeling and sailing adventure for groups sized 4 to 30. Fourteen years strong, the men-only excursion includes lunch and wine/beer (once done swimming and snorkeling) and a rare opportunity for clothing-optional sea bathing and mid-ocean sunbathing! Dutch and French guests seem particularly keen on remaining undressed the entire trip, even following major shrinkage from the cool waters of the Atlantic! Staff are welcoming, knowledgeable (and usually naked), fostering a casual atmosphere without the strict agendas of regular, timed, and straight catamaran trips. Departures take place from the foot of William Street at the Historic Seaport. 201 William Street, (305) 923-7245, BLUEKEY WEST.COM

VENUS CHARTERS FOR WOMEN Women-only snorkel, fishing, dolphin watching, and sunset trips. Departures from Palm Drive in the Garrison Bight City Marina. 2210 Staples Avenue, (305) 292-9403, VENUSCHARTERS.COM

BLUE PLANET KAYAK ECO-TOURS Independently owned and operated by environmental scientist Chad Bryant, Blue Planet ventures with small groups to secluded tidal creeks, tidal pools, and serene waters to explore a world of urchins, starfish, coral, conchs, and baby sharks. At night, shifts change to reveal a world of nocturnal animals such as eels, squid, lobster, and wading birds. Tours are offered during mornings, afternoons, and evenings. This is a brilliant opportunity for adults and kids alike. (305) 294-8087, BLUE-PLANET-KAYAK.COM

FURY WATER ADVENTURES Fury offers daily catamaran departures for an action-packed day of reef snorkeling and water sports on Fury's "floating island," home to a floating rock climbing wall, kayaking, water trampoline, jet skiing, parasailing, and sunbathing decks. Departure point assigned at time of booking. Excursion includes food and drinks. Specific gay sailings happen weekly, sometimes monthly. Check with your hotel concierge. 237 Front Street, (305) 294-8899, FURYKEYWEST.COM

BAREFOOT BILLY'S The best option for water sports enthusiasts, with endless varieties of group-led and independent opportunities of jet skiing, kayaking, paddling, and banana boat diversion. Located at the Wyndham Reach Resort (with an "R") off the only natural sand beach in Key West. 1435 Simonton Street, (305) 296-5000 x6670, REACHWATERSPORTS.COM

EVENING CRUISES

SUNSET CRUISE (LGBT) In the evening, the **BLU Q** transforms into an "all welcome" sunset cruise—a perfect opportunity to watch the dramatic disappearance of the sun in the presence of the entire dysfunctional family. Soft drinks, beer, and wine are included during the two-hour cruise. Departures are from the foot of William Street at the Historic Seaport. Alternatively, **SEBAGO WATERSPORTS** runs a women-only sunset cruise every Thursday. (305) 923-7245, BLUQKEYWEST.COM and KEYWESTSEBAGO.COM/GAY.PHP

LIBERTY FLEET Either the classic 125-foot *Liberty Clipper* or the 80-foot *Schooner Liberty* whisks you away to the open ocean to witness a famous Key West sunset with unlimited champagne, wine, and beer. The sunset cruise is strongly recommended over the dinner cruise. 6:30–8:30 in summer and 5–7 in winter on Wednesday, Friday, and Saturday. Departures are from Schooner Wharf, William Street at the Historic Seaport. (305) 295-0095, LIBERTYFLEET.COM

ISLESCAPES GOURMET YACHTING A wonderful idea for celebrating a milestone or guaranteeing good sex from your partner, this romantic dinner cruise offers a gourmet gastronomic adventure in an intimate setting aboard a private yacht. Start with crabmeat Portobello mushrooms and mango salad, followed by fresh catch of the day, and finish with strawberries served with key lime white chocolate whipped cream. (305) 923-3319, ISLESCAPES.COM

BY LAND

WALKING AND BIKING TOURS For bespoke self-guided tours of arts and history, pick up *Sharon Wells' Walking and Biking Guide to Historic Key West,* free in most shops.

THE SOUTHERNMOST POINT The first Key West essential—a photo in front of the Southernmost Point mega buoy marker. You may have to wait in line, but it's a priceless addition to the photo collection.

MALLORY SQUARE No trip to Key West is complete without a (five-minute) trip to the world-famous and hypertouristy Mallory Square, where the Gulf of Mexico and Atlantic Ocean collide. Mallory still reigns as the most popular spot for watching the sunset, though the roof at La Concha Hotel on Duval Street or a sunset cruise are much better options.

THE GAY AND LESBIAN TROLLEY TOUR OF FABULOUS KEY WEST The only gay and lesbian historic trolley tour in the nation provides an excellent overview of Key West, even for locals, with a LGBT twist that puts the history and the stories you may have heard about Key West in topographical perspective. The tour is both informative and entertaining and strongly recommended for first-time visitors. Check with the concierge at your guesthouse or call (305) 295-4603. Tours usually depart Saturdays at 11:00 AM from South and Simonton streets. Alternatively, the world-famous **CONCH TOUR TRAIN** (CONCHTOURTRAIN.COM) or **OLD TOWN TROLLEY TOUR** (OLDTOWNTROLLEY.COM) are available daily, but be prepared to take it with the masses.

MOPED HOSPITAL AND BIKES Zooming around the 2 × 4 island on a moped is an empowering and exhilarating feeling while biking feels more relaxing and thought provoking. 601 Truman Avenue, (305) 296-1625, MOPEDHOSPITAL.COM

FLORIDA KEYS ECO-DISCOVERY CENTER This $6 million government project brought together coordinated efforts of five major government bodies (imagine that!) but has fallen short on its marketing budget leaving it virtually unknown in the Key West ringside. Within the walls of the center lies over 6,000 square feet of hands-on and interactive exhibits and living reefs. Free. 9 AM–4 PM, Tuesday–Saturday. 35 East Quay Road, (305) 809-4750, FLORIDAKEYS.NOAA.GOV

WHAT TO DO WHEN IT RAINS?

- Take a primer in Keys marine biology by visiting the Florida Eco-Center and Key West Aquarium.
- Indulge in a spa treatment at Prahna Day Spa (see chapter 3, "Pampering: Florida's Top Spas")
- Get a day pass for the Island House and play in the hot tub and swimming pool while sipping cocktails. Rainy days are popular days at the Island House to head to the bar, and the eerrrrghhmmm video room. Sorry ladies. Men only!
- Contemplate life at the Key West cemetery. Outrageous tombstones and plots will be better read in the rain. Wear black.

KEY WEST BUTTERFLY AND NATURE CONSERVATORY Power couple George and Sam toured butterfly conservatories across the world before building their small masterpiece, rated the #1 tourist attraction in the Keys (it's a family favorite). 1108 Duval Street, (305) 296-2988, KEYWESTBUTTERFLY.COM

AIDS MEMORIAL When AIDS hit, it devastated the Key West community and the economy. Pay homage to the 14,000 names on the AIDS memorial, including Key West's first gay mayor. A picnic on the adjacent pier completes a pensive and commemorative afternoon.

LODGING (LGBT)

Staying at a Key West guesthouse is a fundamental ingredient to your key lime vacation pie. Where I find myself torn between boutique hotels, B and B's and big name brands in other cities, the decision to stay in a gay guesthouse in Key West is second nature. In my weeks of research in the Keys, these B and B's housed some of the most interesting, eccentric, and crazy individuals I have ever met, many of whom have now become fabulous friends. With tens of gay guesthouses, individually themed, and equipped with heavy marketing budgets, accommodations exist to suit all tastes and distastes.

Your experience at the guesthouse will change with each visit. Sometimes they are rammed; other times quiet. Sometimes you have a young tour group from France renting most of the rooms, other times it appears that Santa Claus has found his vacation home. In general, the average age of visitors to the gay houses stands around 42 years old. Most come for the welcome, relaxed atmosphere of the Keys that has always enticed different sizes, shapes, and colors. Most people quickly discover their favorite and return year after year. In fact, all guesthouses featured here boast return rates over 50%. Note that LGBT lodging is adults-only unless specified otherwise.

ALEXANDER'S GUESTHOUSE The fresh-cut birds of paradise displayed at reception in the designer vase indicate the tier of establishment you are about to enter. Void of the sexual tension and cruziness of other guesthouses, Alexander's welcomes both gays and lesbians to a stylish lush oasis with expansive rooms adorned with private verandas and decks. Alexander's is a favorite for power couples looking for seclusion but also to meet other successful gays in a casual setting (regardless of gender). An amazing breakfast spread is served in a contemporary kitchen that would make even Martha Stewart jealous. 1118 Fleming Street, (305) 294-9919, ALEXGHOUSE.COM **MODERATE**

BIG RUBY'S GUESTHOUSE Big Ruby has set an international standard for upscale gay guesthouses. With consistently fabulous resorts dotted across the globe, guests are guaranteed an exceptional stay. Ruby's boasts extreme proximity to Duval and the water as well as free breakfast, including unlimited Bloody Marys seven days a week, and mimosas on Sunday. The spacious grounds are very social, clothing optional, and adorned with beautiful flowers and amazing landscaping. 409 Appelrouth Lane, (305) 296-2323, BIGRUBYS.COM **MODERATE**

COCONUT GROVE RESORT/OASIS RESORT/CORAL TREE INN It's guesthouse multiple choice at this triple resort powerhouse, a series of restored Bahamian style homes, tranquil swimming pools, and luxuriant, multitiered rooftop gardens. With a focus on rest, relaxation, and privacy while catering mostly to couples, the clothing-optional resort trio is mildly cruisy at most. The Beyonce of the three, the Coconut Grove Resort, showcases the conceptualization of interior designer Zeke Fernandez with marble floors, glass showers, sky blue walls, flat screen televisions, and cappuccino-colored furniture direct from the Crate & Barrel catalog. Breakfast included. Happy hour includes wine and appetizers and two rounds of frozen drinks daily. 815-823 Fleming Street, (305) 296-2131, COCONUTGROVEKEYWEST.COM, OASISKEYWEST.COM **MODERATE**

EQUATOR RESORT This resort once reigned as the leading all-male guesthouse. Following renovations in 2006, the hotel revives a traditional Key West feel, with pale yellows juxtaposed on richer yellows, a new hot tub, an upper sundeck, and 20 freshly refurbished rooms. 818 Fleming Street, (305) 294-7775, EQUATORRESORT.COM **MODERATE**

ISLAND HOUSE FOR MEN The world's foremost example of a "gay biosphere," the Island House is a self-contained gay man's world, with all the elements necessary to support gay male life—a fully-equipped gym, a full-service bar, a delicious restaurant, raucous happy hours, a 3:1 staff to guest ratio, free Starbucks coffee 24 hours a day, a gregarious and eventful poolside, a sundeck with misting system, sauna on premises, and plenty of nudity. Housed in flawless architecture inspired by Ernest Hemingway's Havana home and inundated with an intoxicating and undeniable sexual vibe, readers of our *Out Traveler* magazine have consistently declared Island House their favorite resort on the planet! It's a fantasy campground for the liberal and the open, and the happy hour is by far the best in Key West. You will undoubtedly return from the Island House with crazy stories, new friends, and amazing memories. While breakfast may not be included, the restaurant dishes up exceptionally affordable plates that rival neighboring restaurants. Note that you can experience the hype without staying by purchasing a day pass for $25 (must have a photo ID). 1129 Fleming Street, (305) 294-6284, ISLANDHOUSEKEYWEST.COM **MODERATE**

PEARL'S RAINBOW FOR WOMEN Even my lesbian friends were shocked to discover an all-women's clothing-optional resort. Where Pearl herself says, "this has to be the best women's paradise in the country," *Out Traveler* readers named it their favorite female resort. Thirty-eight rooms grace the inside of three historic buildings joined by heated swimming pools and hot tubs. With an even mix of couples and singles, it's a welcoming arena for new friends, feminist bonding, and fun in-house events like the annual hippie fest (retro theme with special drinks) and the "Bad Girls Party." 525 United Street, (305) 292-1450, PEARLSRAINBOW.COM **MODERATE**

LODGING (MAINSTREAM)

CASA MARINA Home to some of my favorite childhood memories, Henry Flagler's 1920s luxury resort has changed hands numerous times between corporate giants over the past 20 years. Following Hurricane Wilma in 2005, Marina was a hot, mildewy mess, but a major face-lift in 2007 has revealed a flagship Wyndham property that exudes tropical elegance. The open splendor of this contemporary oceanfront masterpiece is accessorized with swaying palms trees, blooming native flowers, and sweeping ocean views. Descending straight-edged water pools spill out onto 1,100 feet of private beach and with coral heads fit for snorkeling and countless intertidal pools great for exploring (once serving as my living marine doll houses). 1500 Reynolds Street, (866) 397-6342, CASA-MARINARESORT.COM **EXPENSIVE**

SHERATON SUITES The best kid-friendly, pet-friendly, and family option on the island, the Sheraton Suites provides all-suite accommodations across from the beach in a traditional Key West resort setting with all the amenities and services known with a category 4 Starwood property (SHERATONKEYWEST.COM). Starwood's more upscale option, the Westin Key West Resort and Marina, is located in the heart of old town. 245 Front Street, (305) 294-4000, WESTINKEYWESTRESORT.COM **EXPENSIVE**

DINING

EARLY SHIFT

BLUE HEAVEN RESTAURANT A renovated whorehouse in Bahama Village, Blue Heaven offers the quintessential Key West island experience with casual outdoor seating, solid American selections, and the island's notorious chickens run amok. Famed for its "breakfast with the roosters," fresh baked breads, amazing wine selection, and temperature-controlled wine cellar, Blue Heaven is a top choice for breakfast and lunch. Homemade pancakes are the morning favorite, followed by shrimp, beef, bacon, ham, or sausage Benedict with poached eggs, and lime hollandaise sauce. Lunch and dinner dishes blend Caribbean and Southern cooking with a Keys' flair. Drink specials such as the Key West Pink Lemonade concocted with homemade sour mix is a must. Note the remnants of the brothel structures such as the massive peepholes in the toilets. 729 Thomas Street, (305) 296-8666, BLUEHEAVENKW.COM

B.O. FISH WAGON The first time you drive, walk, or bike past the parking lot that houses B.O. Fish Wagon, you are sure to do a double take. The colorful and tactless signs and slabs of ill-placed wood sitting around four defunct tires appear to be a fascinating termite-laden junkyard somehow reminiscent of an aboriginal structure on a deserted island. This strange curiosity lands you at a Key West institution with the freshest fish on the island, a chalkboard menu of daily caught favorites, and an old-school charm among the staff, who serve 'em as fast as they cook 'em. 801 Caroline Street, (305) 294-9272

CAMILLE'S RESTAURANT A great breakfast and lunch spot known for morning specialties (which earned the title "Best Breakfast in the United States" from the fading AOL), homemade soups, salads, sandwiches, and a cocktail, Camille's sports a number of home-made originals such as an ever-changing drink of the day (mine was Camille's Passion Fruit Mimosa), the self-proclaimed "best eggs Benedict ever," and a signature chicken salad sandwich made with a secret combination of raisins, mustard, and homemade mayonnaise. 1202 Simonton Street, (305) 296-4811, CAMILLESKEYWEST.COM

HARPOON HARRY'S A gay-owned and -operated local favorite, this simple, consistent, and inexpensive Key West diner provides all the nutrition and grease necessary to jumpstart the day or cure the worst of hangovers. My favorites include the crispy hash-and-onion omelet and the traditional breakfast dishes with a bit of lobster thrown in the mix. Open only until 3 PM. 832 Caroline Street, (305) 294-8744, HARPOONHARRYS.COM

LATE SHIFT

ALICE'S RESTAURANT Large groups often crowd the simple storefront, eagerly awaiting the latest ingenious taste sensation of Chef Alice Weingarten, such as the Cuban Style Mojo Marinated Ostrich and the Pure Passion Salad (wild baby greens with goat cheese, mango, toasted almonds, and berries in Alice's own passion fruit vinaigrette). Rich in flavors, succulence, and the contrasts of sweets and sours, Alice combines tropical tastes with Latin, American, and Asian distinction to create her own eclectic mouth-watering fusion. 1114 Duval Street, (305) 292-5733, ALICESKEYWEST.COM

CAFÉ MARQUESA Imagine a restaurant so sensational that it was recommended by the *Miami Herald* as a valid excuse for a seven-hour round-trip from Miami with a sole purpose of pure gastronomic indulgence. While the *Herald* may have gone a bit overboard with this statement, Chef Susan Ferry undoubtedly prepares an *entire* menu of food orgasms in contemporary American cuisine, with a heavy focus on seafood, most notably macadamia-crusted yellowtail snapper and conch-and-blue crab cakes. The menu changes regularly according to season and availability of fresh ingredients. 600 Fleming Street, (305) 292-1919, MARQUESA.COM/CAFE MARQUESA

MICHAEL'S RESTAURANT Conchs are very picky about their food and each swears by his or her token favorite restaurant. However, the 100-plus conchs I interviewed while in Key West all had one thing in common—Michael's Restaurant—as one of their three favorite places to dine. Situated in the heart of the historic district, patrons dine in the lush courtyard, starting with a treat from the extensive cocktail list and moving on to culinary divinity. The most popular dish: Michael's veal chop stuffed with prosciutto, basil, fresh mozzarella, and lightly breaded, topped with a mushroom-and-marsala demi-glace. 532 Margaret Street, (305) 295-1300, MICHAELSKEYWEST.COM

915 The luminous star of Duval Street, Nine One Five Bistro and Wine Bar serves up Key West global fusion in tapa and entrée portions alongside complementary whites and reds from around the world. Housed in a restored century-old white-washed Victorian house, the subdued lighting maintained by lights dangling over and around the classical porches fosters an ambience of romance and relaxed elegance. The taste sensations from the menu run the gamut from the signature Tuna Dome (fresh Dungeness crab with a lemon miso dressing wrapped in ahi tuna sashimi) to Serano Ham Carpaccio and Chipotle Conch Chowder. 915 Duval Street, (305) 296-0669, 915DUVAL.COM

SQUARE ONE RESTAURANT Once heralded as a top restaurant in the Keys, Square One's popularity waned when locals felt the menu had grown tired and insipid after 15 years. Owner Michael Stewart heeded the jeers and commentaries, successfully revamping the menu with novel Asian-American fusion under the direction of Executive Chef Andrew Nguyen. The newly inspired creations such as the Chocolate-Espresso New York Striploin Tataki with Papaya Kimichi Salad and Micro Coriander Sprouts constitute an avant-garde cuisine guaranteed to excite the palate. As always, Michael treats every guest as a VIP. 1075 Duval Street, (305) 296-4300, SQUAREONERESTAURANT.COM

NIGHTLIFE

I have met most of my best friends at La Te Da.
—*Mary Jo Da Silva, Key West resident since 1999*

Key West's nightlife centers on a small section of Duval Street, aptly termed the Pink Triangle. Overly inebriated visitors conveniently crawl from one bar to the next before unscrambling the pieces the following morning in a stranger's bed. Sunday starts early a few blocks down from the Triangle but is the most rewarding night on the town.

AQUA NIGHTCLUB The premier nightclub and show club in Key West, Aqua hosts nightly performances from the best drag queens in the Southeast. The riveting impersonations of celebrity favorites such as Celine Dion and Cher (Faith Michael's performance of "I'm Alive" and Randy Thompson's performance of "Turn Back Time" changed my life) coupled with creative, interactive mimed compilations of pop favorites attracts straights and gays alike. Around 9 PM, the club swells with locals and curious tourists ready to unleash their liberal side. The young straight girls comprising nearly 40% of the audience go wild at presumably their first fabulous drag shows, having their very own "I'm so cool, I'm at a gay place moment" and enjoying what most of them describe in valley girl talk as "the best night EVER!" For Aqua regulars,

KEY LIME RAPTURE

Of course a trip to the Keys would never be complete without overindulging in the specialty—key lime pie. While capitalist tendencies have led to key lime products ad nauseam, creativity and secret recipes still dominate the baker's landscape, with countless pie variations across the island.

- The Dining Room, Little Palm Island—cashew crust, thick vanilla bean cream
- Kermit's—traditional, meringue topped, or chocolate dipped (200-A Elizabeth St., (305) 296-0806, KEYLIMESHOP.COM)
- Key lime milkshake at Robert Is Here (near Everglades National Park)
- Alice's Restaurant—chocolate coating on crust
- Joe's Stone Crabs—traditional and fabulous, the best key lime outside of the Keys

the shows stand as predictably funny and entertaining. 711 Duval Street, (305) 294-0555, AQUAKEYWEST.COM

BOURBON STREET PUB The closest thing Key West has to a gay dance club, the Bourbon Street Pub has two bars in the front with male dancers and a poolside bar in the back. 724 Duval Street, (305) 296-1992, BOURBONSTREETPUB.COM

801 BOURBON STREET Another bar with heavy emphasis on the drag entertaining, the nightly 9:00 and 11:00 shows are more raw and less theatrical than Aqua. Different drag queens host each show nightly in a hit-or-miss sequence of entertaining and sometimes shocking cabaret. $5 cover and best enjoyed after copious amounts of alcohol. 801 Duval Street, (305) 294-4737, 801BOURBON.COM

JAZZ IN THE GARDENS AT THE GARDENS HOTEL Fabulous owner Kate Mariano hosts a Sunday live jazz party in an intimate and fairy-tale setting of luxuriant landscaping and exquisite gardens. The sophisticated and upscale nature of the event coupled with the welcoming atmosphere has attracted a large gay population on a weekly basis (roughly 30% gay). 526 Angela Street, (800) 526-2664, GARDENSHOTEL.COM

KWEST MEN Hot strippers entice you into a rectangular sliver of bass thumping and go-go boys, into the only place in Florida where the men can legally flash their willies (though they are not allowed to orgasm). 705 Duval Street, (305) 292-8500, KWESTMEN.COM

LA TE DA, SUNDAY TEA DANCE The Sunday tea dance symbolizes the legend, history, and philosophy of Key West—one human family—a testimony to liberation and freedom in its purest form. Set to the sounds of bad bar mitzvah music (like the Pointer Sisters), this tea dance embraces all who attend with kindness, generosity, and wicked fun. It's an overwhelming congregation of joy, camaraderie, and friendship. 1125 Duval Street, (305) 296-6706, LATEDA.COM

PEARL'S PATIO FOR WOMEN Located within Pearl's Rainbow, the guesthouse bar is open to all women from 5 to 7 PM Monday through Saturday (Fridays are the most popular). On Sunday Pearl's Patio offers discounted drinks and beers, often hosting televised sporting events. 525 United Street, (305) 292-1450, PEARLSPATIO.COM

SALOON 1 Key West's only Levi, leather, and uniform bar. Down the street, Leathermaster sells all your leather paraphernalia. 801 Duval Street, (305) 294-4737

ORLANDO

8

OUT TRAVELER RATINGS GUIDE

GAY-FRIENDLY: ▼▼▼▼
GAY SCENE: ▼▼▼
LESBIAN SCENE: ▼▼▼▼
PRO-GAY LAWS: ▼▼▼▼
HIV RESOURCES: ▼▼▼▼

HELP, I'M IN ORLANDO!

In a land of fairy tales and imagination, Walt Disney himself would be removed from his cryogenic chamber and resuscitated to wake up in the commercial explosion that he unknowingly began over 50 years ago in California. Chances are Pixar already has begun work on this movie!

But more likely, had Walt really been frozen and brought back to life, he would suffer an immediate heart attack from consumerist asphyxiation upon arrival in Orlando. The swamp and wilderness that once served as a backdrop for his dream project has transformed into an incomparable monstrosity of 100 attractions, 112,000 hotel rooms, and 5,300 restaurants spread over a merger of four cities dubbed "Orlando" (Kissimmee, St. Cloud, Lake Buena Vista, and Orlando), all inspired by a little mouse.

The Magic Kingdom opened on October 1, 1971, as the first part of Walt Disney's planned Florida Project with two hotels on the property—Disney's Contemporary Resort (which still considers itself "contemporary") and Disney's Polynesian Resort. Exactly 11 years later, in 1982, the more educational EPCOT (Experimental Prototype Community of Tomorrow) fascinated the big-haired public with fantasies of the future such as solar-powered cars, cordless transportable phones (now called cell phones), space travel, and what life would be like if they lived to "party like it was 1999!" As the '80s progressed, global investments surged in Orlando, hotels and restaurants began to litter the landscape, and new theme parks popped up like unwanted hemorrhoids.

Sea World brought the oceans to Central Florida in 1973, Wet-n-Wild the overgrown Slip 'n' Slide in 1977, Universal the movies in 1990. Inane and poorly designed imposters soon followed—the Holy Land Experience biblical theme park (built by Jews for Jesus), the World's Largest McDonald's Play Place (literally supersized), and Splendid China (the first modern fall of the growing superpower, closed in 2003). The scramble for Orlando between the 1980s and 1990s mirrored the imperialist scramble for Africa between the 1880s and 1914, where each corporate giant/investor (European nation) fought for a piece of the Orlando pie (African continent), effectively destroying the land and the people and changing the entire landscape and culture.

Flash forward to modern-day Orlando, a toppled gaudy sequence of bright lights, oversized outlets, competing theme parks, flashy shopping malls, 50 million visitors annually, and an economic impact of $29.6 billion. While we will never know Walt's feelings on this, for the general public Orlando *is* the American dream. It's the very gluttonous portions, gargantuan rides, recognizable brands, and envy that lure droves of visitors to the most visited place on Earth. In a world where consumerist capabilities constitute success, taking the family to Orlando is a societal and parental pressure from the children once plopped in front of the tube for distraction, now gleefully obsessed with a favorite character (Pluto and Pocahontas in my case). It's even greater pressure to outshine the other kids and neighbors who visit the Mouse et al. on a regular basis, and always return with the same souvenir—the oversized and insurmountable rainbow swirl lollipop that becomes a melted bacterial cesspit of saliva, and then sits in the fridge for a year.

It's arguably a fact of life that for generations born from the 1970s onward, most of your fondest childhood memories will have taken place in Orlando, regardless of where you grew up, and one day you will return to bask in the glory and frivolity of childhood. You will ride "Peter Pan" and long for Never-Never Land and freak out when you feel the tracks of "Space Mountain" nearly decapitate you, now that you're all grown up. You will also notice that the grounds of Disney and all of Orlando are undeniably bouncing with robust populations of homosexuals, a phenomenon you probably never noticed as a child. The fantasy and imagination of Orlando has always attracted a large LGBT population and provided countless jobs for aspiring entertainers and service industry novices and professionals. Disney's progressive domestic partner benefits took root long before it was politically correct or socially forced. It's no surprise that the Gay Days event held every June in Orlando has grown to be one of the largest LGBT congregations in the world.

Though I personally feel the allure of Orlando detracts from the experience of Florida's natural attractions and magnificence, visiting the theme parks and enjoying the world's most vacationed destination is an essential element for a charmed life. Without fail I return annually to Orlando Gay Days, and as a native Floridian, pass through the entrance aisle at Disney Hollywood Studios time and time again to watch my cousin star in the Voyage of the Little Mermaid, followed by some cheap thrills on Tower of Terror and Rock 'n' Rollercoaster. I just always remind those around me that there is much more to Florida! It's more than the mouse!

A COMPLETE GUIDE TO GAY DAYS: THE BEST GAY EVENT IN AMERICA

Loud and proud, 3,000 gay, lesbian, bisexual, and transgender individuals took to the candy-coated streets of the Magic Kingdom in June 1991 to "wear red and be seen," commencing what would become the fiercest and most inclusive gay event in U.S. history—Gay Days. In nearly two decades, Gay Days has swelled into a weeklong, citywide celebration of love, life, sex, and everything G-A-Y. The rightwing protests have faded, and with over 150,000 attendees, Gay Days (now referred to as Gay Disney Weekend) offers events and parties catering to all crowds: muscle boys, bears, crack heads, butch lesbians, fem lesbians, families, pre-ops, post-ops, recovering alcoholics, sports fanatics, teens. It's the most anticipated annual event in Florida and a mind-boggling explosion of gay subcultures.

Most Gay Disney activities center on four themed events—One Mighty Weekend, Gay Days, Girls at Gay Days, and Girls in Wonderland. Each event sponsor offers a host hotel, exhilarating pool parties, and a recommended series of activities and excursions specific to their demographic. Staying at a host hotel provides free admission to the respective pool party.

Choosing the correct themed event is crucial to making the most out of Gay Disney weekend without feeling misplaced. In the most general sense, One Mighty Weekend (ONEMIGHTYWEEKEND.COM) caters to scene queens, muscle boys, circuit partiers, fashionistas, and the general party crowd. Girls in Wonderland (GIRLSINWONDERLAND.COM) offers the female equivalent. Gay Days (GAYDAYS.COM) and Girls at Gay Days (GIRLSATGAYDAYS.COM) celebrates being gay and enjoying Disney World, focusing less on the party aspect and more on the pride aspect. Local venues get in on the action and host outrageous parties! The Parliament House, for example, hosts a popular concert series with acts such as Expose, Sister Sledge, RuPaul, Deborah Cox, and En Vogue. They pack a full

JUST ONE OF MANY POOL PARTIES DURING DISNEY'S GAY DAYS

THEME PARK ATTENDANCE 2007

PARK	2007 ATTENDANCE
Magic Kingdom Walt Disney World Lake Buena Vista, FL, USA	17,060,000
Disneyland, Anaheim, CA, USA	14,870,000
Tokyo Disneyland, Tokyo, Japan	13,906,000
Tokyo DisneySea, Tokyo, Japan	12,413,000
Disneyland Paris Marne-La-Vallee, France	12,000,000
Epcot Walt Disney World, Lake Buena Vista, FL, USA	10,930,000
Disney's Walt Disney World Hollywood Studios Lake Buena Vista, FL, USA	9,510,000
Disney's Animal Kingdom Walt Disney World, Lake Buena Vista, FL, USA	9,490,000

THEME PARK ATTENDANCE 2007

PARK	2007 ATTENDANCE
Everland Kyonggi-Do, South Korea	7,200,000
Universal Studios Japan Osaka, Japan	8,713,000
Universal Studios Universal Orlando, Orlando, FL, USA	6,200,000
SeaWorld Florida Orlando, Fl, USA	5,800,000
Disney's California Adventure Anaheim, CA, USA	5,680,000
Pleasure Beach, Blackpool, UK	5,500,000
Islands of Adventure Universal Orlando, Orlando, FL, USA	5,430,000

Source: Themed Entertainment Association/Economic Research Associates' Attraction Attendance Report 2008

house on Saturdays and Sundays to a strong mix of Central Florida locals and visitors. Make sure you choose the correct host hotel that coincides with your ideas of Disney "fun!" This will prevent disappointment and the blank faces of the multitudes who previously thought there was only one host hotel during Gay Disney weekend and chose the wrong one!

ONE MIGHTY WEEKEND (HOST HOTEL: BUENA VISTA PALACE HOTEL AND SPA) Each year the first weekend of June marks the official commencement of gay summer. In the ultimate showcase of male dominance, territoriality, superficiality, and courtship, tens of thousands gather during One Mighty Weekend to initiate the start of the summer breeding season. The overt psychological and biological intensity of One Mighty Weekend reduces to a primitive definition common to behavioral ecology—the *lek*—a gathering of males for the purposes of competitive mating display.

Leks are a common breeding behavior among certain birds, amphibians, and hot gay men. Within a lek, the same group of males congregates on a daily basis at an instinctually established location (the Buena Vista Palace) and adheres to individual positions within an arena (the pool area), each occupying and defending a small territory. The males spar sporadically and engage in physical contest in a showcase of supremacy, often resorting to extravagant visual or vocal displays. While peacocks display their tails, gay men flaunt pecs and packages. In a lek mating system, no permanent pair bonds are formed, and exclusively within the homo lek does procreation fail to take place.

For a first-timer, One Mighty Weekend undoubtedly results in sensory overload—a plethora of hot men, scantily clad, hot and bothered, ready to party is the gay version of every straight man's

Miller Lite big-breasted fantasy. An ornate display of six packs, nine packs, and the occasional beer can itself down the pants, the sensory excess is physically inspirational for some and emotionally destructive for others. Where half the crowd thrives and relishes in the mayhem, many return home to diet pills and laxatives.

One Mighty Weekend officially begins on the first Thursday night of June in Downtown Disney at the House of Blues. Prior to the close of the Pleasure Island nightclub enclave, Mannequinn's was the stage for eager crowds lining up at sunset to size each other up for what is surely the lamest party at One Mighty Weekend (which I skip to reacquaint myself with old friends and bond with my Gay Disney roommates). By late night Thursday, the hot tub cauldron at the host hotel, the Buena Vista Palace, becomes a stew of scantily clad men. All in all, it's a low-key, predictable start to a chaotic and fun-filled weekend.

Friday at noon begins Reunion Pool Party, a daily event which carries to Saturday, and Sunday too between the hours of 12 to 6 PM. As the hours pass, the gays get wetter and filthier, multiplying like Gremlins in the murky water, vying for space in sardine-packed swimming pools and patios! Saturday boasts the most well-attended party and the best concerts, with Sunday a close second, followed by Friday.

Friday, Saturday, and Sunday peak at nighttime circuit parties (8 PM–2 AM) and late night events that carry on into early morning (1 AM–8 AM). The late night events at Arabian Nights are hardly feasible without substance abuse; Arabian Nights II on Saturday indisputably constitutes the pinnacle of the circuit party hysteria. Friday night's event, Beach Ball at Typhoon Lagoon, deserves the superlative for the best and most arousing gay event in America. Imagine an entire mega water park crammed with beautiful men in Speedos, the sounds of world-renowned DJs, dance floors of powdery sand, copious amounts of alcohol, and exhilarating slides at your leisure—this, believe it or not, is the reality of Beach Ball. Saturday night's party at Disney Hollywood Studios focuses more on the music and talents of top-named DJs and live performances (such as Donna Summer and Kathy Griffin in previous years), signature rides, and dancing. Similarly, Universal hosts a party of equal content but lesser magnitude on Sunday.

Most leave One Mighty Weekend with many fewer brain cells than when they arrive but with some of the most incredible memories of the year. Monday morning feels almost like camp, where you don't want to say good-bye to the names and places, both old and new. But alas, it's time to start a new workout plan for next year and to start eyeing the new swimsuits!

GIRLS IN WONDERLAND (HOST HOTEL: MARRIOTT VILLAGE)

Meanwhile, cross town . . . the young and trendy female demographic mirror the insanity of One Mighty Weekend through Girls in Wonderland at Marriott Village. They party to the same homo-thumping beats echoed down the street and strut the poolside runway in fashionable two-pieces. The nighttime party on Friday forks into two themes (clubbing and live music) at separate rotating venues. Saturday's bash at the House of Blues packs 2,300 women to the backdrop of a Carnival-themed contemporary circus set aglow with seductive go-go girls and mesmerizing sounds.

GAY DAYS AND GIRLS AT GAY DAYS (HOST HOTELS: ROYAL PLAZA HOTEL AND REGAL SUN RESORT, RESPECTIVELY)

Though One Mighty Weekend may feel like gay judgment days, this is only one event among many during Gay Disney weekend. The original Gay Days itself is a place where gays of all genders, shapes, sizes, and ages bask in the gayness of the happiest place on Earth. Surely the original intention of Orlando's gayest week was not to conjure inner demons of insecurity.

The host hotel for Girls at Gay Days, the Regal Sun Resort, hosts daily pool parties, a fabulous Friday night pool party, and a riotous Gay Days Comedy Show on Saturday night. The host hotel for Gay Days, the Royal Plaza, hosts three-day pool parties and three-night pool parties as well as the best exposition. The expo itself is a fantastic way to collect lots of cool goodies, to learn about what's going on in Florida (culturally, travel-wise, politically), and to meet some pretty awesome people who work damn hard to make gay life better for all of us. Each year booths distribute innovative marketing products such as memory sticks shaped like conch shells (from Key West Business Guild) or personal martini shakers (from Delta Airlines).

The Gay Days and Girls at Gay Days crowd divides time between socializing at pool parties, the exposition, visiting the theme parks, and visiting local Orlando nightlife venues. The official daily lineup begins with Thursday at Animal Kingdom, Friday at Disney Hollywood Studios, Saturday at Magic Kingdom, and Epcot on Sunday. It's recommended to buy a multiday pass if you wish to experience more than one theme park.

Saturday at the Magic Kingdom marks the actual "Gay Day" where everyone wears red to commemorate pride and the park fills to capacity early in the day. This is probably the one day of the year you won't rush to use a Fast Pass. Standing in line is almost as fun as going on the rides. The crowd is warm and welcoming, strong and united. Strangers approach you. New friends are made. It's a beautiful sight to witness children from loving gay homes in a day-long safe haven. Even most token straight couples with children who unknowingly came to Magic Kingdom this fateful Saturday fall in love with the "gay day."

8 THE STRAIGHT GUY AT GAY DAYS

Being a 40-year-old businessman with a gorgeous 31-year-old wife and two terrific boys, ages four and five and a half, I was really looking forward to taking a weekend off and having some family fun at Walt Disney World. I have been working out of the country on and off for the past three and a half years, so I have missed plenty of milestones during my commuting. Business has been slow, so I decided to seize the moment to spend some family time.

On June 7, 2008, we leave our resort at a casual 10 A M and get to the gate to buy tickets by 10:30. I am studying all the different ticket offerings—park hoppers, buy three days, get one free, plus four water park days—too many decisions! Then, I notice a group of people wearing red T-shirts in line in front of us. At the next window, a larger group of red shirts. Must be a big tour group, I thought, probably from Ohio State. In front of us were two guys in their twenties, obviously with their dad. It was obvious because I read the father's red shirt. The back of it was imitating a Mastercard advertisement: TRIP TO DISNEY $600. RAISING TWO CHILDREN $200,000. BOTH OF THEM BEING GAY, PRICELESS!!! Not being in the loop, I was just fascinated by the sea of red T-shirts, most of them displaying a catchy phrase or two: STOP PICTURING ME NAKED! HI! YOU'LL DO! LOOKING FOR A BEAR! It took us another five minutes to realize that this was the famous Gay Days during gay and lesbian week.

There was a big guy with his family in front of us, not

THE STRAIGHT GUY AT GAY DAYS

gay and clearly uncomfortable, wearing a red shirt. Not intentionally (I presume). He immediately asked the ticket counter where the nearest T-shirt store was. He wanted to represent Mickey Mouse and quick. And not in red!

I will say my family and I had the greatest time at the Gay Days at the Magic Kingdom. My kids made friends with everyone they were standing next to in every line. My sons' desires to lick the poles and railings were entertainment for the long lines. The lesbian shirts were particularly amusing: LOOK! A LESBIAN! OH NO!, WOMEN ARE THE NEW MEN! GREAT TASTE, LESS FILLING. I AM A LESBIAN AND I NEVER PLAYED SOFTBALL! There were also some hot, size zero bi/lesbian strippers that had "bang bus" shirts. Definitely they were the straight crowd pleasers.

The only disappointment was debunking the myth of the perfect gay man. Having grown up in South Florida, most gay men I meet make the stereotype. Neat, well groomed, attractive, lean. I was exposed to a whole new world of the heavy, unattractive, too short, too tall, too skinny, too old—well normal, imperfect people I guess! Even still, truth be told, a very handsome blond guy waiting in Small World wore a shirt that said STOP PICTURING ME NAKED. Well I just can't!!! I even told my wife he looked kind of hot . . . I still keep some pictures on my camera phone from the line at It's a Small World of boatloads of guys in red. Now those were boatloads of happiness.

—JULIAN SIEGAL

ORLANDO GAY PRIDE

Most are not aware that Gay Disney weekend is not Orlando's official pride event. In actuality, Orlando Pride takes place every October with a weekend chock full of events, including a parade around Lake Eola Park in downtown Orlando. The event draws an estimated 30,000, mostly from Central Florida. COMEOUTWITHPRIDE.ORG

TO DO AND SEE

THEME PARKS

Describing a theme park in a few sentences would unjustly reduce ingenuity to a blasé blueprint of rides and recreation. I am confident that the parks listed below (and their opening dates) are not virgin territory for 99% of readers. To find out details about individual parks ad nauseam, please visit the respective Web sites and note that multiday passes and Florida residency grant visitors deep discounts.

SEUSS LANDING AT UNIVERSAL STUDIOS' ISLANDS OF ADVENTURE

WALT DISNEY WORLD RESORT Including Magic Kingdom (1971), Epcot (1982), Disney's Hollywood Studios (1989), Disney's Typhoon Lagoon (1989), Disney's Blizzard Beach (1995), Disney's Animal Kingdom (1998). WALTDISNEYWORLD.COM

UNIVERSAL ORLANDO RESORT Including Universal Studios Florida (1990), Islands of Adventure (1999), Wet 'n' Wild (1977).

SEAWORLD ORLANDO RESORT Including SeaWorld Orlando (1973), Aquatica Water Park (2008), and Discovery Cove.

HALLOWEEN HORROR NIGHTS For the same reason we pay money to see scary movies, Floridians flock to Universal Studios starting as early as late September to be terrorized and freaked out through living tales from crypt. Transforming the Studios into a giant haunted house, the featured "scare zones," attractions, and shows feed on the morbid fascination with horror and gore and are guaranteed to give you a few sleepless nights and make you question every creak and noise you hear late at night. Nevertheless, the intense adrenaline rush and terrifying exhilaration keeps us coming back for more! No way for the faint at heart! 6000 Universal Blvd., Universal Studios Orlando, HALLOWEENHORRORNIGHTS.COM

OTHER

KENNEDY SPACE CENTER Grounds of the U.S. space mission's billions of investments, the Kennedy Space Center is NASA's most advanced work station here on Earth. The accompanying esoteric and adult-oriented attraction, 45 minutes from Orlando, allows visitors to tour launch areas, view giant rockets, launch into space via spaceflight simulators, and dine with an astronaut. (321) 867-5000

THEME PARK RHAPSODY— LATEST THRILLS!

THE WIZARDING WORLD OF HARRY, UNIVERSAL ORLANDO RESORT While there are no plans for nude horse rides with our favorite cut Brit, Daniel Radcliffe, fans of J. K. Rowling's young wizard and his magical posse can enter the bewitching world of Hogwarts Castle, Hogsmeade Village, and the Forbidden Forest in the latest addition to the Lost Continent at Universal Studios' Islands of Adventure.

AMERICAN IDOL, DISNEY HOLLYWOOD STUDIOS It's every show mom's dream come true—a chance to get her mildly talented child on the waning television hit series *American Idol*. Considering the lackluster performances in recent seasons, the chances of striking gold with a daily grand prize of an audition are high! Unfortunately, you will not be graced by the kind and encouraging words of Paula, which stress perseverance and determination, so Texas moms, heed two words of advice: bring Kleenex and don't wear mascara!

AQUATICA PARK, SEA WORLD Getting splashed by a 2-ton killer whale was once glorious enough to make a theme

CIRQUE DU SOLEIL: LA NOUBA The contortions, acrobatics, special effects, and visual splendor of Cirque du Soleil resides permanently in Downtown Disney West Side in a custom-designed, 1,500 plus-seat theater. Roughly the same price as a theme park, but more rewarding and awe-inspiring, Cirque defies boundaries of body and

THEME PARK RHAPSODY—
LATEST THRILLS!

park successful in Orlando. Not anymore! Sea World has upped the stakes in recent years to add mechanical attractions that augment the splashes with screams and thrills. Now Sea World's Aquatica Park takes on Typhoon Lagoon Shamu style with the park's signature attraction, the Dolphin Plunge—two enclosed tube slides passing through a pool containing a pod of dolphins, in addition to wave pools, rafting rides and slides, and a lazy river.

THE SIMPSONS RIDE, UNIVERSAL STUDIOS Remember the Back to the Future Ride at Universal? Well it's gone, re-accessorized, and re-opened as the new Simpsons Ride. Homer, Bart, Marge, and Lisa join you on your motion-based stimulator through the low-budget Krustyland, which is sure to please avid Simpsons fans!

MANTA, SEA WORLD RESORT In Sea World's largest investment yet, the flying roller coaster, Manta, feigns the gliding movement of manta rays through an adventure of mind and sea focused on these graceful giants of the sea.

gravity in a stunning display of magnificence. 1478 E. Buena Vista Drive. Call Walt Disney World Resort for tickets (407) 939-7600, CIRQUEDUSOLEIL.COM/CIRQUEDUSOLEIL/EN/SHOWSTICKETS/LANOUBA/INTRO/INTRO.HTM

VISIT THE MEDIUMS OF CASSADAGA Twenty minutes north of Orlando, Cassadaga is a small community of mediums that functions as a Spiritualist camp offering readings, classes, church services, and informative sessions. Though still well off the beaten path, tourist ventures to Cassadaga have surged in tandem with popularity of the Most Haunted/Travel Channel and TAPS Ghost Hunter fans. Established as a Spiritualist community over 115 years ago, the 57 acres home to the Southern Cassadaga Spiritualist Camp Meeting Association was designated a historic district on the National Register of Historic Places in 1991. Twenty-five of the camp's residents offer counseling and readings from their homes. The camp "welcomes not only believers, but the curious and skeptical, as well." Information center located at 1112 Stevens Street, Cassadaga, (386) 228-2880, CASSADAGA.ORG

WORLD'S LARGEST MCDONALD'S PLAY PLACE (BIG DISAPPOINTMENT) I have never been one to jump on the anti-McDonald's bandwagon. In fact when *Supersize Me* came out, I criticized the poor documentary for lack of a scientific control in the juvenile experiment, fooling the gullible world into believing that eating 10,000-plus calories at McDonald's causes health problems (well it will make you ill wherever you engage in this caloric and fat intake!). The pièce de résistance of McDonalds, an overgrown and overhyped Frybox called the World's Largest McDonald's Play Place, features the standard McDonald's menu plus paninis, deli sandwiches, pasta, soup, desserts, and hand-dipped ice cream. Truth be told, there is nothing exciting or special about consuming your trans fats in the arcade, the 1950s room, or alongside MacTonight (one of my favorite advertising campaigns). 6875 Sand Lake Road, (407) 351-2185, MCFUN.COM/RESTAURANTS/VIEW/7

LODGING

BUENA VISTA PALACE HOTEL AND SPA Outside of One Mighty Weekend, Buena Vista Palace is a luxurious yet affordable option year-round. Sitting on 27 beautifully landscaped acres across from "Downtown Disney," the resort recently underwent a major renovation to resurface as one of the nicest hotels on Disney property (though strangely maintaining a 3-star rating). With elegantly pimped-out rooms, bird's-eye views, free shuttle service to all Disney theme parks, massive pools, tennis courts, a kiddy pool, a decent gymnasium, and a playground, it's every frugal holiday maker's dream come true. 1900 Buena Vista Drive, Lake Buena Vista, (866) 397-6516, BUENAVISTAPALACE.COM **MODERATE**

DOUBLETREE HOTEL The Doubletree is one of the few hotels in Orlando that actively seeks gay and lesbian travelers outside of event weekends. Twelve million dollars into their renovation, they still boast their TAG approval and welcome the LGBT community as "one of Orlando's finest gay-friendly hotels." Located across from Universal Studios. 5780 Major Boulevard, Orlando, (407) 351-1000, DOUBLETREE.HILTON.COM **INEXPENSIVE**

MARRIOTT VILLAGE Three Marriott properties joined as a village one mile from the Walt Disney World Resort in Lake Buena Vista, the Marriott Village consists of three corporative economical favorites: Fairfield Inn and Suites, Courtyard, and Springhill Suites. You get free transportation to all the Disney fun—Disneyworld, Universal Studios, and Sea World—plus guests have the choice of utilizing the amenities of all three hotels. For those looking to economize, the Fairfield Inn and Suites, as well as the Springhill Suites, also offer free breakfast daily. 8623 Vineland Avenue, Orlando, (407) 938-9001, MARRIOTT.COM **MODERATE**

REGAL SUN RESORT In changing from the Grosvenor Resort to the new Regal Sun Resort, the 626 guest rooms of the Cold War eyesore underwent a complete overhaul with the addition of a fabulous, custom windmill-shaped swimming pool. Like its Downtown Disney neighbors, Regal provides free transportation to the four theme parks in Disney World, and houses numerous recreational facilities. 1850 Hotel Plaza Boulevard, Lake Buena Vista, (800) 624-4109, REGALSUNRESORT.COM **INEXPENSIVE**

ROYAL PLAZA HOTEL Also located across from Downtown Disney in the Walt Disney World Resort, Royal Plaza offers a family-friendly environment, spacious and modern rooms, and overall superior comfort. Free shuttle service to Disney theme parks, heated pool, and fitness center. 1905 Hotel Plaza Boulevard, Lake Buena Vista, (407) 828-2828, ROYALPLAZA.COM **MODERATE**

DINING

CAPITAL GRILLE The supreme American steakhouse, Capital Grille is the rare example of a culinary imperialist that has expanded its food empire without compromising the utmost quality and service on which it was founded. Indeed, service and savor are institutionalized at Capital Grille. Every dish is cooked to perfection and meticulously displayed. The rich, dark woods spread across intimate dining rooms lends to a traditional, upscale "Old America" feel complemented by one of the finest wine cellars in the business. While various cuts of steak constitute the majority of specialties, the sushi-grade tuna steak reigns supreme over all seafood restaurants I have tried (including Joe's Stone Crabs), and the signature drink, the Stoli Doli (vodka marinated in pineapple for two weeks then drained) both soothes and excites the palate. 9101 International Drive, (407) 370-4392, THECAPITALGRILLE.COM

EMERIL'S ORLANDO The dream of eating a meal from the kitchen of the Food Network's Chef Emeril Lagasse once seemed distant and nonsensical. However, Emeril has spread the love and taste of his "new" New Orleans cuisine around the United States, including a location at Universal Studio's CityWalk. A break from tired Italian and sushi options, Emeril's cuisine is an innovative pan-American classic. Feast on fried green tomatoes with jumbo lump crabmeat and andouille-crusted redfish with grilled vegetable relish, then finish off with banana cream pie baked in a banana crust, topped with caramel sauce and chocolate shavings. 6000 Universal Boulevard #702, (407) 224-2424, EMERILS.COM

SEASON'S 52 "Celebrating living well through seasonally inspired healthier dining 52 weeks a year," Season's 52 caters to both the calorie and taste conscious with all menu items under 475 calories, including homemade Sonoma goat cheese ravioli, grilled chipotle prawns, four different flatbreads, and caramelized sea scallops. Ordering just one item is the real challenge; my typical meal at Season's 52 tallies to a whopping 2,375 calories (without alcohol). The main culprit—mini-indulgences at the end of the meal (small desserts in shot glasses). The full tray of nine mini-indulgences is perfect for celebrating milestones and occasions (unless commemorating your latest Weight Watchers goal!). 7700 Sand Lake Road, (407) 354-5212, SEASONS52.COM

SHARI SUSHI LOUNGE Once upon a time, I used to drive from Fort Lauderdale to Orlando for the sole purpose of dining at Shari Sushi Lounge. Gas prices now prevent this lunacy, but the sentiments have not changed. Removed from the ostentatious settings of Lake Buena Vista and Kissimmee, Shari is tucked into a small corner of historic downtown Orlando among historical homes.

Hands down the hottest, sexiest restaurant in Orlando, their sushi rolls and sashimi specialties are masterpieces of taste and sight. Their ginger dressing is my favorite outside of Japan; their desserts keep me scraping the plate even when none is left (and sometimes even licking it). 621 E. Central Boulevard, (407) 420-9420, SHARIS SHILOUNGE.COM

WOLFGANG PUCK GRAND CAFÉ Located in Downtown Disney across from the Cirque du Soleil Theatre, world-famous chef (circa 1990) Wolfgang Puck uses the finest, freshest ingredients to deliver his signature recipes, combining French techniques with Asian and California cuisines. My personal favorites include the marinated tuna sashimi, pumpkin ravioli, and the famous smoked salmon pizza (smoked salmon, dill cream, red onion, chili oil, and chives). 1482 E. Buena Vista Drive, (407) 938-9653, WOLFGANGPUCK.COM

NIGHTLIFE

PARLIAMENT HOUSE "P" House originally opened its doors in 1975 and has evolved into Florida's largest gay institution. A monstrous complex set deep in the heart of the ghetto, it boasts six bars/clubs under one roof as well as a restaurant, a dodgy hotel, an enormous outdoor patio, and a quaint little theater, which showcases some very smart theater. Parliament House is no-frills guaranteed fun with big crowds, live DJs, drag shows, and dancers. Watching a performance by Darcel Stevens is a highlight of any trip to Orlando! Weekends are best. Sundays are indestructible. 410 N. Orange Blossom Trail, (407) 425-7571, PARLIAMENTHOUSE.COM

PULSE Orlando's most upscale option, Pulse attracts a good mix of gays and lesbians to its three-room conundrum—a hoity-toity white lounge perfect for sipping martinis, a hip-hop dance room ripe for getting your freak on, and a dark stripper room where strippers swing from the ceiling and plant their crotches smack in your face. Most crowded on the 18-plus Tuesday and Wednesday college nights. 1912 S. Orange Avenue, (407) 649-3888, PULSE ORLANDO.COM

REVOLUTION NIGHTCLUB/HYDRATE VIDEO BAR/MAJESTIC THEATER AND LOUNGE The former location of Southern Nights, Revolution has sufficient square footage and potential to put Orlando back in the nightlife spotlight. Thus far, the club has gained a loyal college night following, a strong gay/lesbian mixed crowd for Unity Saturdays, and has hosted high-profile events that cater to the transgendered community. Supermodel duo Shaun and Paul present special events, called Evolution, on the second Friday of each month. 375 S. Bumby Avenue, (407) 228-9900, REVOLUTIONORLANDO.COM

SAVOY ORLANDO This gay hotspot features chic, upscale décor, indoor and out, but its true claim to fame is its hot, hunky bartenders and heaps of male dancers six days a week. 1913 N. Orange Avenue, (407) 898-6766, SAVOYORLANDO.COM

TAMPA BAY AREA

9

OUT TRAVELER RATINGS GUIDE

GAY-FRIENDLY: ▼▼▼▼
GAY SCENE: ▼▼▼▼
LESBIAN SCENE: ▼▼▼▼
PRO-GAY LAWS: ▼▼▼▼
HIV RESOURCES: ▼▼▼▼

A TALE OF TWO CITIES

Comebacks aren't always successful, but in the case of the Tampa Bay, second time's a charm. Revitalization efforts throughout the Bay area have revived not one but two major cities, Tampa and St. Petersburg, through an arduous and protracted process of demolition, gentrification, and determination. Since good news travels at a pace far slower than its counterpart, the word is only just spreading around the state and around the country—Tampa Bay is *the* place to be right now.

Tales of industrial wasteland, high crime, uncontrollable ghettos, and a paucity of investment opportunity are stories of the past. Tampa Bay, present day, is the perfect blend of Orlando attractions and Miami nightlife, a city of progress and originality, without claims to being a major U.S. cosmopolitan center like LA, New York, or even Miami. The general vibe is reminiscent of the Midwest, with sentiments of community, commitment to hospitality, and stories of endearment. The lower cost of living compared to other parts of Florida has attracted a young professional crowd and a blossoming gay community. The streets of downtown are fresh with paint, lined with contemporary urban living spaces, and completely refurbished historical buildings from the late 1800s.

Tampa's first gayborhood took root in Hyde Park, a former "up and coming" neighborhood-cum-Wisteria Lane, all thanks to the LGBT community. While the gay population has now moved on to other parts of town such as Ybor City and Downtown, the heart of Hyde Park remains rich with our presence and influence. Cash n Carry has lost its reputation as Cruise n Carry, but the Starbucks on Howard Avenue ontinues to draw scores of gay men and women for skinny lattes, day or night.

Heavy LGBT investment and elaborate coordination have facilitated the success of South Tampa's most recent revitalization attempt to Ybor City—the GaYbor District. The historic cigar-manufacturing district has embraced the concept of a one-stop GaYbor shop—continuous blocks of gay interest stores, nightclubs, bars, restaurants, and coffee shops, similar to Halstead (Boys Town) in Chicago and Canal Street in Manchester, England. Within a five-minute walk, the possibility of entering separate worlds of cuisine, dance, trance, line dancing, leather, hip-hop, and drag exudes a sense of gay unification and embraces the subcultures that define our community. The beauty, character, and rich past of the historic

Ybor District instill an element of class and distinction into the landscape. The original bricks, paintings, and style send you back in time to Tampa's 19th century glory and wealth. Contemporary interiors line classic buildings once home to casinos, cigar factories, and prohibition movements. This inspiration has fostered a young, vibrant arts scene most visible through the impressive art and collectible galleries, rotating art shows, and displays of live artists.

The avant-garde art scene of Tampa has also been attributed to the deep-rooted cultural awareness of its sister city, St. Petersburg. Long overlooked as a just a borough within the Tampa Bay area, St. Petersburg houses the premiere cultural gems of Florida, namely a series of top-tier museums and possibly the largest LGBT population outside of Fort Lauderdale. The relaxed and artsy feel of St. Petersburg has welcomed tens of thousands of gays and lesbians from around the globe. Most of these individuals are "invisible," living married lives with their two pets and tending to the garden. Unlike Fort Lauderdale, the LGBT community focuses much less on segregation and more on integration. Of the 110 neighborhood associations in St. Petersburg, each has active "out" members. These members are respected and admired, equally content engaging in social interaction with nongay community members. The dwindling obsession with gay versus straight means that more restaurants and bars are mixed, and boundaries are fading.

St. Petersburg enjoyed its first golden age in the 1920s as a campground for baseball legends, politicians, and Hollywood divas. The blustering pink Vinoy Hotel was the heart and soul of the young town during the Big Boom Era. The Mediterranean revival-styled hotel charged $20 a night for its all-star cast, including Babe Ruth, Herbert Hoover, Calvin Coolidge, Scott Fitzgerald, and Jimmy Stewart. The city survived the atrocities of the Great Depression through large Public Works Administration projects and resur-

INTERESTING, RANDOM, AND USELESS FACTS

- Over 15,000 boxes of live fish are flown out of Tampa International Airport weekly, making it the most valuable air freight item leaving the airport annually.
- Florida fish farms produce over 95% of aquarium fish grown in the United States, many of which are raised in concrete burial vaults.
- Tampa's Bayshore Boulevard is touted as the world's longest continuous sidewalk.
- St. Petersburg holds the record in the *Guinness Book of World Records* for the longest period of continuous sunshine—768 consecutive days of sunshine beginning in 1967.
- St. Petersburg averages 361 sunny days every year.
- The Ku Klux Klan in Dunedin operates as the "Crusader Church of Florida."
- The first scheduled airline flight with a passenger (on a biwing Benoist seaplane) was flown by Tony Jannus January 1, 1914 from St. Petersburg to Tampa.
- St. Petersburg is home to the world's first floating wedding chapel.
- The Hideaway in St. Petersburg, formerly known as Marilyn's closet, is the oldest women's bar in the United States.

faced as a stylish vacation destination following the New Deal. The advent of air conditioning in the 1950s permanently altered the landscape as northerners flocked down to retire in the Florida sun, and vacationers began to go elsewhere. By the 1970s interest in St.

Petersburg had completely waned, the Vinoy was literally deserted, and the streets lacked rule of law. The city suffered through a very painful and economically distressing time for nearly 20 years before the community grabbed the city by the balls and fought to bring back the glory of the 1920s. The perseverance, investment, and determination paid off. By the dawn of the millennium, St. Petersburg was entering a second golden age, fresh from Florida's finest face-lift and offering a pedestrian-friendly downtown, beautiful waterfronts, 370 different events per year, an exploding arts scene, and museums on par with New York.

Domestically, the achievements of Tampa and St. Petersburg go largely unrecognized to this day. The museums, nightclubs, and restaurants are largely filled with locals. Until researching and traveling for this book, I was not even aware of the spectacular and incomparable Dalí Museum that graces the Tampa Bay waterfront, or of the tapas delicacies and the divine sangria served in Columbia Restaurant, the oldest restaurant in Florida in its original location since 1903. But the magic exists and indeed, it thrives. Tampa and St. Petersburg are two cities on the move that have retained small-town feels while embracing both history and modernity in the same breath.

EVENTS

GASPARILLA (JANUARY) The Gasparilla Pirate Fest draws a crowd of over 500,000 annually to Tampa each January/February to indulge in Johnny Depp–esque fantasies of looting, drinking, and roughing the high seas. Not necessarily a LGBT event, but a raucous crowd nonetheless. GASPARILLAPIRATEFEST.COM

ST. PETE PRIDE (JUNE) The largest gay pride event in Florida held every June, St. Pete pride has grown from 10,000 during its inaugural year in 2003 to nearly 100,000 in 2008! Naturally an entire weekend of mega events in both Tampa and St. Petersburg form around the actual festive street parade on Saturday afternoon. STPETEPRIDE.COM

GAY DAYS TAMPA BAY (OCTOBER) A much smaller Gay Days event, Tampa Gay Days Weekend in October features a three-day sequence at three of Tampa's most popular tourist destinations: Busch Gardens and Adventure Island (Friday), Lowry Park Zoo (Saturday), the Florida Aquarium (Sunday). GAYDAYSTAMPABAY.COM

CLIP TAMPA INTERNATIONAL GAY & LESBIAN FILM FESTIVAL (OCTOBER) Since 1989 the Tampa International Gay & Lesbian Film Festival has infused gay films, events, and videos into the Bay area every October with nearly two weeks of screenings focusing on homosexual themes, gay love stories, transgender issues, and harsh truths such as the murder of Ryan Skipper. Seventy films from more than 20 countries were included in the 2008 lineup. The Clip Film Festival proudly honors the achievement as one of America's most popular independent gay film festivals. TIGLFF.COM

TO DO AND SEE: TAMPA

SMOKE CIGARS IN HISTORIC YBOR CITY Ybor City was once known as the Cigar Capital of the World with nearly 12,000 tabaqueros (cigar makers) employed in 200 factories that produced 700 million cigars a year. Though the city comes to life at night with nonstop partying, a daytime photo safari and walking tour provides a glimpse into the fascinating past of the former Cuban social colony. Revel in the glory days with a nice fat (non-Cuban) cigar at King Corona Cigars and a café con leche. 1523 E. 7th Avenue, Tampa, (813) 241-9109, KINGCORONOCIGARS.COM

BAYSHORE BOULEVARD The world's longest sidewalk, Bayshore Boulevard is graced by a series of upscale Southern-style homes catering to the lifestyles of Tampa's rich and famous. Eleven miles long, the boulevard offers serene water-side jogging and countless contemplative thought spots.

FLORIDA AQUARIUM Had Walt Disney had a say in designing the Living Seas exhibit in Epcot, his grandiose vision would have probably closely resembled the stunning Florida Aquarium. More fun than a theme park and one-quarter of the price, a plethora of exhibits keeps both adults and kids entertained for hours on end. Exhibits begin with an educational focus on Florida marine biology and ecology, stressing the exotic and glorious in Florida's backyard. The flagship exhibit, Sea Dragons: Sorcerers of the Sea, boggles the mind as it allows patrons to enter the world of these mythological creatures whose males give birth and rear young. One of the top "kid-friendly aquariums" in the country, kids can't decide whether to spend time petting stingrays at the 5,000-gallon

TAMPA'S HISTORIC YBOR CITY

A DAY OF REHAB

The Tampa Bay Area is home to a number of animal rescue and rehabilitation facilities, led by dedicated teams of altruistic individuals. The stories of courage and endurance of both the staff and the animals at these facilities are truly inspirational and spellbinding.

BIG CAT RESCUE (BCR) The largest big cat rescue in the United States, BCR serves as a sanctuary for abused and confiscated felines. Open to the public only on organized tours, BCR's Web site meticulously describes the variety of options for interacting with the 150 carnivores that call BCR home. The debilitated residents have suffered heinous acts of abuse, mostly in the name of tourism and photo opportunities at makeshift tourist attractions in Central Florida. Unfortunately, the big cats are at the mercy of weak and defunct permitting laws in Florida, condoning deplorable conditions, crude and cruel veterinary procedures (such as complete tooth extraction by farmers), and allowing people to harbor these deservedly wild animals in neighborhood backyards. Money for tours goes directly to helping the animals and promoting laws for better animal welfare. An excellent investment of time. Must be over 15 years old. 12802 Easy Street, Tampa, (813) 920-4130, BIGCATRESCUE.ORG

SUNCOAST SEABIRD SANCTUARY Tucked between miles of condominiums and hotels, the largest wild bird hospital in the United States, the Suncoast Seabird Sanctuary, cares

A DAY OF REHAB

for over 600 injured birds on any given day. Open 8:00 to sunset 365 days a year, entrance is always free; but tours on Wednesday and Sunday at 2 PM are essential to appreciate the individual stories of bravery and fortitude. The facility may appear small and frenetic, but rescuing 25–30 severely injured birds per day and maintaining an 85% release rate requires hundreds of volunteers and devoted individuals. Many of the released birds have built homes in and around

THE BIG CAT RESCUE

A DAY OF REHAB

the sanctuary—shacked up with other local birds and started families—making it sometimes difficult to constantly clean the copious quantities of poo! The exemplary commitment of owner Ralph Heath, who goes home to even more birds on the mend scampering around the house, has resulted in the survival and second chance for tens of thousands of hit-and-run victims, fishing accident atrocities, and general injuries. 18328 Gulf Boulevard, Indian Shores, (727) 391-6211, SEABIRDSANCTUARY.COM

CLEARWATER AQUARIUM A relatively nondescript and clearly nonprofit facility, the Clearwater Aquarium gained worldwide attention after rescuing Winter, the dolphin who had lost her tail after getting caught in a fishing net. Winter's heroism and determination inspired people across the globe when she taught herself an alternative swimming method and then became fitted with a pioneering prosthetic tail. Once given seven days to live, Winter thrives in her home at the aquarium, the focus of a therapeutic methodology for adults and children around the world coping with prosthetic limbs. The Florida aquarium works closely with injured Iraq war veterans from the nearby War Veterans Memorial Hospital. It also houses a strong rehabilitation program for other dolphins for future releases as well as sea turtles and other marine creatures. 249 Windward Passage, Clearwater, (727) 447-0980, CMAQUARIUM.ORG

lobby touch tank, playing with starfish in the gargantuan critter tank, or splashing around the massive outdoor water adventure park (bring swimsuits for kids). 701 Channelside Drive, Tampa, (813) 273-4000, FLAQUARIUM.ORG

FLORIDA AQUARIUM NATURE TOURS The Aquarium offers eco-tours to view the 400 resident wild dolphins of Tampa Bay, manatees, and bird sanctuaries as well as a "Dive with the Sharks" experience where you brave the shark tank in a wetsuit. 701 Channelside Drive, Tampa, (813) 273-4000, FLAQUARIUM.ORG

BUSCH GARDENS The biggest attraction in Tampa and the most thrilling rides of any theme park in Florida, Bush Gardens entertains nearly 5 million visitors annually with its global animal themes and gravity-defying roller coasters. The latest edition in 2008, Jungala, sports exhibits of orangutans, gibbons, and flying foxes as well as the paramount crowd pleaser—tug-of-war with a Bengal tiger. 10001 N. McKinley Drive, Tampa, (888) 800-5447, BUSCHGARDENS.COM

BUY SOME GAY KNICK KNACKS AT MCFILMFEST A campy and festive novelty store in the heart of GaYbor, McFilmfest carries the full range of gay gifts from clothing to nude cards to DVDs and poppers. More importantly, owners Mark and Carrie always make your shopping experience one to remember with silly anecdotes, outrageous outfits, or just plain amazing hospitality. 1901 N. 15th Street, Ybor City, (813) 247-6233, MCFILMFEST.COM

EXPERIENCE THE ARTS *Gallery Live* features five hand-selected local artists cast behind glass shields through moments of conceptual creativity and actual works in progress. The historic and palatial **RITZ THEATER** hosts an art show every three months which showcases cutting-edge designs and affordable paintings by young artists from the Tampa Bay Area. 1901 N. 15th Street, and 1503 E. 7th Avenue, Ybor City, THERITZYBAR.COM

TO DO AND SEE: ST. PETERSBURG

CATCH THE SUNSET Indulge in West Florida's ideal geography and topography to enjoy some of the most beautiful sunsets in the country. Whether on the beach, on the road, or at a restaurant, St. Petersburg offers endless opportunities for sunset rapture.

SUNSHINE SKYWAY BRIDGE The impressive structure of I-275, the Sunshine Skyway Bridge, wows drivers as it spans over 5 miles of deep blue with a symphony of yellow cable pilings upon entrance to St. Petersburg. Not quite the Golden Gate, Sunshine still merits a few snapshots, most easily achieved from the adjacent park and pier on either side of the bridge. Unfortunately there are no pedestrian walkways over the bridge itself.

SUNKEN GARDENS St. Petersburg's first roadside attraction, a former sinkhole turned subterranean botanical garden and zoo opened in 1935, was saved from ruin in 1999 when it was purchased by the City of St. Petersburg. Now (thankfully) void of caged wildlife, the gardens provide a tropical maze 15 feet below street level. There were once rumors of turning it into a male nude swimming hole, but this never went through. The adjoining Great Explorations Children's Museum is great to wear out the kids. 1825 4th Street, (727) 551-3102, STPETE.ORG/SUNKEN

THE PIER St. Petersburg's proud landmark pier stretches a half mile into Tampa Bay from the center of downtown, offering five levels of mediocre tourist shopping, but very good photo opportunities.

MUSEUM OF FINE ARTS Situated on prime waterfront property, St. Petersburg's Museum of Fine Arts espouses the vision of founder Margaret Acheson Stuart (1896–1980) to provide outstanding examples of world art in an inviting, elegant setting. With the addition of the new Hazel Hough Wing, this home for ensembles of European art, American art, photography, Greek and Roman antiquities, and pre-Columbian and Asian art has doubled in size. Georgia O'Keeffe's *Poppy* and Claude Monet's *Le Parlement, effet de brouillard* (Parliament, Effect of Fog) continue to serve as anchors for an ever-growing collection of global splendor. 255 Beach Drive, N.E., St. Petersburg, (727) 896-2667, FINE-ARTS.ORG

THE PIER IS THE PERFECT PLACE FOR SOUVENIR PHOTOS

HOLOCAUST MUSEUM Indisputably depressing but irrefutably important, remembering the Holocaust and its victims seems more important than ever as the last remaining survivors pass away. At the Holocaust museum in St. Petersburg, the atrocities of the Holocaust are presented in a tactful and subtle manner, even suitable for children (10+). The visual timeline chronicles the years before and after the Holocaust through news stories, propaganda pictures, personal accounts, and artifacts. The intimate and personal nature of the museum is reminiscent of its Washington, DC, counterpart. Volunteers provide fascinating and educational tours, emphasizing an overall theme of genocide that has continued to plague the globe even to present day. 55 Fifth Street S., St. Petersburg, (727) 820-0100, FLHOLOCAUSTMUSEUM.ORG

SALVADOR DALÍ MUSEUM The museum in St. Petersburg showcases his largest and most comprehensive collection in the world.

THE HALLUCINOGENIC TOREADOR, BY SALVADOR DALI

The first-class Euro-museum experience allows patrons to enjoy the lunacy and genius of Salvador Dalí, leaving inspired and fascinated by the multifaceted and contentious artist most noted for surrealism. Dalí's sinister and dark works exude sexual anxiety and moribund creativity through easily recognized flagship pieces such as the *Persistence of Memory* (1931) and lesser-known splendor such as the *Metamorphosis of Narcissus, Hallucinogenic Toreador, Involuptate Mors,* and *Spellbound*. Even an entire bottle of absinthe and space cake barely provides a personal breakthrough to Dalí's mental brilliance. Over 25 years strong, the Dalí is the only museum in Florida unable to close on Mondays due to high demand. Guided tours available. 1000 Third Street, S. St. Petersburg, (727) 823-3767, SALVADORDALIMUSEUM.ORG

SUNSET BEACH The strip of beach once famous for housing double-story foam parties at the club Bedrocks now keeps the gay momentum alive with regular Sunday beach parties. Parties are most intense on Sundays between Memorial Day and Labor Day when Tampa hot spots even set up beachfront booze outlets. The crowd at the only LGBT beach in the Tampa Bay tends to be young, hot, somewhat cliquish gay men peppered with butch lesbians and Miller Lites. Beyond Sundays, Sunset Beach is hit or miss, but almost always occupied with a few stragglers. Situated down Gulf Boulevard West directly in front of the "Tern Lot," the beach is located on southern tip of Treasure Island; don't get confused and park at Treasure Island Park Access or municipal beach. Pay meters in lot. Bring quarters. W. Gulf Boulevard and 79th Avenue at end of W. Gulf Boulevard, before yellow arrows leading you left.

GULFPORT BEACH Not the prettiest stretch of beach adjacent to the Gulfport casino, but a popular lesbian destination for Sunday

DAY TRIPS FROM TAMPA BAY

The West Coast of Florida is blessed with some of the most enchanting, quaint, and splendid small cities in the state. Most of them are less than two hours from the Tampa Bay Area, and worth a day trip if time and interest permits.

SIESTA KEY BEACH Siesta Key Beach near Sarasota boasts arguably the finest and purest sand in the country (it's 99% pure quartz), plenty of room for beach shenanigans, and a parade of sand sculpture artists.

VENICE BEACH Known as the Shark Tooth Capital of the World, visitors can easily stroll the beach and collect mountains of prehistoric sharks' teeth as souvenirs.

ACADIA AND WAUCHULA Starting points for the fossil tours in chapter 3, "Forgotten Florida," these towns are the major starting points to the placid waters of the Peace River and the underground paleontological paradise of Central Florida.

CAYO COSTA STATE PARK Isolated 7 miles offshore west of Fort Myers, the secluded barrier island Cayo Costa is reachable by a small public ferry. For those who want to stay overnight in rustic conditions, 12 primitive cabins and 18 campsites are available. Reservations necessary. (800) 326-3521; cabin reservations (239) 283-0015

DAY TRIPS FROM TAMPA BAY

SANIBEL ISLAND A shell collector's dream come true, the unique seabed structure off the coast of this barrier island lends to massive distribution of shells and sand dollars along the coastline and along sand bars.

TARPON SPRINGS The Greek stronghold of Florida, Tarpon Springs remains a small Greek fishing village frozen in time with the world's most active sponge harvesting industry. Indeed, the sponge docks are a working reality complete with rusty old boats, sponge divers, and sponge auctions. Naturally, cheesy tourist shops have cropped up and diminished the aesthetic authenticity. The highlight of Tarpon Springs, however,

TARPON SPRINGS, WHERE BOATS RULE

DAY TRIPS FROM TAMPA BAY

is authentic Greek food, the best I have sampled outside of Greece. Mykonos (628 Dodecanese Boulevard, (727) 934-4306) stands out as the most exceptional in a sequence of gastronomic showstoppers.

SAWMILL CAMP RESORT Situated off I-4 between Tampa and Orlando, Florida's only all-gay campground is a favorite among Central Florida locals. 21710 U.S. 98, Dade City, (352) 583-0664, FLSAWMILL.COM

---

beachside parties that revolve around volleyball. 5730 Shore Boulevard, Gulfport (727) 893-1068

FORT DE SOTO After garnering the title of #1 beach in the USA for 2007, Fort de Soto is now well on the beaten path. The county park is jam-packed with families and couples, a historic fort, ferry services to Egmont Key (for snorkeling), boat ramps, kayaks, bikes, and canoes for rent. Though de Soto no longer sports a gay beach, its still boasts 7 miles of refined quartz, winding trails, two fishing piers, and a campground. 3500 Pinellas Bayway, Tierra Verde, (727) 582-2267, FORTDESOTO.COM

CALADESI ISLAND STATE PARK After two years as the runner-up (2006 and 2007), Caladesi Island was rated America's #1 beach in 2008. Accessible only by ferry from Honeymoon Island, Caladesi bears striking similarity to Fort de Soto, with picturesque sunbathing opportunities, snorkeling, a three-mile nature trail, and the added bonus of good shelling. An undisturbed barrier island, Caladesi offers more seclusion than Fort de Soto but the two are nearly indistinguishable. 1 Causeway Boulevard, Dunedin, (727) 469-5918, FLORIDASTATEPARKS.ORG/CALADESIISLAND

EGMONT KEY Across from Fort de Soto, Egmont Key houses a working lighthouse and harbors the underground remnants of Fort Dade. The ferry to and from Egmont is half the fun—an opportunity to see wild dolphins, marine turtles, and marine birds. The ferry leaves Fort de Soto at 10 and 11 AM and returns at 2 and 3 PM (year-round except December and January). HUBBARDSMARINA.COM

STROLL AROUND DUNEDIN AND GULFPORT An overwhelming LGBT acceptance is ever-present in a number of Tampa Bay's smaller cities, namely Dunedin and Gulfport. With LGBT representation on par with Key West, these small cities amended their human rights ordinances and provided small-town homo sanctity long before the sentiment was taken to the county level in 2008. Both Dunedin and Gulfport retain a small-town, welcoming feel with cute downtowns adorned with boutiques, one-of-a-kind restaurants, and bars with an even mix of local gays and straights.

LODGING: TAMPA

DON VICENTE HISTORIC INN Located in the historic Ybor City, this boutique hotel was originally built in 1895 by the City's founder, Vincente Martinez Ybor, as a planning and development office. After serving as two different healthcare clinics and then sitting idle for several years, the property was refurbished from 1998 to 2000 as the Don Vicente Historic Inn with 16 guest rooms featuring four-poster canopied beds, down comforters, and Persian rugs. The Don Vicente hosts numerous private events, allowing guests to rent out the entire hotel and common areas for weddings and commitment ceremonies. Corner of 14th Street and 9th Avenue, 1915 Republica de Cuba, (813) 241-4545, DONVICENTEINN.COM **MODERATE**

HAMPTON INN, YBOR CITY With a company-wide motto "We Love Having You Here," the Hampton Inn Ybor City shines as the global model for Hampton Inns worldwide for its superior customer service, genuine interest in customer satisfaction, general vibe of kindliness, and irrefutable LGBT friendliness. The exterior of the property softly integrates into the historic landscape; the interior is fresh and functional, even sporting a small cardio room and a welcoming pool to complement 138 comfortable and spacious rooms. The property is ideally located one block from the main gay bars and nightclubs (the GaYbor District), the perfect affordable weekend party getaway or an alternative to a DUI on those late weekend nights. Rates include breakfast, high-speed Internet, and transport via shuttle within 5 miles of the hotel. 1301 E. 7th Avenue, (813) 247-6700, HAMPTONINN.HILTON.COM **MODERATE**

TAMPA MARRIOTT WATERSIDE HOTEL AND MARINA Located along the Channel Riverwalk and adjacent to the Tampa Convention Center, this bayfront downtown hotel demonstrates typical Marriott excellence with over 681 guest rooms and 36 suites. The dramatic lobby impresses with high ceilings and swaying Washingtonian palm trees in excess of 20 feet. 700 S. Florida Avenue, (813) 221-4900, MARRIOTT.COM **MODERATE**

LODGING: ST. PETERSBURG

DICKENS HOUSE Owner and first-class host Ed Caldwell offers "casual refinement" in his downtown oasis—a former apartment

and boarding house-cum-crumbling shack of wood and termites—finally restored and refined over a number of grueling years to become the neighborhood masterpiece in the heart of downtown. Unveiled at the turn of the 21st century, this 1912 arts and crafts home promises modern comforts in a traditional B and B setting, complemented by peace, quiet, and serenity of the surrounding bamboo and fern gardens. A top pick by other travel guides and Travel Advisor (and myself), Ed deservedly takes pride in his award-winning B and B, which caters to a large LGBT following. Breakfast changes daily but never fails to impress. 335 8th Avenue Northeast, St. Petersburg, (727) 822-8622, DICKENSHOUSE.COM
MODERATE

GAY ST. PETE HOUSE (LGBT) In the wake of Suncoast Resort's demise and the gay guesthouse fever in South Florida, the Gay St. Pete House pioneers the gay guesthouse experience in St. Petersburg. Entering the market at an exceptionally affordable price point, St. Pete House is the best deal in Florida—12 comfortable rooms, a clothing-optional pool and hot tub, a full bagel breakfast, beer and wine, and a relaxed, homey feel complemented by the extreme kindness of owner Brian Longstreth and his crazy dog, Urban. 4505 5th Avenue N., St. Petersburg, (727) 365-0544, GAYSTPETEHOUSE.COM **INEXPENSIVE**

SNUG HARBOR INN A small inn with direct beach access overlooking Boca Ciega Bay, this budget accommodation caters mostly to families for longer-term stays. Owners Susan and T. J. Gill readily welcome alternative families, making this a great choice for cost-conscious couples with children and pets. 13655 Gulf Boulevard, Madeira Beach, (727) 395-9256, SNUGHARBORFLORIDA.COM
INEXPENSIVE

THE VINOY HOTEL The Pepto Bismol pink powerhouse shares a splendid and sordid history with roots as the premiere hotel during the Big Band Era; a dilapidated and abandoned wasteland by the 1970s, and the superlative revival of the St. Petersburg 1990s following a $93 million makeover. The arduous efforts to restore a living piece of history from the Great Gatsby era combined with an acquisition for Marriott Corporation, this Renaissance property offers all the amenities of a 4-star hotel with the grandeur of the 1920s (including the authentic Augusta Block bricks lining the front driveway). 501 5th Avenue, (727) 894-1000, MARRIOTT.COM
MODERATE

DINING: TAMPA

COLUMBIA RESTAURANT No trip to Tampa is complete without a meal at the oldest and most authentic Spanish restaurant in the state of Florida. Over 100 years under the same family ownership, Columbia Restaurant stands as a living piece of history that has enchanted generations with its bona fide charm and superior cuisine. Combining original recipes with evolving flavor fusions, Columbia's chefs travel to Spain throughout the year to share and learn with their European counterparts, keeping abreast of the latest taste sensations. The results are extraordinary. The tapas burst with flavor and variety; dishes, both simple and complex, exceed expectations with authenticity and robustness. Ordering the signature white or red sangria almost seems a prerequisite until perusing the best wine list in the state of Florida. Expanding over an entire city block, Columbia is a living and breathing piece of Spain that has stood as the heart and soul of Ybor City for more than a century. Do not miss it! 2117 E. 7th Avenue, Tampa, (813) 248-4961, COLUMBIARESTAURANT.COM/YBOR.ASP

MEMA'S ALASKAN TACOS Ybor's fiercest budget dining option, the Alaskan-style tacos from Mema's will leave you craving more and longing for your 2 AM hangover cure long before you are even drunk. The homemade white corn tortillas, lightly fried and filled with meat or veggies, delicately crunch in your mouth upon impact, exciting the salivary glands and inducing an inner feeding frenzy. Choose from traditional veggies and carnie options or more exotic gator and lobster choices, as well as healthy and extra fattening alternatives. Great as cheap eats for lunch and dinner as well. Open for lunch and dinner all nights and until 3 AM Wednesday through Saturday. 1724 E. 8th Avenue, Tampa, (813) 242-8226

NEW YORK, NEW YORK PIZZA Countless pizza joints dot the length of La Setima (7th Avenue) eager to fill hunger fixes and

TRY THE TAPAS AND SANGRIA AT THE COLUMBIA

to appease the inebriated. The conveniently located New York, New York Pizza, in the heart of the GaYbor District, continues to support and give back to the gay community; plus they serve up the best local pizza! 1512 E. 7th Avenue, Tampa, (813) 248-1845, MYSPACE.COM/GAYBOR

PACH'S PLACE In the heart of South Tampa, the family tradition of good eating has persevered since 1983 in this supergay-friendly daily breakfast/brunch hot spot. Pronounced "Patch," the quaint diner is the kind of place tourists search far and wide to discover as a "local secret." Open daily until 2 PM, crowds from around Tampa converge at Pach's for conventional breakfast favorites and massive skillets (such as the chicken skillet—huge pilings of home fries, peppers, onions, chicken, eggs, and Swiss cheese). The diner is a true mom-and-pop operation (actually mom and daughter); at 4 AM they are making hollandaise sauce from scratch and serving it up together 3 hours later. 2909 W. Bay-to-Bay Boulevard (off Bayshore Boulevard), Tampa, (813) 831-7122, PACHSPLACE.COM

SQUARE ONE BURGERS A steakhouse ambience with contemporary style, the fun and funky Square One uses nine types of burgers as a starting point, from sashimi tuna to buffalo to Meyer's 100% Angus, to commence an individual mouth-watering masterpiece. With three types of buns, 25 toppings, 12 cheeses, and 13 sauces to choose from the possibilities are endless (actually not endless but calculable with a simple statistical formula). Those who do not feel inspired can opt for the predetermined house specialties like the chili cheeseburger with innovative sides such as sweet potato fries with cinnamon and sugar. 3701 Henderson Boulevard, Tampa, (813) 414-0101, SQUARE1BURGERS.COM

STREETCAR CHARLIE'S Tampa's equivalent of DC's Duplex Diner or an upscale version of Fort Lauderdale's Hamburger Mary's/Rosie's, StreetCar Charlie's doubles as a bar and restaurant serving salads, burgers, and grilled tuna as quickly as the pints and martinis. The atmosphere is relaxed yet cruisy; the food surprisingly well prepared. An integral dining stop during any given weekend in Tampa, you are likely to run into your future, past, or dream hook-up at some point in your meal. The endearing yellow streetcar monopoly man theme and the work of Cuban artist, Alex Ruix, add an element of camp and cuteness. Tuesday is 2-for-1 dinner night. 1811 N. 15th Street, Tampa (corner of 8th Avenue and 15th Street), (813) 248-1444, MYSPACE.COM/STREETCARCHARLIES

DINING: ST. PETERSBURG

BELLA BRAVA This urban trattoria in the gay-friendly Grand Central District exudes urbanity as a refined double-story architectural masterpiece of crisp wood designs and glass accents, suave lighting and the subsequent stylish atmosphere. With a new chef focused on the fresh and seasonal, Italian classics are prepared with a neo-American Whole Foods-esque twist. Some of the more notable items include the Strozzapretti Incrostati (a heaping portion of fresh pasta with family recipe lamb meatballs, roasted veggies, and ricotta in a spicy tomato sauce then accented with zambuca and baked in the grilled oak fire oven with a layer of pizza dough) and the Tuna alla Puttanesca (fresh ahi tuna smothered in balsamic roasted onions, basil vinaigrette, and olives to create a robust mouth sensation). 515 Central Avenue, St. Petersburg, (727) 895-5515, BELLABRAVA.NET

GEORGIE'S ALIBI Surprisingly delicious cheap eats, Georgie's menu hardly features dishes more than $10 but still delivers hearty portions of American classics. A popular spot for lunch, dinner, and even Sunday brunch, Georgie's food is best enjoyed outdoors on the rocking tables with the daily drink specials. 3100 3rd Avenue N., St Petersburg, (727) 321-2112, GEORGIESALIBI.COM

KELLY'S JUST ABOUT ANYTHING RESTAURANT For the past six years, gay-owned and operated Kelly's has been voted one of the best restaurants in the Tampa Bay area. Located in the quaint and LGBT-friendly small town of Dunedin, Kelly literally serves up—well, you guessed it—just about anything in its own eclectic style. Dismissing the notion of a particular fusion, void of any culinary restrictions, this kitch neighborhood restaurant emanates an Old Florida gay touch in all facets of ambiance, service, and presentation. 319 Main Street, Dunedin, (727) 736-5284, KELLYSCHICABOOM.COM

MFA CAFÉ The latest addition to the Museum of Fine Arts includes the breathtaking glass conservatory, home to a flourishing contemporary lunch café. Chef James Canter creates his own culinary art through hefty-sized paninis and mixed green favorites with homemade salad dressings, such as the tantalizing lavender honey vinaigrette. Gourmet sandwiches such as the chargrilled chicken scaloppini with roasted piquillo peppers, smoked provolone, and dried tomato caper alioli on roasted garlic ciabatta means sophisticated flavor fusions at reasonable lunch prices. Dining also available on the outdoor patio facing the landmark St. Petersburg Pier. 255 Beach Drive. N.E. St. Petersburg, (727) 896-2667, FINE-ARTS.ORG

NIGHTLIFE: TAMPA

CITY SIDE City Side's proximity to Tampa's original gayborhood, Hyde Park, ensures a reliable happy hour crowd and nightly groupies. Frequented by a more established and mature crowd from Hyde Park,

City Side maintains a familiar pub feel with occasional new faces. 3703 Henderson Boulevard, (813) 350-0600, CLUBCITYSIDE.COM

THE FORGE AND 714 Long overdue, the Forge carries the leather scene to a more mainstream arena by situating the intimate venue in the heart of Ybor City. Relaxed and welcoming, this soft-core leather bar provides an excellent meeting ground for varying degrees within the leather subculture, including curious novices. The Forge spills out into the colossal sister bar, 714, which caters primarily to a weekday crowd, namely during Monday karaoke with Stormin Normie and Thursday's amateur strip contest. 1327 E. 7th Avenue, (813) 247-2711, LOUNGE714.COM. Those looking for a harder leather scene, try 2606 in West Tampa. 2606 N. Armenia Avenue, (813) 875 6993, 2606.COM

G. BAR Hands down the hottest spot in Tampa with packed Fridays for women and the largest congregation and concentration of Florida studs on Saturday nights. Glass mirrors and original walls from the late 1800s separate the massive dance palladium, split between two decadent rooms of dance music and pop hits. Lipsticks rule at G-Spot Fridays, but the party fever still draws 40% men for a wild, refreshingly mixed gay and lesbian throw down! G. Bar Saturdays achieve the grandeur, allure, and sex appeal only matched once upon a time by China White in Fort Lauderdale. Worth a drive from miles away, scores of hotties dominate the dance hall and fulfill their "party like a rock star" ambitions. Check their Web site to see if currently hosting any mid-week events. 1401 E. 7th Avenue, (813) 247-1016, GBARTAMPABAY.COM

THE HONEY POT The multimillion dollar palatial venue houses three stories of nightlife decadence embellished with cutting-edge audio and visual technology. On holiday weekends, high profile parties and big-name DJ's pack the expansive dance floor, the plush couches, and the elaborate bars spread over 13,000 square feet. Breezy crowds clamor along the balcony, sipping cocktails while overlooking La Setima. During nonholiday weekends, Steam Fridays and Tease Saturdays (replacing both Flirt Saturdays at the Honey Pot and Flirt Saturdays at Flirt Nightclub, which is now closed) still lure healthy crowds. While not filling to capacity, the sheer elegance and eminence of the venue beguiles a target audience of party boys on Friday and lesbians on Saturdays. 1507 E. 7th Avenue, (813) 247-4663, MYSPACE.COM/TAMPAHONEYPOT

POP N WAVE THURSDAYS AT THE CASTLE A long-standing Goth club housed in a castle-style tower, The Castle hosts Goth-goes-camp Thursday nights with all the videos you can handle from the dawn of music television to present. Though not an official gay night, Pop n Wave Thursdays has a staunch LGBT following. 2004 N. 16th Street, Ybor City, (813) 247-7547, CASTLE-YBOR.COM

SPURS Originally picking up where Wranglers left off, Spurs opened as a country line dancing bar catering to the venerable cowboy population of west Florida. It has since spread into other realms including hip-hop and dance nights, but remains steadfast to its roots most days of the week with free country line dance lessons, feel-good organized dance, and the predictably mellow and friendly line dancing crowd. 1701 E. 8th Avenue, (813) 247-7877, SPURSCOUNTRYBAR.COM

STREETCAR CHARLIE'S The popular restaurant consistently woos the thirsty to its central bar before, after, and sometimes instead of dinner. Sunday afternoons are standing room only for the traditional post Sunset Beach T-dance, which then continues either in the adjoining room or a rotating venue. Drink specials change nightly. 1811 N. 15th Street, (813) 248-1444, MYSPACE.COM/STREETCARCHARLIES

NIGHTLIFE: ST. PETERSBURG

BEAK'S OLD FLORIDA A bit off the gay beaten path, the gay-friendly Beak's Old Florida welcomes all sexual orientations for innovative experiences in mixology such as the Huck Finn and the Tiramisu martini. In an eclectic setting of "unpretentious over-the-top vintage old Florida décor" the alternative bar captivates with the bizarre, the tasteful, and the tacky (like the life-sized Captain Hook figure). Food also served in the outer bamboo dining bar and garden patio. 2451 Central Avenue, (727) 321-9100, BEAKSOLDFLORIDA.COM

CHIQ BAR A popular lesbian bar among fems and butches alike, Chiq Bar blasts pop favorites over a series of rooms that include a main dance floor, a principal bar, pool room, and a spacious patio. 4900 66th Street N. (727) 546-7274, CHIQBAR.COM

DETOUR A location rich in LGBT history, Detour began as the gay-friendly lounge the Stuffed Pepper in the early '70s before re-opening as DTs, then Grand Central Station and Platform in 2001, and now Detour in 2008. A neighborhood bar with some room to dance, Detour is a quieter alternative to the rowdiness of Georgie's. 2612 Central Avenue, (727) 327-8204

GEORGIE'S ALIBI The St. Pete location of Alibi outperforms its Fort Lauderdale counterpart, espousing the same "come as you are" philosophy but also serving as a welcoming arena for lesbians and hip-hop homos, a sizeable dance floor, more square footage, and the absence of that horrible throw up smell. Every night draws a decent crowd but Long Island Iced Tea Thursdays and Saturdays are busiest. 3100 Third Avenue N. (727) 321-2112, GEORGIESALIBI.COM

MIAMI

CLUB BOI
726 Nw 79th St
305.836.8995

SANDAL CLUB
1060 NE 79th St
305.758.3556

DISCOTEKKA
950 NE 2nd Ave
305.371.3773

AZUCAR
2301 Sw 32nd
305.441.6974

SOUTH BEACH

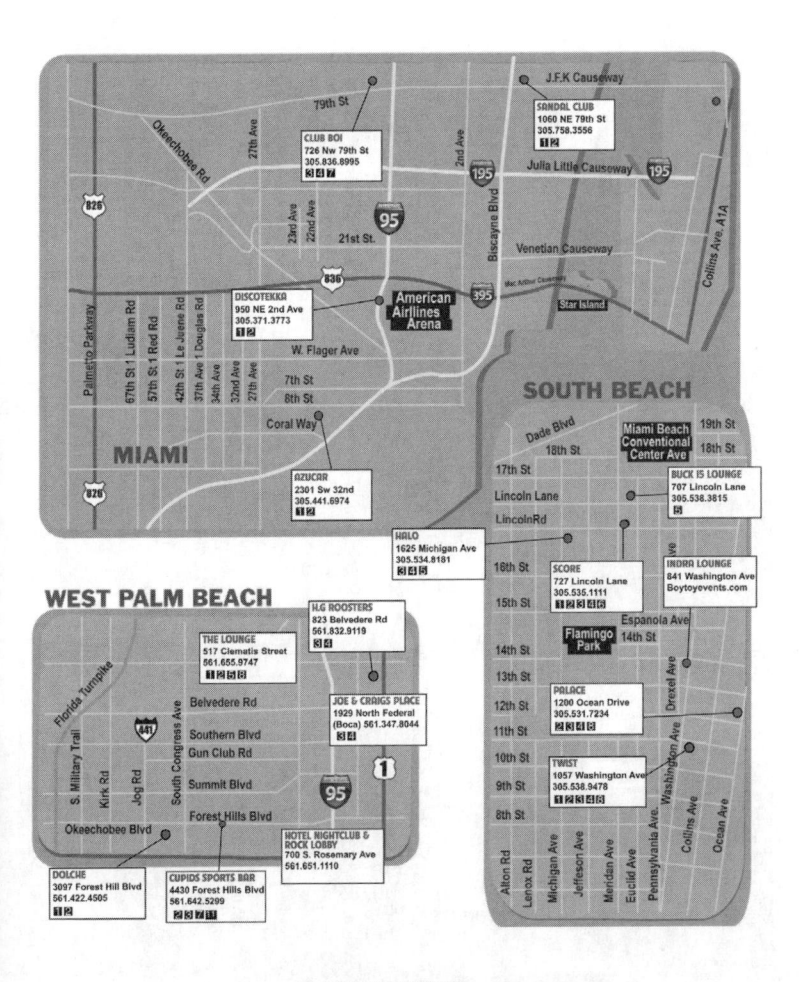

BUCK 15 LOUNGE
707 Lincoln Lane
305.538.3815

HALO
1625 Michigan Ave
305.534.8181

SCORE
727 Lincoln Lane
305.535.1111

INDRA LOUNGE
841 Washington Ave
Boytoyevents.com

PALACE
1200 Ocean Drive
305.531.7234

TWIST
1057 Washington Ave
305.538.9478

WEST PALM BEACH

H.G ROOSTERS
823 Belvedere Rd
561.832.9119

THE LOUNGE
517 Clematis Street
561.655.9747

JOE & CRAIGS PLACE
1929 North Federal
(Boca) 561.347.8044

HOTEL NIGHTCLUB & ROCK LOBBY
700 S. Rosemary Ave
561.651.1110

DOLCHE
3097 Forest Hill Blvd
561.422.4505

CUPIDS SPORTS BAR
4430 Forest Hills Blvd
561.842.5299

MAP KEY

1. DANCING
2. LIVE ENTERTAINMENT
3. HAPPY HOUR
4. NEIGHBORHOOD BAR
5. MIXED CROWD
6. LESBIAN
7. MALE DANCERS
8. FOOD
9. MEMBERSHIP REQUIRED
10. LEATHER
11. SPORTS
12. COUNTRY WESTERN

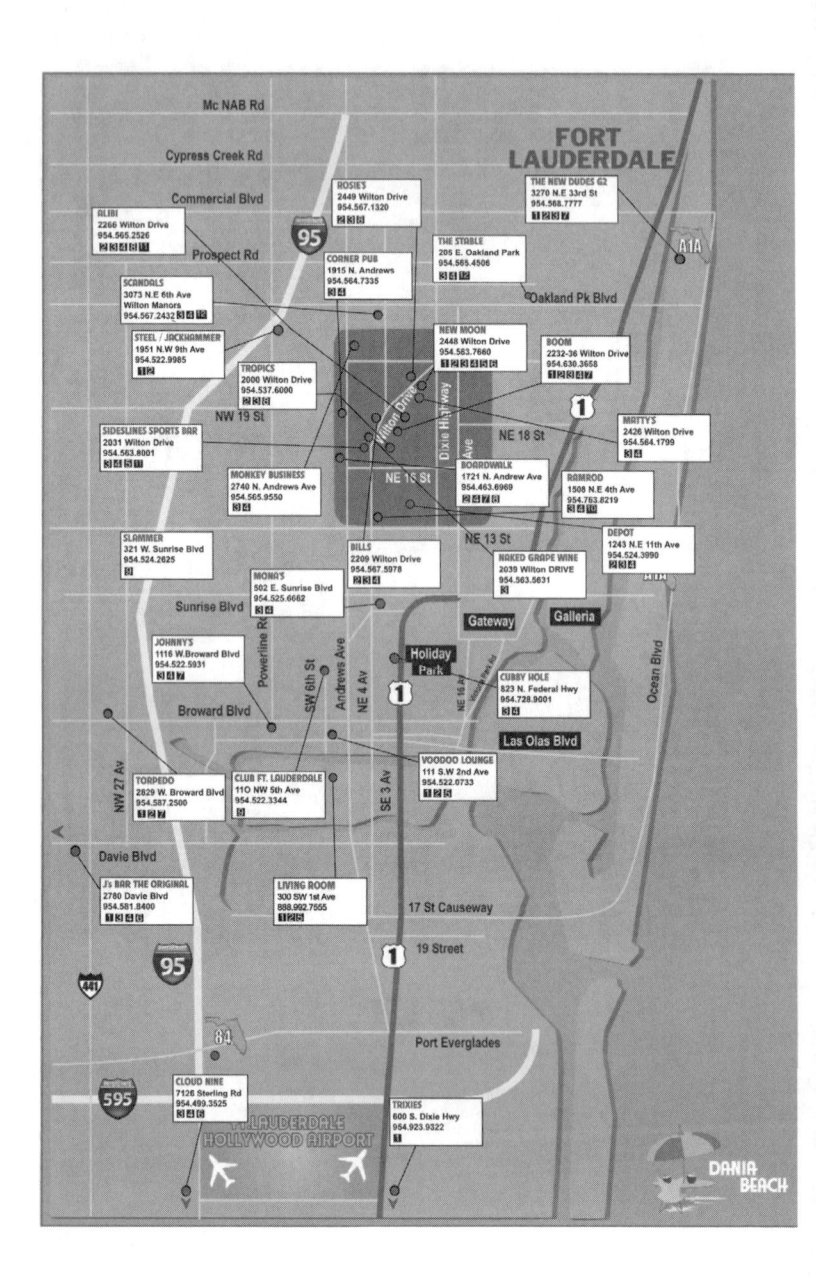

FORT LAUDERDALE

ROSIE'S
2449 Wilton Drive
954.567.1320

THE NEW DUDES G2
3270 N.E 33rd St
954.568.7777

ALIBI
2266 Wilton Drive
954.565.2526

CORNER PUB
1915 N. Andrews
954.564.7335

THE STABLE
205 E. Oakland Park
954.565.4506

SCANDALS
3073 N.E 6th Ave
Wilton Manors
954.567.2432

NEW MOON
2448 Wilton Drive
954.563.7660

BOOM
2232-36 Wilton Drive
954.630.3658

STEEL / JACKHAMMER
1951 N.W 9th Ave
954.522.9985

TROPICS
2000 Wilton Drive
954.537.6000

MATTY'S
2426 Wilton Drive
954.564.1799

SIDELINES SPORTS BAR
2031 Wilton Drive
954.563.8001

BOARDWALK
1721 N. Andrew Ave
954.463.6969

RAMROD
1508 N.E 4th Ave
954.763.8219

MONKEY BUSINESS
2740 N. Andrews Ave
954.565.9550

DEPOT
1243 N.E 11th Ave
954.524.3990

SLAMMER
321 W. Sunrise Blvd
954.524.2625

BILLS
2209 Wilton Drive
954.567.5978

NAKED GRAPE WINE
2039 Wilton DRIVE
954.563.5631

MONA'S
502 E. Sunrise Blvd
954.525.6662

JOHNNY'S
1116 W.Broward Blvd
954.522.5931

CUBBY HOLE
823 N. Federal Hwy
954.728.9001

TORPEDO
2829 W. Broward Blvd
954.587.2500

CLUB FT. LAUDERDALE
110 NW 5th Ave
954.522.3344

VOODOO LOUNGE
111 S.W 2nd Ave
954.522.0733

J's BAR THE ORIGINAL
2780 Davie Blvd
954.581.8400

LIVING ROOM
300 SW 1st Ave
888.992.7555

CLOUD NINE
7126 Sterling Rd
954.499.3525

TRIXIES
600 S. Dixie Hwy
954.923.9322

DANIA BEACH

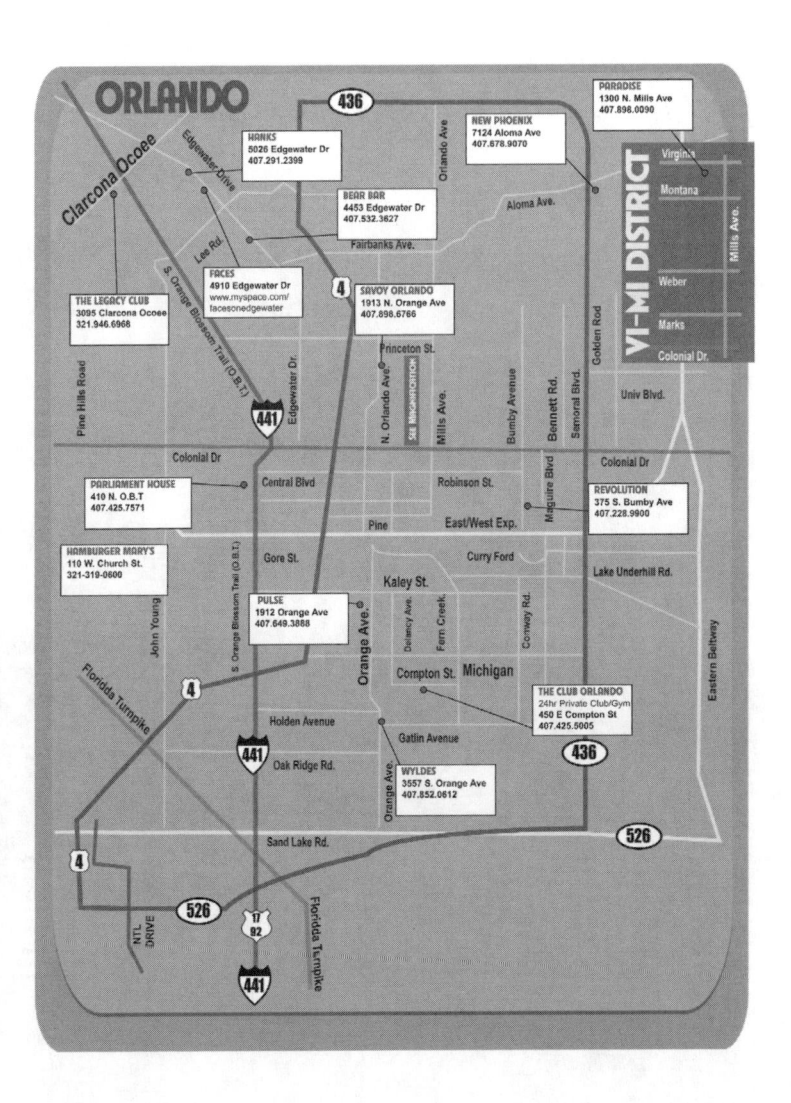

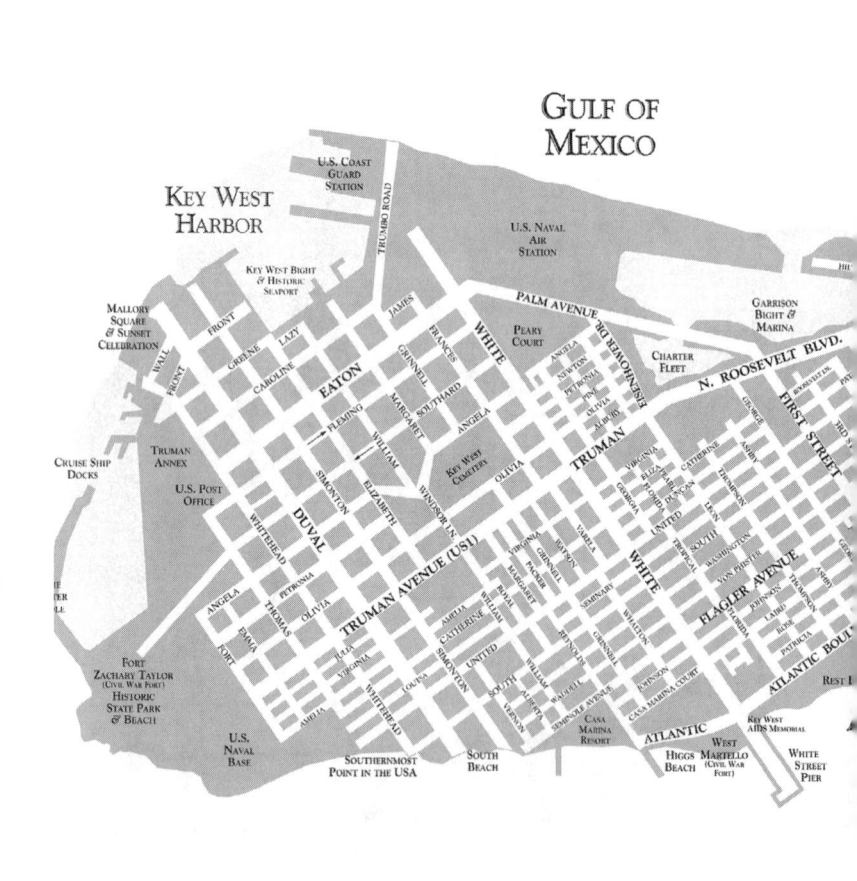

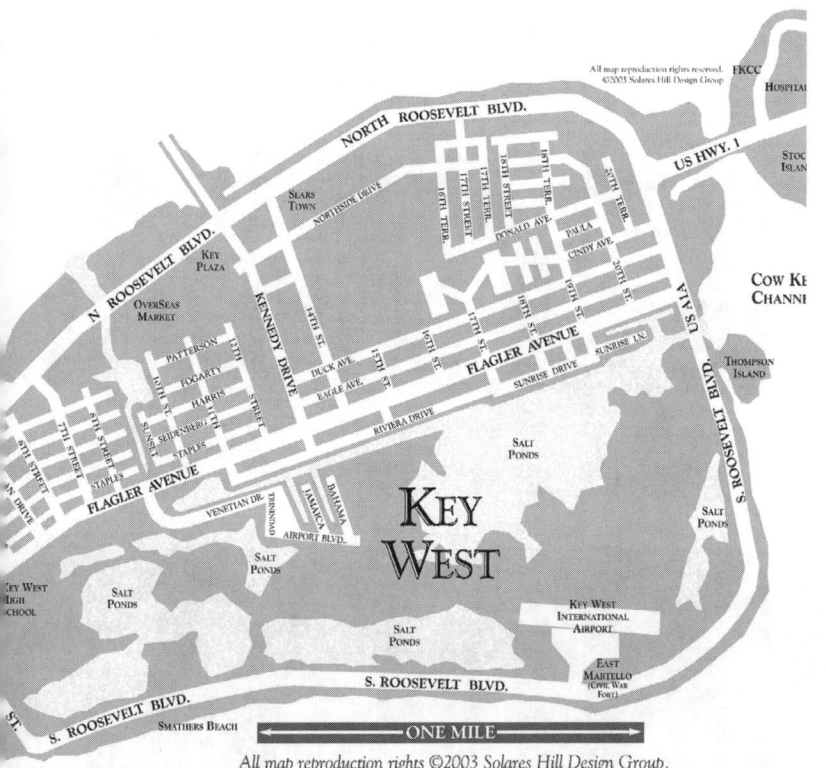

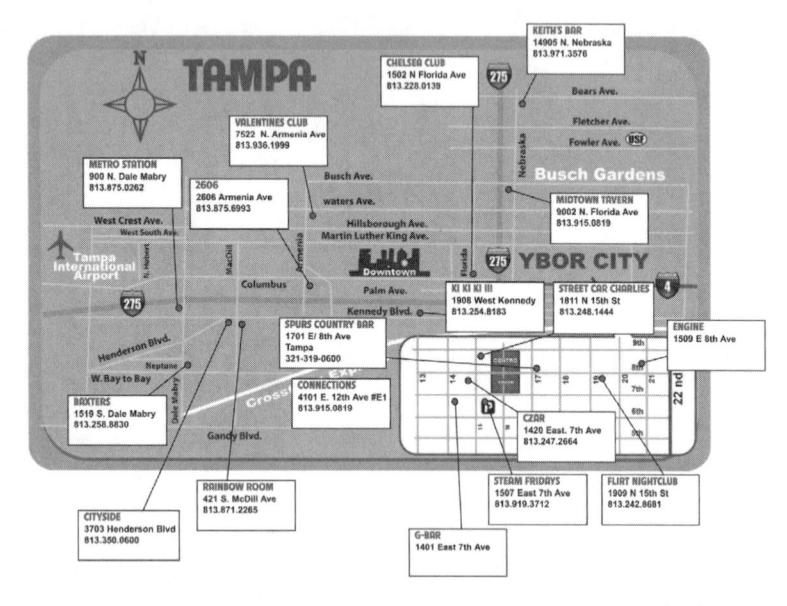

TAMPA

KEITH'S BAR
14905 N. Nebraska
813.971.3576

CHELSEA CLUB
1502 N Florida Ave
813.228.0139

VALENTINES CLUB
7522 N. Armenia Ave
813.936.1999

METRO STATION
900 N. Dale Mabry
813.875.0262

2606
2606 Armenia Ave
813.875.6993

MIDTOWN TAVERN
9002 N. Florida Ave
813.915.0819

KI KI KI III
1908 West Kennedy
813.254.8183

STREET CAR CHARLIES
1811 N 15th St
813.248.1444

ENGINE
1509 E 8th Ave

SPURS COUNTRY BAR
1701 E/ 8th Ave
Tampa
321-319-0600

CONNECTIONS
4101 E. 12th Ave #E1
813.915.0819

CZAR
1420 East. 7th Ave
813.247.2664

BAXTERS
1519 S. Dale Mabry
813.258.8830

RAINBOW ROOM
421 S. McDill Ave
813.871.2265

STEAM FRIDAYS
1507 East 7th Ave
813.919.3712

FLIRT NIGHTCLUB
1909 N 15th St
813.242.8681

CITYSIDE
3703 Henderson Blvd
813.350.0600

G-BAR
1401 East 7th Ave

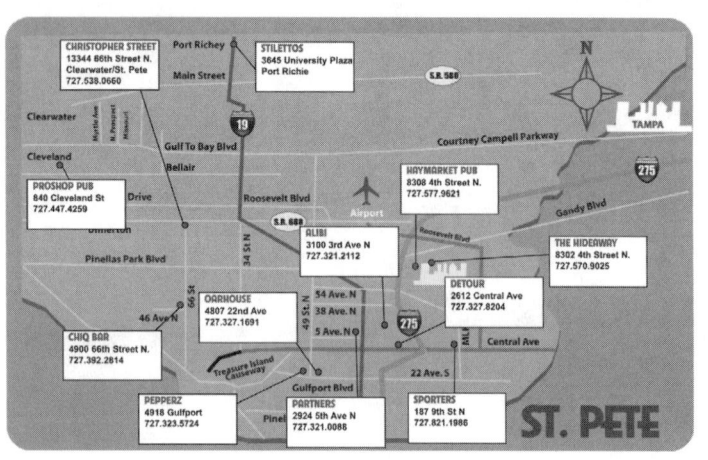

ST. PETE

CHRISTOPHER STREET
13344 86th Street N.
Clearwater/St. Pete
727.538.0660

STILETTOS
3645 University Plaza
Port Richie

PROSHOP PUB
840 Cleveland St
727.447.4259

HAYMARKET PUB
8308 4th Street N.
727.577.9621

ALIBI
3100 3rd Ave N
727.321.2112

THE HIDEAWAY
8302 4th Street N.
727.570.9025

OARHOUSE
4807 22nd Ave
727.327.1691

DETOUR
2612 Central Ave
727.327.8204

CHIQ BAR
4900 66th Street N.
727.392.2614

PEPPERZ
4918 Gulfport
727.323.5724

PARTNERS
2924 5th Ave N
727.321.0088

SPORTERS
187 9th St N
727.821.1986

INDEX

Aardvark Kayak Company, 76
Acadia, 238
Ace Ventura, Pet Detective, 40–41
adoption, by gays and lesbians, 13–14, 16–17
African-Americans, Miami Urban Beach Week and, 101
AIDS memorial, 182
AIDS walks/events, 61, 99
airboats, 136
airline flights
  economical/popular, 52–53
  first scheduled, 226
airports, 52–53
Alcazar Resort, 140
alcohol consumption in Fort Lauderdale, 129–130
Alexander's Guesthouse, 183
Alice's Restaurant, 188, 191
alligator attacks, 27–28
alternative nightlife, Fort Lauderdale, 153–154
American Idol, 212
Amnesia, 45
Angler's Boutique Resort, 109
animal rescue/rehabilitation facilities, Tampa Bay Area, 230–233

Anthony's Coal Fire Pizza, 142, 145
antiquing in Palm Beach, 161–162
Anushka Day Spa, 68
Aqua Foundation for Women, 98
Aqua Girl, 48, 98
Aqua Nightclub, 190–191
aquarium fish, 226
Arabian Nights II, 48, 205
Art Basel Miami, 22, 101
Art Deco Photo Safari, 103
Art Deco Pub Crawl, 123
art galleries, South Beach, 104
arts in Tampa Bay, 233–234
The Atlantic, 141
Atlantic Shores Resort, 44
Automatic Slims, 153
Aventura Mall, 69–70
Azaria, Hank, 39

Babylon T-Dance, 152
Bahia Honda State Park, 174
Bal Harbour Shops, 95, 103
Barefoot Billy's, 179
Barton G, 113–114
Bayshore Boulevard, 228–229
Beach Ball at Typhoon Lagoon, 48, 205–206

beaches, 71–72. *See also specific beaches*
Beach on 12th and Collins, 48
Beak's Old Florida, 251
Bella Brava, 247
Belle and Maxwell's, 164
Big Cat Rescue, 230
Big Pink, 114
Big Ruby's Guesthouse, 184
biking, 162, 180
Billionaire's Row, 159
Bill's Filling Station, 149
Billy's Swamp Safari, 136
The Birdcage, 38–39
black gay events, 98–99
Blue Heaven Restaurant, 186–187
Blue Moon Fish Co., 142, 145
Blue Planet kayak eco-tours, 178–179
Blue Spring State Park, 75–76
Blu Q cruises, 178, 179
Boardwalk, 149–150
B.O. Fish Wagon, 187
Bond Street, 114
Bonnet House, 137
books about South Beach, 100
Boom, 150
booty music, 31–33
Bourbon Street Pub, 191
boutiques, 103
bowling, 154
the Breakers, 163
Britton Hill, 28
Bryant, Anita, 10–13, 16
Buck 15 Lounge, 119
Buena Vista Palace Hotel and Spa, 211, 215
Burger King Corporation, 28
Busch Gardens, 232–233
Bush, President George W., 14, 24
bus service, public, 103

Café Emunah, 142, 145
Café Marquesa, 188
Caladesi Island State Park, 240–241
Calle 8 (Carnival weekend), 99–100
Camille's Restaurant, 187
Cantina Beach, 115
Canyon, 142–145
Cape Canaveral, 84–85
Capital Grille, Fort Lauderdale, 144
Capital Grille, Orlando, 217
Care Resource, 17
Carrey, Jim, 40
cars, rental, 53–55, 105
Casa Marina, 186
Castle, Pop 'n Wave Thursdays, 250
Catalina Hotel and Beach Club, 110
Cathode Ray, 44–45
Cayo Costa State Park, 238
celebrities, 41–43
Central Florida. *See also* Orlando
    Gay and Lesbian Community
        Center, 17
    shopping, 70–71
Chambers, 45
Cher, 28
China Grill, 143, 144
China White, 45
Chiq Bar, 251
cigar smoking in Ybor City, 228
Cioppino, 115
Cirque du Soleil, 213–214
City Side, 248–249
civil unions, 16
Clearwater Aquarium, 232–233
Clinton, Hillary, 25
Clinton, President Bill, 14
Coconut Grove, Miami, 107–108
Coconut Grove Resort, Key West, 184
Cocowalk, 107
Coliseum, 45
Colombia Restaurant, 244
Colony Hotel, Thursdays at, 166
community centers, gay and lesbian, 17
Compass: Gay and Lesbian Community
    Center West Palm Beach, 17
"Conch Republic," 170, 177. *See also* Key
    West
conch train tour, 181
"Conga," 29–30
conga line, world's largest, 95
COPA, 44

Coral Castle, 106
Coral Tree Inn, 184
Cox, Courtney, 40–41
Crème Lounge, 119
Crockett, James "Sonny," 35–36
crocodiles, 29
cruises, evening, 179–180
"Crusader Church of Florida," 226
Cruz, Celia, 30, 99–100
Crystal River Wildlife Refuge, 75–76
CSI: Miami, 37
Cuban food in Little Havana, 118
Cuban immigrants, 104
culture, in Florida, 21–23
Cunanan, Andrew Phillip, 24

Dalí museum, 22, 78–79, 236–237
Deering, James, 105
Defense of Marriage Act (DOMA), 14–15
Dek 23, 122
Delano Hotel, 110
Democratic National Committee, 25
Design District, 108
Dessange Paris, 68
Detour, 251
Dickens House, 242–243
Dilido Beach Club, 114–115
Dine Out Lauderdale, 62
dining, 56–57
    cost categories, 58
drag, 154
    Fort Lauderdale, 142–147
    Key West, 186–190
    Miami, 113–118
    Orlando, 217–219
    Palm Beach, 164–165
    St. Petersburg, 247–248
    Tampa, 244–247
Discotekka at Metropolis, 123
discrimination based on sexual orientation, 5, 12
Disney, Walt, 33, 197–198
Disney Channel, Mickey Mouse Club, 37
Disney Hollywood Studios, 212
Disney World Magic Kingdom, 11, 32–33, 198, 207
D-list celebrities, 41–43
dolphin encounters, 83–84, 178
Dolphin Research Center, 173–174
DOMA (Defense of Marriage Act), 14–15
domestic partner protections, 11
Don Vicente Historic Inn, 241–242
Doubletree Hotel, 215–216
Doubletree Surfcomber, 110
Downtown Pizzeria, 147–148
drag cabaret, 120–121
drag dining, 154
Dry Tortugas National Park, Key West, 73–74, 178
Dunedin, 241
Dune Oceanfront Burger Lounge, 115

Egmont Key, 241
801 Bourbon Street, 191–192
El Gordo Y la Flaca, 96
El Goya, 45
El Show de Cristina, 96–97
Emerill's Orlando, 217
EPCOT, 198
Equality Florida, 17
Equator Resort, 184
European Guesthouse, 109
events
    food-related, 61–62
    Keys, 175–176
    LGBT exclusive, 59–61, 98–99
    Miami, 98–101
    Palm Beach, 159–160
    St. Petersburg, 227–228
    Tampa Bay, 227–228
Everglades, 79–81, 107
Everglades Holiday Park, 136
Everglades National Park, 175

Fairchild Tropical Gardens, 107
Fantasy Fest, 176
fast food, introduction of, 28
ferry service to Dry Tortugas National Park, 74
Flamingo Inn, 139

flamingos, 32
Flight of the Navigator, 40
Florida. *See also specific cities and vacation destinations*
    facts/figures about, 28–29, 56
    homo-hypocrisy of, 5–6
    myths about, 32–33
    packing list for, 52
    stereotypical images of, 47–48
    as vacation destination, 23
Florida Aquarium, 84, 229, 232
Florida Keys Eco-Discovery Center, 181, 182
Florida Keys National Marine Sanctuary, 176
Florida Legislative Investigation Committee, 7
Florida4Marriage, 15
Florida politics, homosexual issues and, 15–17
Floridian, 148
Food Amongst the Flowers, 154
food-related events, 61–62
the Forge, 249
Fort De Soto, 240
Forte di Aspirino, 164
Fort Lauderdale, 127–154
    coffee shops and 24-hour eateries, 147–149
    dining, 142–147
    events, 131–134
    facts/figures about, 58, 130
    gyms, 65
    housing prices, 131
    lodging, 138–141
    nightlife, 149–154
    past gay bars, 44–45
    religious organizations, 64–65
    sightseeing, 134–138
    spas, 66–69
    spring break, 127–129
    yachting community in, 128
Fort Lauderdale Beach, 48
Fort Lauderdale International Boat Show, 22, 133
fossil expeditions, 81–83
Foster, Steven, 29
411 Magazine, 58
The Four Rivers, 143–144
Freedom Tower, 104
From Justin to Kelly, 40
Front Porch, 115–116
Fury water adventures, 179

G. Bar, 48, 249
Galanga Restaurant, 143
Galleria Mall, 70
Gallery Live, 233–234
Gansevoort South, 111
Gasparilla Pirate Fest, 227
Gatorade, 28–29
Gator attacks, 27–28
gay adoption, 11
Gay and Lesbian trolley tour of fabulous Key West, 181
gay bars. *See also specific gay bars*
    historical background, 6, 10, 44–47
gay beaches, 102
GaYbor District, Hampton Inn, Ybor City, 242
Gay Days, 59
    in Orlando, 199–201, 206–207
    straight guy's view of, 208–209
    in Tampa Bay, 228
gay/lesbian organizations, 17
gay life
    in Florida, during 1980's and 1990's, 13
    locations of interest, 63–64
    of 1950's, 8–9
gay marriage. *See* same-sex marriage
gay pride events, St. Petersburg, 227–228
gay publications, 62–64
Gay St. Pete House, 243
gay travel budget, statewide, 28
gender-reassignment surgery, 15
Georgie's Alibi, 150, 247–248, 251–252
GIE (gender identity and expression), 15
Girls at Gay Days, 206–207
Girls in Wonderland, 206
Golden Girls, 36

golf courses, 29
Gonzalez, Elian, 26
Gonzalez, Juan Miguel, 26
Gore, Al, 24
The Grand Resort and Spa, Fort Lauderdale, 139
The Grand Spa, 67–68
Grandview Gardens Bed and Breakfast, 163
Gran Forno, 145, 146
ground transportation, 53
guesthouses, gay, 55, 183
Gulfport, 241
Gulfport Beach, 237, 240
Gumby Slumber, 77
gyms, 65–66

Halloween Horror nights, 211
Halo Lounge, 119
Halo Night Club Fort Lauderdale, 152
Halouver Beach, 103, 135
Hampton Inn, Ybor City, 242
Harpoon Harry's, 188
Henry Flagler museum, 162
Heyman, Richard, 10
H.G. Roosters, 166
Hilton Fort Lauderdale Beach Resort, 141
hip/hop music (booty music), 31–33
HIV resources, 17
Hogan, Brooke, 43
Hollywood Beach, 135
Holocaust Museum, 22, 236
Homosexuality and Citizenship in Florida ("Purple Pamphlet"), 6, 8–9
homosexuality in Florida, 5–7
the Honey Pot, 249–250
housing prices, Fort Lauderdale, 131
Human Rights Ordinance, 11
Hydrate Video Bar, 219–220

Ice Box Cafe, 116
Ikea, 70
"I'm Going to Disney World" commercial, 37–38
International LGBT events, 59–60
International Plaza, Tampa, 70–71

International Swimming Hall of Fame and Aquatic Complex, 48, 138
Islamorada Fish Company, 173
Island House, Miami, 109
Island House for Men, Key West, 182, 185
Islescapes gourmet yachting, 180

J. Alexanders, 146
Jackie Gleason Show, 36–37
January, Tony Jannus, 226
Java Boys, 148
Jazz in the Gardens at the Gardens Hotel, 192
Jet Set, 152
Jewish congregations, 65
Jewish residents, in Palm Beach, 161
Jimenez, Yovy Suarez, 27
Joe's Stone Crabs, 116, 191
Johnny's Boys, 152
John Pennekamp State Park, 174–175, 177
Johns, Charley Eugene, 7
Johns Committee, 7–8, 10
Jolly Mamma, 77
Juanes, 31
jumponmarkslist.com, 58

kayaking, 76, 136
Kelly's Just About Anything Restaurant, 248
Kennedy Space Center, 84–85, 213
Kermit's Key West Key Lime Shop, 191
Key Biscayne, 93–94, 112, 115
Key Largo Conch House, 173
key lime pie, 191
The Keys, 169–193. *See also* Key West
    driving through, 172–173
    events, 175–176
    food options, 173
    nature options, 173–175
    rainy-day activities, 182
    sightseeing, 176–182
Key West
    dining, 186–190
    driving to, 172–173
    Dry Tortugas National Park, 73–74
    facts/figures on, 58, 177

Gay and Lesbian Community Center, 17
gyms, 66
lodging, 182–186
nightlife, 190–193
past gay bars, 44
religious organizations, 64–65
spas, 68–69
Key West Butterfly and Nature Conservatory, 182
Key West cemetery, 182
Ku Klux Klan, 226
Kwest Men, 192

Lane, Nathan, 39
Langbehn, Janice, 14
La Nouba, Cirque du Soleil, 213–214
Las Olas Boulevard, Fort Lauderdale, 137
Las Olas Wine & Food Festival, 62
La Te Da, Sunday Tea Dance, 192
law, 5
Lawrence v. Texas, 11
Leedskalnin, Edward, 106
legal protections for gays, 5
leks, 204
Les Beans, 164
Le Tub, 146
Liberty Fleet, 180
"liger," 106
Lightening Capital of the World, 25–26
Lighthouse Court, 44
Lincoln Road, 48
Lincoln Road Mall, 103
Lips, 154
Little Havana, Cuban food in, 118
Little Palm Island, 77–78, 178, 191
lodging
Fort Lauderdale, 138–141
Key West, 186
LGBT exclusive, 55, 138–140
Miami, 109–113
Orlando, 211, 215–216
Palm Beach, 163
St. Petersburg, 242—244
Tampa, 241–242

the Lounge, 165
love bugs, 32

"Macarena," 30
magazines, gay scene, 58, 62–63
Magic Kingdom, 11, 32–33, 198, 207
Majestic Theater and Lounge, 219–220
Mall at Millenia, Orlando, 70–71
Mallory Square, 180–181
manatees, 75–76
Manor Lanes, 154
Manta, Sea World Resort, 213
March on Washington, 10
Marilyn's closet, 226
Marlin Beach Resort, Fort Lauderdale, 12
Marriage Protection Amendment, 15–16
Married to the Mob, 39–40
Marriott Village, 206, 216
Marshall, Vickie Lynn Hogan, 24–25
Martini Tuesdays, 123
Mary Brickell Village, 108
McAulife, Christa, 26
McDonald's Play Place, 214
McDuffie, Arthur, 95
McFilmfest, 233
Mediums of Cassadaga, 215
Mema's Alaskan Taco's, 245
MFA Café, 248
Miami, 89–123. *See also* Miami Beach; South Beach
dining, 113–118
downtown, 108–109
events, 98–101
facts/figures, 33, 58
gyms, 65
as "Hollywood of Latin America," 94–97
iPod playlist, 93
lodging, 109–113
nightlife, 119–123
past gay bars, 6, 45–46
spas, 67
Miami bass (booty music), 31–34
Miami Beach, 64, 90. *See also* South Beach
Miami-Dade public bus service, 103

Miami freestyle music, 34–35
Miami Herald, 7, 120
Miami Sound Machine, 29–30
Miami Spanish Monastery, 106–107
Miami Spice, 62
Miami Urban Beach Week, 101
Miami Vice, 35, 95
Michael's Restaurant, 189
Mickey Mouse Club, 37
"Miss Cleo," 43
Monster, 44
moped hospital and bikes, 181
Morikami Gardens, 162
Morrison, Jim, 95
movies shot in Florida, 38–41
Muscle Beach Party, 48
Museum of Art, Fort Lauderdale, 137
Museum of Fine Arts, 235
museums. *See specific museums*
Mushroom, Merrill, 8–9
music, 29–35, 93
myths, about Florida, 32–33

Naked Grape, 153
NASA, 84–85
National Gay and Lesbian Task Force, 98
National Inquirer, 29
NativeVacations, 76
"Naturist beaches" (nude beaches), 102–103
New Moon, 150
news headlines, sensational, 24–28
newspapers, gay, 63–64
New Year's Shoe Drop, 175
New York, New York Pizza, 245–246
nightlife, 57–58
  Fort Lauderdale, 149–154
  Key West, 190–193
  Miami, 119–123
  Orlando, 219–220
  Palm Beach, 159, 165–166
  St. Petersburg, 251–252
  Tampa, 248–251
  Wilton Manors, 149–151
  915, 189

Oasis Resort, 184
"Old Folks at Home (Suwannee River)," 29
Old Town Trolley tour, 181
"One Human Family" concept, 170
One Mighty Weekend, 204–210
Orlando, 197–220
  attractions, 210–211
  dining, 217–219
  facts/figures, 58
  gyms, 66
  lodging, 211, 215–216
  nightlife, 219–220
  past gay bars, 46–47
  religious organizations, 64–65
  spas, 69
Orlando Gay Pride, 210
Orlando Youth Alliance, 17

Pach's, 246
packing list, for Florida, 52
Palace Bar, 121–122
Palm Beach, 157–166
  dining, 164–165
  events, 159–160
  facts/figures, 23, 58, 161
  gyms, 66
  homes, 157–159, 160
  lodging, 163
  nightlife, 159, 165–166
  sightseeing, 160–162
  spas, 68
Palm Beach County Human Rights Council, 17
Palm Beach Daily News, 161
Palm Beach Jewelry, Art, and Antique Show, 22, 159
Pangea at Hard Rock, 153
parking, 55
Parliament House, Orlando, 12, 219
Parrott Jungle Island, 105–106
Peace River, 81–83
Pearl's Rainbow for Women, 185, 192–193
Pensacola, 48
people-watching, on South Beach, 102

Peter Pan, 148
The Pier, 235
Pineapple Point, 140
Pleasurdome, 45
Pleasure Island, Mannequin's Thursdays, 46–47
Pond, Lisa, 14
Pop 'n Wave Thursdays, 250
porn Industry, 41
Prana Spa, 68–69, 182
presidential election of 2000, 24
prices, 58
Pridefest
    Fort Lauderdale, 131
    Key West, 175
    Palm Beaches, 160
public transportation, 54
Pulse, 219
Pump, 45

"Queen of the Night" column, *Miami Herald,* 120

rail system, 53
rainy-day activities, 182
Ramrod, 150
Raphael: Food and More, 117
reading materials, on South Beach, 100
Regal Sun Resort, 206–207, 216
religious organizations, 64–65
rental cars, 53–55, 105
Reunion Pool Party, 205
Revolution Nightclub, 219–220
Rhythm Cafe, 165
riots, 95
Ritz-Carlton, Key Biscayne, 94, 112, 115
Ritz-Carlton, South Beach, 111
Ritz-Carlton Spa, Miami, 67
Ritz-Carlton Spa, Orlando, 69
Ritz Theater, 234
Robert Is Here, 175, 191
Rodman, Dennis, 43
Romero Britto gallery, 104
Romer v. Evans, 11

Rooftop at Townhouse Hotel, 122
Rosie's, 150–151
Rosie's Bar & Grill, 146
Royal Palms, 140
Royal Plaza Hotel, 206–207, 216
Rush, Matthew, 43
Rybolovlev, Dmitry, 161

Sábado Gigante, 96
Saloon 1, 193
Salvador Dalí museum, 22, 78–79, 236–237
same-sex marriage, 14, 16
Sanibel Island, 239
"Save Our Children" campaign, 12–13
Savory Orlando, 220
Sawgrass Mills Outlet Mall, 70
Sawgrass recreation park, 136
Sawmill Camp Resort, 240
Scandals Saloon, 151
Scarface, 39
Schwarzenegger, Arnold, 39
Score, 119
Sea Experience Snorkel Cruise, 136–137
Sea Monster, 45
seaplanes, to Dry Tortugas National Park, 74
Season's 52, 217–218
SeaWorld, 198, 212–213
SeaWorld Orlando Resort, 211
Sebago watersports, 179
Sebastian Beach, 134
Setai, 111–112
714, 249
Shack, Ruth, 12
Shari Sushi Lounge, 218
shark attacks, 27
Sheraton Suites, 186
Shikira, 31
shopping
    mainstream, 69–71
    outdoor, 103
shuttle services, 53
Sidelines, 151
Siesta Key Beach, 238

sightseeing, 55–56
    Fort Lauderdale, 134–138
    The Keys, 176–182
    Palm Beach, 160–162
    St. Petersburg, 234–241
    Tampa, 228–234
Sizzle, 98–99
Skipper, Ryan, 15
smear campaign against gays, 6–7
Smith, Anna Nicole, 24–25
Smith, Nadine, 16
snorkeling, 136–137
snow flurries, 33
Snug Harbor Inn, 243
sodomy statutes, gay, 11
Solomon, Tara, 120–121
South Beach
    art/culture, 90–92
    car rentals, 105
    reading materials on, 100
    sight-seeing, 102–104
South Beach Wine & Food Festival, 62
Southernmost Point, Key West, 177, 180
South Florida. *See also* Fort Lauderdale; Miami
shopping, 69–70
Southwest 8th Street (Calle Ocho), 93
Space Shuttle Challenger tragedy, 26
Spanglish, 97
"Spanish Oprah," 96–97
spas, 66–69
Spurs, 250
Square Grouper Bar & Grill, 173
Square One Burgers, 246
Square One Restaurant, 189–190
St. Pete Pride, 227–228
St. Petersburg, 225–227
    dining, 247–248
    events, 227–228
    facts/figures, 58, 226
    lodging, 242–244
    nightlife, 251–252
    religious organizations, 64–65
Salvador Dalí museum, 22, 78–79, 236–237
    sightseeing, 234–241
The Standard Spa, 67
Stanton, Steve, 16
Starbucks Wilton Manors, 148
stone crabs, 29
Stonewall Riots, 10, 12
Stonewall Street Festival, 132–133
Storks, 149
Storms, Rhonda, 14
Streetcar Charlie's, 247, 250–251
Sublime, 146–147
Suncoast Resort, 45
Suncoast Seabird Sanctuary, 230–232
"sun cuisine," 114–115
Sunken Gardens, 234
Sunpass/E-Z pass, 54
sunset, at St. Peterburg, 234
Sunset Beach, 237
Sunset cruise, 179
sunshine, consecutive days of, 226
Sunshine Skyway Bridge, 234
Sunshine Stampede Rodeo, 132
SuperShuttle, 53
Sushi Samba Dromo, 117
Swap Shop Flea market, 138

Table 8, 117–118
Tampa Bay area, 223–252
    animal rescue/rehabilitation facilities, 230–233
    avant-garde art scene, 225
    Bayshore Boulevard, 226
    cost of living, 224
    day trips, 238–239
    dining, 244–247
    events, 227–228
    facts/figures, 58
    GaYbor district, 224–225
    gyms, 66
    LGBT population, 224–225
    lodging, 241–242
    nightlife, 248–251
    past gay bars, 46
    religious organizations, 65

sightseeing, 228–234
Tampa International Gay & Lesbian Film Festival, 228
Tampa Marriott Waterside Hotel and Marina, 242
Tarpon Springs, 239–240
Taverna Opa, 147
taxi service, 53, 105
television
    commercials, Florida-based, 35–38
    shows, Florida-based, 35–38
    Spanish-speaking, 94, 96–97
temperatures, in Florida, 52, 177
theme parks. *See also specific theme parks*
    attendance at, 202–203
    Orlando, 210–214
There's Something about Mary, 38
Tides Hotel, 112–113
Torpedo, 153
Townhouse Hotel, 113, 122
Tracks, 45
Trannie Palace, 151
transportation
    air, 52–53
    bike, 162, 180
    cars, 53–55, 105
    ground, 53–55
    public bus service, 103
    rail system, 53
    taxi service, 53
    water taxi, 135
Trina, 145, 147
Tri-Rail, 53
Tropical Heat, 175–176
True Lies, 39
Trump, Donald, 159, 161
Tubbs, Ricardo "Rico," 35–36
Twist, 120
2 Live Crew, 31

Unitarian universalism, 65
Universal Orlando Resort, 211, 212
Universal Studios, Simpsons Ride, 213

University of Miami, 106

Vanilla Ice, 42–43
Venice Beach, 238
"Venice of America." *See* Fort Lauderdale
Venus Charters for women, 178
Versace, Gianni, 24
Versailles Restaurant, 118
Vinoy Hotel, 244
Vizcaya Museum and gardens, 104–105
Voodoo Lounge, 153

The W, 141
walking tours, 180
Walt Disney World Resort, 211
The Warsaw, 45–46
water taxi, 135
Waycyka, 238
Wearstler, Kelly, 113
weather, 52
web sites, 63
West Palm Beach, 65, 158, 159
Where the Boys Are, 38
White Party, 59, 99, 104
Wicked Manors, 133
Wild Things, 39
Wilton Manors, 130–131, 148–151
wine tastings, 153–154
Winterfest Boat Parade, 133
Winter Music Conference, 95, 100–101
Winter Party, 98
Wolfgang Puck Grand Café, 218–219
woman's bar, oldest, 226
Womenfest, 176
Womyns Words, 10
World Erotic Art Museum, 104
Worth Avenue, 161
Worthington Guesthouse, 140
Wynwood, 108

Ybor City, cigar smoking in, 228

Zona Fresca, 147

PHOTO CREDITS

The photo on page 120 is courtesy of Tara Solomon. The photos on pages 158 and 165 are courtesy of the Palm Beaches Convention and Visitor's Bureau. The photo on page 235 is courtesy of the St. Petersburg Convention and Visitor's Bureau. The photo on page 236 is courtesy of the Dali Museum. The photos on page 253, 254, 255, and 258 are courtesy of *411 Magazine*. The photo on page 256 is courtesy of J.T. Thompson.